# THE
# BANBURY & CHELTENHAM
# RAILWAY

F. R. PACKER

*Chipping Norton station during the early Edwardian period.*

# THE
# BANBURY & CHELTENHAM RAILWAY

## VOLUME ONE

BY

WILLIAM HEMMINGS

'The commencement and carrying out to its present state of completion ... would be a little history in itself. It had many phases. It sometimes looked promising and sometimes gloomy, and I am convinced that it would be a very interesting history, and perhaps a profitable and useful one to trace out in its various stages ...'

*John Fowler, speaking at the opening of the Chipping Norton Branch, 10th August 1855.*

WILD SWAN PUBLICATIONS

Hook Norton from the Church Tower.

# CONTENTS

*The Ports-to-Ports Express near Adderbury c.1908.*          COLLECTION KIDDERMINSTER RAILWAY MUSEUM

ISBN 1 874103 88 7

FOR JOHN MANN
with appreciation for a childhood friendship

F. R. PACKER

Designed by Paul Karau
Printed by Amadeus Press, Cleckheaton

Published by
WILD SWAN PUBLICATIONS LTD.
1-3 Hagbourne Road, Didcot, Oxon, OX11 8DP

# INTRODUCTION

In 1966, at the age of six, I began attendance at a small, friendly school in Churchill, a village situated three and a half miles south-west of Chipping Norton, in Oxfordshire. My home was two miles away at Sarsden Gorse, in a prominent red-brick semi-detached cottage, one of a group of four properties situated beside a lane, surrounded by fields.

The course of the Banbury and Cheltenham Railway or, to be more precise, the part of it that had started out as the Chipping Norton Branch of the Oxford, Worcester and Wolverhampton Railway in 1855, passed a mile to the north. The railway was not visible from the house, as a rise in the landscape called Rynehill, half a mile away and surmounted by a farm of the same name, blocked it from view.

Churchill was not the first school I attended. My experience at Holy Trinity School in Chipping Norton preceded it through the previous two years, and it was during the first journey to the school that I encountered the railway. Mrs Ahern arrived in her taxi, one of a small fleet of Ford Zephyrs, which operated from Station Garage at Kingham, and I and my twin brother, Mark (later joined by my sister, Barbara), were bundled in to the accompaniment of loud wailing from us, and anxious farewells from my mother, to experience the unknown world that lay outside.

The route took us along the Lyneham Road and into Kingham village, passing over the railway via the 'New Line Bridge' near the Mill Hotel. The long approach embankments offered clear views through the post-and-wire fencing. To the left was the site of Kingham East Junction, with the sweep of the branch curve round to the left and the grey trackbed of the old loop on a rising embankment to the right. Around and between the two, were scattered the buildings associated with a once-vibrant industry: a water tank to the left, permanent way and signals and telegraph huts in the centre, an engine shed to the right and, in the middle, the long, grime-covered red-brick wall of a signal box. The scene impressed itself upon my mind. Soon after, perhaps within a matter of days, as we passed again, the view was empty; the buildings had simply disappeared. The days of the Banbury and Cheltenham Railway were over.

At Kingham we transferred to a regular bus, and again the route crossed the railway, at Churchill Crossing, where a fire in the little lodge always seemed to burn. As we passed over the bumpy crossing, I could see that the indentations in the ballast, marking the positions of the recently-lifted sleepers, were still clearly visible. I turned and looked back over my shoulder, at the crossing with its gates – complete with red warning discs – now permanently closed to the railway, staying with the scene until it disappeared from view.

There were to be no frequent trips over the old railway when I moved to Churchill School. However, it was there

that my interest in the line grew through the friendship of a pupil who also had an enthusiasm for it. John Mann lived at Kingham Hill School, close to Churchill, and he knew about the railway. Firstly, his father, Ralph Mann, had begun some research into it and John would tell me things he had learnt from him. For instance, he explained to me that an express used to run over the line from Newcastle to Swansea and back, twice a day, and that there had at one time been a thriving iron ore industry associated with the railway, along with a regular passenger service. All these elements of a vanished history fuelled my growing interest. Secondly, and importantly, John had actually seen the last train to pass over the line between Chipping Norton and Kingham, at the little crossing and stopping place between Kingham Hill and Churchill, known as Sarsden Halt. Try as I might to match it, this was an experience I could never equal and, what is more, John even had a photograph to prove it!

Trips to John's house were always exciting – the highlight for me was invariably when he would ask his father's permission, at my request, to look at his book, *Kingham the Beloved Place* by Ernest Lainchbury, which he dutifully handed over. We immediately turned to the chapter called 'The Coming of the Railway', which described the story of the Oxford, Worcester and Wolverhampton Railway as it entered the district in 1853, and studied the two photographs of Chipping Norton Junction, spanning two centuries, taken some thirty years apart. The experience was like unearthing some long-hidden, buried treasure.

Later, into the early teens, our railway interest continued unabated. John and I, accompanied by my brother Mark, often went on visits to explore old railways, with cameras and tape recorders at the ready and to watch occasional steam specials passing through.

My interest in the Banbury and Cheltenham Railway continued, intermittently, over the years. Of course, other interests and responsibilities developed and took a place of rightful importance. Many years later, my mother told me she was nursing one of the railwaymen who used to work on the line. I did not take much notice until she informed me one day, that the gentleman, whose name was Bert Lane, had died. Fortunately, Bert's story was already secure – a dedicated railway enthusiast had interviewed Bert some years previously. I wondered how many stories had gone unnoticed and how few there were left to tell. It was at that moment that my occasional interest became transformed into a deep, unquestioning resolve to tell the story of the Banbury and Cheltenham Railway.

My priority was to find out what the railway had been like for those who remembered it; so, not knowing how else to begin, I sent a press release to a local newspaper...

AUTHOR'S NOTE

The orientation of the Deposited Plans of the Banbury and Cheltenham Direct Railway is generally east to west, that being the direction of travel between the two centres. Therefore, with the exception of Hook Norton, the Deposited Plans featured in this study assume south is towards the top of the page.

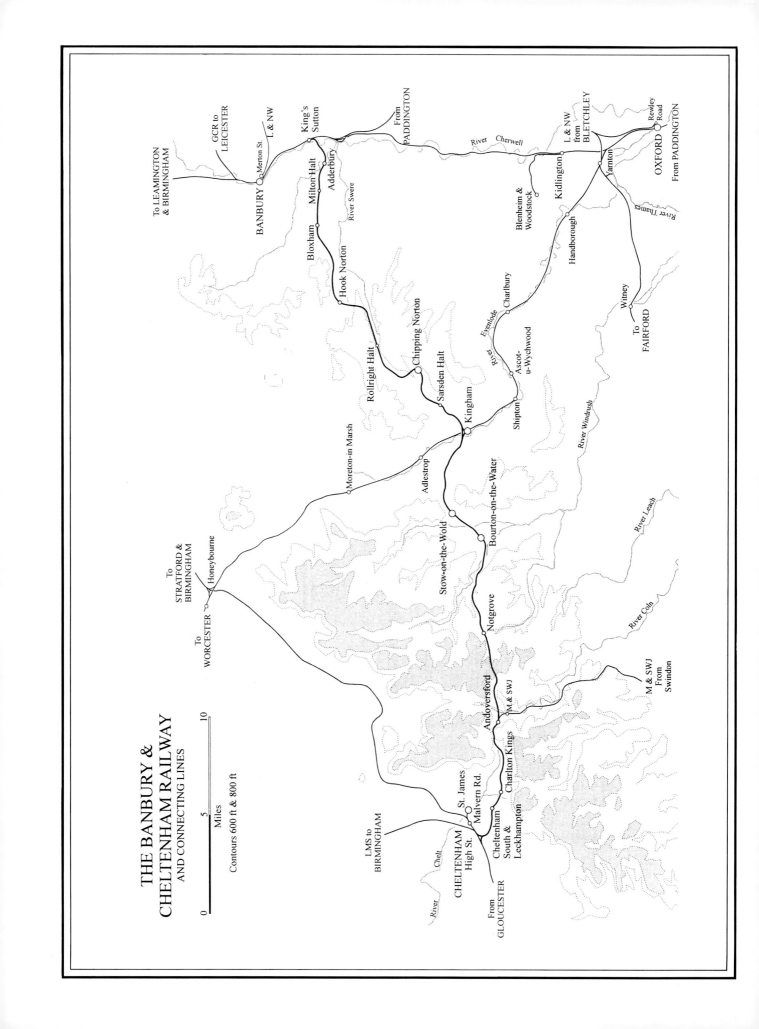

THE BANBURY &
CHELTENHAM RAILWAY
AND CONNECTING LINES

Miles
0    5    10

Contours 600 ft & 800 ft

To LEAMINGTON & BIRMINGHAM

GCR to LEICESTER

L & NW

King's Sutton

Merton St

BANBURY

Milton Halt

Adderbury

Bloxham

River Swere

Hook Norton

Rollright Halt

Chipping Norton

Sarsden Halt

Kingham

Moreton-in-Marsh

Adlestrop

Stow-on-the-Wold

Bourton-on-the-Water

Notgrove

Andoversford

M & SWJ

Charlton Kings

Cheltenham South & Leckhampton

St. James

Malvern Rd.

CHELTENHAM High St.

LMS to BIRMINGHAM

From GLOUCESTER

River Chelt

To WORCESTER

To STRATFORD & BIRMINGHAM

Honeybourne

From PADDINGTON

River Cherwell

Blenheim & Woodstock

Kidlington

Handborough

Charlbury

River Evenlode

Ascot-u-Wychwood

Shipton

River Windrush

River Leach

River Coln

M & SWJ From Swindon

To FAIRFORD

Witney

River Thames

Yarnton

L & NW from BLETCHLEY

OXFORD

Rewley Road

From PADDINGTON

CHAPTER ONE

# THE BEGINNINGS

THE Cotswolds are a ridge of limestone hills extending some 50 miles across the southern part of central England, a section of the lengthy Jurassic uplands that cross the country from south-west to north-east. Rising sharply from the clay vales of the lower River Severn and its tributary, the River Avon, the Cotswold hills then slope gradually down eastward toward the vale of Oxford. The highest ground is mostly around 700 feet above mean sea level, but reaches 1,083 feet in the west, near Cheltenham. The oolitic limestones are fine building stones, and are still widely used in the district.

To the north-east of the Cotswolds, the higher ground continues towards Banbury and Northamptonshire. Historically, the area supported farming, though a valuable mineral lay dormant beneath the rolling hills: iron ore from the Oxfordshire Field would be mined in commercial quantities during the late 19th and early 20th century in the district between Chipping Norton and Banbury.

In the Middle Ages, the Cotswolds were open sheep runs. Between the 14th and 18th centuries, the grazing of the Cotswold breed of sheep (a breed with long wool, now nearly extinct) brought great prosperity to the wool traders and cloth merchants of the district, a wealth that is illustrated in the churches and other fine buildings that are still to be found in the villages and market towns strung mostly along the easterly edge of the hills. The name 'Cotswold' derives from the 'cotes' or sheep pens (or shelters) in the hills. Arable land was mostly to be found associated with individual parishes, generally in the form of large, open fields, divided into owner's strips.

The Cotswold sheep produced wool unlike any other; a medieval phrase summed up the common belief:

'In Europe, the best wool is English.
In England, the best wool is Cotswold'

The hallmark of this quality is not easily recognized today, but the texture was probably finer than present-day sheep's wool. Cotswold wool, in the form of fleeces, was being exported in significant quantities during the late 13th century, and this originated largely from estates owned by monastic orders and landed gentry. Much of this was exported to the continent, frequently to Flanders and Lombardy, with Antwerp and Florence being the largest cloth manufacturing centres.

By the late 15th century, cloth making was well established as a rural industry over much of the Cotswolds. This was organized by clothiers, who bought the wool, but arranged for all the work – except fulling – to be done in the workers' own houses, usually with their own tools and looms.

Around the middle of the 16th century, English wool became longer and coarser. This was more suitable for making worsted than the familiar broadcloth, so that from this time, the local trade moved towards worsteds, with most of the clothing industry shifting geographically towards Somerset, Devon, East Anglia and the West Riding.

In the Cotswolds, the industry had largely died out in the north and east, but was expanding in the southern regions, particularly around Stroud and Painswick, Dursley and Wotton-under-Edge. The deep-sided valleys near Stroud were admirably suited to the building of small reservoirs needed to conserve water for the fulling mills and dyeing sheds. In 1757, Bishop Pocock described Stroud as 'a sort of capital to the clothing villages'.

The clothing industry of the southern Cotswolds was organized on an essentially capitalistic basis from Tudor times to its decline early in the 19th century. As Joseph Tucker wrote, also in 1757:

'One person with a great stock and a large credit buys the wool, pays for the spinning, weaving, milling, dyeing, shearing, dressing, etc. – that is, he is master of the whole manufacture from first to last, and probably employs a thousand persons under him!'

In 1757, the sheep population of Gloucestershire was 400,000, but the cloth industry around Stroud required a colossal 2 to 3 million fleeces annually. Dealers bought wool from all over the country – the Midlands, Kent, and Ireland, with regular visits to the marches of Hereford, Leominster and Ross-on-Wye.

If the buying of the raw fleeces was a massive undertaking, so too was the selling of the final product. Most of the Cotswold cloth seems to have been directed to the growing New World colonies, and the East India Company's trade with India and the Far East, but a great deal was for the home market. Dealers required stamina, for they travelled many miles to different markets in order to sell their cloth.

One such dealer was a young man by the name of Thomas Bliss, whose task it was to travel to Cotswold markets in order to sell cloth for his father, a clothier from Chalford, in the Stroud Valley. Sometime during the middle years of the 18th century, when Thomas Bliss was landlord of the 'Ram' in Chipping Norton, he met and began a romance with Ann Insall, whose father, Thomas, was the landlord of a neighbouring ale house, the Crown and Cushion. The couple married, and, as it was customary at the time for the bridegroom to endow his bride, Thomas Bliss endowed Ann Insall with Green Court, at Chalford in Gloucestershire, which he had inherited from his mother. Some years later, Thomas Bliss took the risk of moving to the Swan Inn, Chipping Norton's largest inn. Thomas Bliss could not make the business pay, due to the high cost of the lease. After about eight years, he was effectively bankrupt, and sold up. He then became a full-time clothier, the trade in which he had been apprenticed, and in which he probably continued while he was an innkeeper.

From these humble beginnings would emerge Chipping Norton's largest industry.

1

For many years, Bliss collected wool from local farms and delivered it to spinners and weavers in their cottages, then took the yarn to Swinbrook mill, near Burford. Completing the cycle, he sold the manufactured cloth in Cotswold markets.

Bliss was not the only industrialist in the district to utilise wool. Some ten miles to the south of Chipping Norton was Witney, home to a thriving blanket-making industry. A similar distance to the south-east was Woodstock, renowned for its glove-making. It has been said that textiles were the cottage industry of the north-western corner of Oxfordshire, all dependent upon the abundance of good grazing land for the sheep which provided the ready-made supply of raw material.

Although the raw materials and means of manufacture were readily available, transportation within the area was difficult. Existing methods had remained largely unchanged for hundreds of years. The roads were poor, which meant that journeys were long and uncomfortable, tolls were levied by the turnpike trusts, and there was always a danger of attack by highwaymen out in the countryside.

In 1820, within the Cotswold area and that immediately to its east, only the Cheltenham district could be termed populous, with around 13,400 inhabitants, followed by Banbury with about 5,300. Of the intermediate towns and villages, Adderbury and its surrounding district amounted to around 2,300 souls, Bloxham 1,500, Hook Norton 1,400, Chipping Norton some 2,600, Stow 1,700 and Bourton around 750. Supporting the surrounding agricultural areas in the provision of goods and services, and often containing related rural industries, the Cotswold towns tended to be smaller than average. Villages were inhabited mostly by craftsmen and labourers, who found employment on increasingly-larger farms.

The age of railways was still some way off, and the advantages to industrial concerns such as that of Thomas Bliss would not yet have been recognised. But as the 19th century progressed, the potential of that mode of transport, along with its effect on society – cultural, economic and physical – began to make itself known. Most of the railway development in those early years was associated with heavy industry in Northern England and South Wales. The Cotswolds was somewhat isolated from these advancements. Then, in 1820, the region was woken up to the exciting possibility of a railway entering the district; the scheme in question was an early contender in the great railway race, the grandly-titled Central Junction Railway & Tramroad. This ambitious project was the brainchild of William James, a West Midland colliery owner of outstanding visionary character, who proposed a railway to link the Midlands with London, providing improved markets for his coal. The route, which was surveyed in 1819/20, was to run from Stratford-upon-Avon to Moreton-in-Marsh, then along the Evenlode valley, passing midway between the towns of Chipping Norton and Stow-on-the-Wold, each some five miles distant. Continuing through Oxford and Thame, the line was to terminate at Uxbridge. A short branch, leaving the main line near Shipston, was to serve James's colliery interests around Coventry. Only the first sixteen miles of line – between Stratford and Moreton – were built, incorporated as the Stratford & Moreton Tramway, and opened on 5th September 1826.

William James's cherished hopes of reaching London were never fulfilled, though subsequent proposals took advantage of the easy route and gentle gradients afforded by his scheme.

The railway network expanded modestly during the third decade of the century, whilst the next saw the London & Birmingham company setting out north-westwards from London, in 1837. The Great Western Railway reached Reading in 1840, and completed their line to Bristol in the following year. A move in the general direction of the Cotswolds was made by the Great Western in 1841, with a line from Swindon to Cirencester.

Although the railways were making advances across the country, there were still considerable distances between adjacent companies, and this ensured that the demand for horse-drawn transport was kept high. This was the era of the packhorse and carriers cart, which also saw the pinnacle in the development of that ultimate in horse-drawn passenger vehicles – the stagecoach. *Piggot's Directory* of 1844 gives us some idea of the stagecoach working at the time.

On weekdays, ten coaches stopped at Chipping Norton. The earliest, at 4.30 a.m., was the Royal Mail running from London and Worcester, which called at the Crown and Cushion. Fifteen minutes later came the Royal Mail to Birmingham, which stopped at the White Hart.

At 7.15 a.m., the *Blenheim* departed from the Royal Oak for London.

Travellers had a choice of two coaches at 11 o'clock: the *Sovereign* at the White Hart, or the *Tantivy* at Chapel House, both of which were routed via Enstone, Woodstock, Oxford and Abingdon to the railway at Steventon. Half-an-hour later, the *Day* passed through from Oxford to Birmingham.

At 4.0 p.m., the *Tantivy* stopped at Chapel House on its return to Birmingham, whilst the *Sovereign* called at the White Hart on its way to Worcester.

Passengers who missed the *Sovereign* could still take the *Day* to Worcester at 6.30 p.m. Finally, at 10 p.m., the Royal Mail arrived at the Crown and Cushion on its way from Worcester to London.

Coach routes therefore linked Chipping Norton with Enstone, Woodstock, Oxford, Wycombe, Beaconsfield and Uxbridge; northwards with Shipston-on-Stour, Stratford, Henley-in-Arden and Birmingham; and westwards with Moreton-in-Marsh, Broadway and Worcester.

There was no cross-country coach service linking Chipping Norton with either Banbury or Cheltenham, although local carriers did run to Banbury, as well as to London and Birmingham, and to many surrounding towns and villages.

The coaches *Sovereign*, *Tantivy* and *Day* did not go all the way to London; as described, their route took them via

Oxford and Abingdon to the new Great Western station at Steventon. A footnote to the stagecoach timetable indicated that 'The STEVENTON STATION is about thirty miles from Chipping Norton. From this station, passengers may proceed to London and intermediate places, and westward to Bath, Bristol, Bridgwater etc. There are regular conveyances to the above station in the preceding coach list.'

In 1844, the Great Western opened its branch between Didcot and Oxford, and Steventon was no longer the nearest railway station to Chipping Norton. The opening of the new station on the southern outskirts of Oxford had reduced the distance to about 21 miles, but more importantly, it had opened up the opportunity to provide a rail link into the heart of Oxfordshire. With its tentative introduction to the Great Western Railway at Steventon, interest in the possibility of railway communication increased as its routes were extended ever nearer. If railway travel was of some interest to the people of Chipping Norton, its haulage capability was of much greater significance to the commercial and industrial aspects of the region, and to the Bliss tweed manufacturing in particular.

The cloth-weaving industry had expanded steadily since Thomas Bliss had set up business as a full-time clothier. It had continued to grow under Thomas's son, William, who, firstly, established a factory in a redundant warehouse in New Street, and then, in 1810, purchased an old flour mill in the valley below the town. Utilising the Over Norton Brook which flowed past, he converted the mill into a water-powered factory for spinning and fulling.

William and his wife Hannah had at least eight children, though around 1830, for medical reasons, he stepped down from the business. William's eldest son, Robert, took over and ran it for a further eight years. In 1838, Robert decided to emigrate, leaving no obvious member of the family to take over the manufacturing company.

With its future now in the balance, and in some desperation, Robert's four aunts turned to his younger brother, also named William, to take over the business and keep it in the family name. William Bliss (II) was born on 16th September 1810, the third son and eighth child of William and Hannah. He was educated at Radley Academy, and when he reached the age of thirteen, was apprenticed to an uncle in London in the merchanting trade. He began his career in a lowly fashion, sleeping under the counter with the other apprentices.

William, however, knew nothing of the textile industry, and was reluctant to come to Chipping Norton to undertake the management of what was only a small family business with an annual turnover of slightly more than £10,000. There were only eleven employees at the mills, and their total weekly wage bill amounted to £17.

Using all their powers of persuasive negotiation, Robert Bliss and his aunts convinced William to return to Chipping Norton and take up the textile trade. So, in 1838, William took up residence in his father's house, which had been built onto the front of the Upper Mill in New Street. Also in that year, William married Esther Cleaver of Saffron Walden, by whom he had four children. One wonders how future events would have unfolded had William resisted his family's pressing request to take up the business; not only did his influence change the status of the town, transforming the rustic settlement into a positive and dynamic centre affecting the whole of the north-eastern Cotswold district, but his determination was also the primary driving force that brought the railway into Chipping Norton.

It was an inspired appointment. William Bliss brought to Chipping Norton not only his own growing acumen for business, but also his knowledge of the developments that were taking place in trade and industry elsewhere. This passage from *A Brief History of the Manufacture of Cloth in Chipping Norton* gives an illuminating insight into the mind of the man:

'Young William soon saw the possibilities of expanding his business if he could introduce new fabrics and methods. It was his ambition to get £10,000 in the bank, when he felt he would be independent of everybody. The fashion for more fancy tweeds, as opposed to broad cloths and Kerseys, was being developed by London merchants, notably by one James Lock of Regent Street.

'For seven years (1838–1845) James Lock and William Bliss joined forces and the result was a tremendous increase in trade for Chipping Norton.'

The horse clothing was developed, but to expand his business William Bliss had cloth manufactured for him outside of Chipping Norton. One letter to Messrs. Fox Bros. & Co. of Wellington, Somerset (who eventually became the parent company) dated July 1846 reads as follows:

Chipping Norton
Messrs. Fox Bros.                                    15th July 1846

Gents;

In addition to the 1000 yards Grey mix. Tartan (7), you now have on order, 500 yards of which you will fwd to London directed as before soon as ready – the other 55 pec. of 50 yards each 27" wide to weigh 9oz. (yard for 37") and to be exact to the enclosed pattern in colour and must be firm and well put together in the loom.

A sample piece to be forwarded in a week and the whole to be delivered in three weeks from this time – per Rail to London directed as before.

If the colour of the shoot you have on order for 1000 yards will do – you can use it for the above. The colour must not be at all more lavender than the enclosed pattern but must be an exact match. Now worsted yarns are lower I should hope you will be able to reduce my price ½d per yard to meet other houses that are supplying it.

Your most prompt and best attention to this order will oblige.

Gents
Your ob. Servant
Wm. Bliss

P.S. Since writing the foregoing I have in yours of the 13th with your sample for the piece of cloth and must say I am much disappointed abt. it. To prevent further delay you had better have the piece well buried and cold pressed, and sent off to London all possible despatch.'

In 1877, Bliss wrote:

'At this time [about 1838] … the manufacture of tweeds and shawls were introduced which afterwards led to become the staple and most important part of the trade.'

Following his learning of the practical duties, William Bliss applied his knowledge, being both manager and salesman.

The above account continues:

'From 1838 to 1851, his business grows by leaps and bounds, producing not only tweeds for trouserings, horse clothing of various descriptions, and shawls of various sorts, but also special rugs for the users of the new mode of travel, the railway train.'

As Bliss's business began to expand, he was faced with the technological problem of a power supply. For a number of years – certainly since the establishment of the Lower Mill in 1810 – the cloth manufactory had been adequately served by the available water supply fed to it from the Over Norton brook. Chipping Norton, unusually for a town its size, was not founded near a particularly abundant water source. Most of the supplies were springs within a band of limestone strata separating layers of clay along the hillside. During hot summer months, the brook flowed at barely a trickle. As the workload expanded, the mill's consumption of water did likewise; ever-increasing demands were made on the supply, and soon problems began to reveal themselves. In describing the situation at the Lower Mill, William Bliss reported that 'during four months of the year each year the mill was still for water power.'

Bliss was well aware of the benefits of steam power, and by 1851 he had begun to introduce this new technology into his mills. The completion of the Oxford Canal in 1790 had brought Warwickshire and Moira coal southwards to the canal basin at Banbury, just thirteen miles away. Even so, purchasing and transporting the coal required was costly, and the difficulties of conveyance were immense – there were steep gradients both sides of South Newington and down Wyckham Hill. Nevertheless, the inconvenience was a price that Bliss and manufacturers of similar mind were prepared to pay in order to keep abreast of the technological advances.

However, changes were on the way. A new railway was currently under construction and heading into the district. It originated in the Midlands and was to pass through Worcester and Evesham, entering the Thames watershed near Moreton-in-Marsh before gently descending towards Oxford. Its route was to pass through the valley of the River Evenlode, 4½ miles from Chipping Norton. The Oxford, Worcester & Wolverhampton Railway was a long time coming, and its drawn-out construction had provided the people of Chipping Norton with plenty of time to think about the benefits and disadvantages of having a railway passing through – besides the obvious talking point of whether or not it would be finished at all. Undoubtedly, some were anxious about the new technology; after all, there was danger involved. Perhaps others harboured a greater fear of the change that the new would bring, understandably reluctant to give up traditional ways established and unchanged over hundreds of years. Others may have broadly welcomed the railway, recognizing its advantages to society.

Finally, for a few like William Bliss, the steadily-advancing construction and its army of navvies sharpened an already certain resolve that the continuing prosperity of their town depended upon being connected to the railway system. Now, for the first time, there existed the means to bring direct communication between the town and the outside world. Importantly, coal and other freight would be transported quickly and at a much-reduced rate of carriage, whilst travel times would be reduced, and business responsibilities would expand. The coming of the railway into the district would also change society; social limitations, for so long an accepted norm, would cease to apply as townspeople and those in the locality would be enabled to travel quickly and efficiently throughout the country.

*'Top Side', Chipping Norton, and the Town Hall c.1848.* CTY. GREEN PASTURES NURSING HOME, BANBURY

# CHAPTER TWO
# THE CHIPPING NORTON BRANCH
## 1845–1863

THE 1850s were a period marked by contrasts. It was an era of imperial colonialism, and Britannia dominating the waves. 'Dark, satanic mills' hugged the valleys in the North of England, children laboured, brown drinking water came from the standpipes in London, and the Thames smelled. The year 1851 – the mid-point of the nineteenth century – also marked the period of the greatest optimism in Victorian Britain. It was the year of Prince Albert's Great Exhibition in Hyde Park, and of the Crystal Palace – Joseph Paxton's glorious celebration of possibilities in glass and cast iron – which housed it. The decade also saw massive technological advancement; that most powerful device, the steam engine, and its mobile derivative, the steam locomotive, were in full production.

This period was popularly termed the 'Railway Mania'. With hundreds of miles of iron rails being laid down throughout the land, the fastest and most efficient transportation system known was steadily transforming the environment. One of the lines caught up amongst all this frantic development was the Oxford, Worcester & Wolverhampton Railway, which, since its authorisation in August 1845, had been beset with difficulties. The effects of its problems, evidenced by its stop-start construction, were plain to see. But the bulk of the problems and their causes remained unseen. As it was, a legacy of bad management, the effects of a grossly-inadequate estimate for construction of its 90-mile length, together with difficult relations with the Great Western Railway (who had made an agreement to lease the line in perpetuity), had seriously damaged the OW & W's reputation.

Two dominant problems originated in the company's 1845 agreement with the Great Western. In the first instance, soon after the authorisation, the estimate for construction was amended from the original £1½ million to just under £2½ million. The Great Western duly amended the lease agreement between the two companies to stipulate that the GWR would guarantee the OW & W to a sum not exceeding £2,500,000, with interest of 4 percent. When the OW & W Board met and discussed the terms, they understood that the Great Western's guarantee was 4 percent on an unlimited sum – or hoped that it was – and presented it as such to the shareholders. All went well for the next three years until, in the grip of a recession in 1848, the OW & W were forced to curtail their expenditure and stop work along the line. Now the Great Western's guarantee became public knowledge, and when the OW & W approached them for assistance, the Great Western refused. Various attempts to bring about a resolution failed, including arrangements put forward by the OW & W to lease a section of the line upon its completion on favourable terms to the Great Western, and the intervention of the Railway Commissioners to mediate, but the Great Western would not move.

Various changes in the early 1850s, including a new issue of shares, a change among the board of directors, and the opening of the first short section of the route near Worcester, brought a degree of optimism. Meanwhile, at the Oxford end of the route, a positive step had been taken with the opening of the Great Western (Oxford & Rugby) line from Millstream Jct., Oxford to Banbury on 2nd September 1850, over which the OW & W trains were to run the three miles between Wolvercot Jct. and the new Oxford station on the western outskirts of the city. The line at this stage was broad gauge.

In January 1851, after the contracting firms of Peto & Betts and Treadwells had been appointed, the company believed itself to be sufficiently buoyant to declare the intention to continue on an independent footing, and therefore avoid suffering wasted negotiations with other companies. The gap between the GWR and the OW & W widened. Soon, other companies began to take an interest in the OW & W, amongst them the London & North Western and Midland Railway Companies, who like the Great Western, were all looking to expand into other territories. The outcome was an agreement whereby the OW & W would allow the L & NW (the Buckinghamshire Railway, from Bletchley to Oxford, which had been opened in May 1851) direct access to their line at Yarnton.

This action highlighted a second problem relating to the agreement with the Great Western back in 1845 – that of gauge. To the railway user between London, the South Midlands and the West Country during the mid-nineteenth century, the issue of gauge was of some importance. Two recognized operating gauges prevailed in the area: the 4 ft 8½ in 'narrow' gauge, and the Great Western's dedicated broad gauge of 7 ft 0¼ in. Broad gauge was the unique feature of the Great Western Railway, used by Isambard Kingdom Brunel in the construction of the main line from London and Bristol between 1838 and 1841, and subsequently on other routes connected to it. However, its proven advantages of stability, speed, comfort and increased payload were not sufficient to convince everyone that the broad gauge should be universally adopted. The broad gauge system was of course incompatible with the surrounding 'narrow' gauge railways, requiring passengers, and more significantly, goods, to be transhipped on a journey where a change of gauge occurred, causing great inconvenience. Understandably, the Great Western sought to extend their broad gauge network as deeply as possible into the territory of 'foreign' systems, thereby maximising their investment. The OW & W had provided the Great Western with an opportunity – by virtue of the running rights that the GWR would hold over that line – to extend the existing broad gauge out of Oxford and obtain a foothold in the Black Country.

Under the enabling Act of 1845, the OW & W was to be a broad gauge railway throughout, though with mixed gauge (broad and narrow in combination) northwards from a point just to the south of Worcester. However, the OW & W did not consider the laying of broad gauge to be a matter of priority, particularly around the northern part of its line where use of the 'narrow' gauge was influenced by the requirements of local industries. In a proof, which was to be given by one Captain Hickman, the reasons for the preferred use of the 'narrow' gauge were laid out:

> Captain Hickman will state
>
> that he is a magistrate for Stafford and Worcester – he resides near Stourbridge and close to the line of the OW and WR.
> that he has extensive fire clay and coal works.
> that the narrow gauge is the gauge which is most convenient for the South Staffs mineral districts.
> that almost all witness' traffic goes to the north, consequently the narrow is the only gauge of benefit to him.
> that witness would not lay down the broad gauge into his works.
> that this is the case with a great many other mineral owners.

Evidence such as that given by Captain Hickman served to persuade the OW & W that the 'narrow' gauge was the best option at the northern end of the line; further, the agreement made between the OW & W and the London & North-Western proved the value of that gauge on the southern section, too. The Oxford Worcester & Wolverhampton, interpreting the Act of Parliament for their own ends, readily – and illegally – laid down 'narrow' gauge rails over the southern section in addition to a minimum amount of the broad, though with clearances to provide for further broad gauge.

As may be expected, the Great Western were irritated by the outright flaunting of the Act by the OW & W. One cannot avoid thinking that on the part of the OW & W, this may have been, to some extent, a deliberate reaction against past failures. However, in responding to a later memorial given by the Great Western, the OW & W summarised the reasons for laying the 'narrow' gauge in the south, stating that the directors …

> '… during the summer of 1851 … could look for no aid or friendly co-operation from the Great Western Railway Company on terms satisfactory to their Proprietors, and it was therefore determined not to rely solely on the broad gauge system in their traffic arrangements. The railway was consequently laid out as a mixed gauge line … of sufficient capacity for a double line on the mixed gauge, but to lay down ready for opening one line of mixed gauge rails.'

Some twelve miles north-west of Chipping Norton, the course of the OW & W line descended from the Cotswold Hills onto the Vale of Evesham, in the course of which it was to pass through the half-mile length of Mickleton (later, Campden) tunnel. It was here that another battle was taking place.

From the outset, the tunnel had been a constant source of trouble, and work had been suspended on it during 1849, soon after a heading, or horizontal passage, had been carried through, and a little brickwork at either end completed. Two years later, work began again, but soon halted when a

dispute broke out between the OW & W and the contractor. The company decided to seize the workings and hand them over to the new contractors, Peto & Betts, but the tunnel contractor, Mr Marchant, kept his man there on guard. Following some minor clashes, Brunel, who was at the time preoccupied with early developments on his steamship, the *Leviathan* (later, *Great Eastern*), soon arrived on the scene with an army of navvies, intent on taking whatever measures were necessary. After consultation with two magistrates, who had in the meantime been called by the contractor, Brunel decided to delay the onslaught until the next day.

Early the next morning, Brunel's army confronted Marchant's reinforced body of navvies with a view to taking the workings, but the magistrates, supported by a large body of armed police, read the Riot Act, and violence was avoided. This was, however, only a prologue, for Peto & Betts then began to collect its workforce from all points of the compass, including other locations along the line, to gather at Mickleton in order to convince Marchant that further resistance was futile.

So, on that Monday morning in late July 1851, battle was joined. In the process, a few heads and limbs were injured, though no fatalities were recorded. As the morning wore on, Brunel's army was continuously reinforced by Peto's men until some 2,000 of them faced Marchant's navvies. It became clear to Marchant that he could no longer hold out in the face of these overwhelming odds, and agreed to consultations with Brunel; arbitration was decided upon. The conflict had been defused before the arrival of troops, who had been called for by the overstretched police, and the seriousness of the matter was subsequently played down.

In May 1852, the section between Evesham and Worcester was opened for traffic; again, the line was narrow gauge, but with provision made for the broad. The GWR had previously lodged a Bill of Restraint against the laying of 'narrow' gauge between Evesham and Abbott's Wood Jct, Worcester, which was to have been broad gauge only. The OW & W responded by stating that a mixed gauge would be laid, by the addition of the third rail, for which moneys had become available. Nevertheless, the OW & W continued to lay only the 'narrow' gauge. Once more, the Great Western responded with a Bill of Restraint to Chancery on the construction of further 'narrow' gauge north of Wolvercot until the broad gauge had been completed.

During the winter of 1851–52, construction on the railway in north-west Oxfordshire was under way. This was a phenomenon which the rural communities were totally unprepared for, and the villages were thrown into turmoil as hundreds of navvies descended on them. The son of J.W. Lockwood, the rector of Kingham, vividly recorded the event:

> 'The railroad which joins Oxford with Worcester, passing through the Rectory glebe, was being constructed, and hundreds of navvies found a lodging here. They were a strange, rough lot, such as one might expect to meet in a new gold or diamond field abroad. The village constables

were powerless to stop any disturbance which they chose to make, and our chief safety lay in their getting high wages for piece-work, so, as a rule most of their buoyant spirits were consumed in a praiseworthy direction. But when the snow lay deep upon the ground in Winter and work was stopped, they passed most of their time in the public houses, from which they would at length emerge well primed for mischief. It was at such a time as this, when late one night we were startled by a loud hammering at the Rectory door accompanied by shouts outside, and my father, who was reading by the fire, started up, closely followed by my brother and myself. Somewhat rashly, the door was opened, when a stalwart navvy attempted to effect an entrance, cheered on by comrades from below. My father was about to collar the man, when I handed him an oaken hat-stand which was near, and then all three of us, using this engine of war as a battering-ram, drove it straight against the waistcoat of our assailant, and sent him flying down the stone steps much faster than he came up. Seeing this, and noticing that a crowd of men were coming on, I flew upstairs, and in less than no time handed my father the loaded gun which he always kept in his bedroom in those troubled times. Then the navvies, seeing ours was a formidable stronghold to attack, prudently withdrew, contenting themselves with a burst of boisterous laughter at the discomfiture of their mate.'

The process of construction continued slowly, and the line was opened in sections as each was completed. By the end of 1852, construction work over the Wolvercot and Evesham section was well advanced and had been almost completed by the spring of 1853. The opening of the line was announced for 21st April, but following engineering problems, the event was postponed until 7th May.

Captain Galton, the Board of Trade Inspector, duly visited the line, and found that the broad gauge was unfinished in several places, though the 'narrow' had been completed. Broad gauge loops had been provided at four intermediate stations, though with seven for narrow gauge traffic; at completion, Great Western broad gauge traffic would not therefore be physically prevented from using the route between Oxford and Evesham. Nevertheless, another postponement was announced.

However, despite the further delay, the decision was made to celebrate the opening on the previously-announced 7th May. Stations along the route were decorated with flowers, flags and evergreens to welcome the train conveying representatives of the OW & WR, which ran on the 'narrow' gauge line from Dudley to Wolvercot Junction, at which point the change was made into a broad gauge train for the last three miles along the Great Western into Oxford. Crowds turned out at the stations, where local bands inevitably played 'See the Conquering Hero Comes' despite the steady downpour of rain that continued all day.

When the broad gauge line was completed, along with some repairs, at the end of the month, the section between Wolvercot and Evesham was once more ready for inspection by the Board of Trade. On 2nd June, Captain Galton visited the line and duly inspected the works, riding in a broad gauge train; it was the only known occasion that a broad gauge train ran over the entire section. Galton sanctioned the opening of the mixed gauge single line as two traffic sections, with one pilotman over the ten-mile length between Wolvercot and Charlbury, and the second between Charlbury and Evesham, a distance of thirty miles; clearly the traffic flow was envisaged to be light.

The broad gauge Oxford & Rugby Railway had been converted to the mixed gauge northwards from Oxford station during the previous autumn, and the OW & W trains were now able to gain access from Wolvercot Junction into Oxford.

Meanwhile, the L & NW's Bill for a connection from their Buckinghamshire line to the OW & W route at Yarnton, four miles to the north of Oxford, was passed, and became an Act. This success gave the OW & W the prospect of a direct connection to London via Bletchley, and offered an alternative to the despised Great Western's route.

On 4th June 1853 the Oxford, Worcester & Wolverhampton Railway finally opened its line throughout to the public, with running operations in the hands of a contractor. The OW & W had received some new locomotives from Hawthorns, and had previously acquired or borrowed others from various sources.

Great interest was generated throughout the district as villagers gathered upon the bridges and at the lineside to watch the first trains pass through. This was, of course, something quite new to them, and the people of Chipping Norton were given ample choice of where to observe the event. The nearest stations at Charlbury, Shipton and Adlestrop were each six miles distant, though the closest point was at the bridge carrying the Kingham to Bledington road over the railway, within sight of Bledington Mill, where perhaps a number of inhabitants from those villages had also gathered. This bridge bore no features to distinguish it from any of the other country road bridges along the route; however, within a few weeks of opening, the people of Chipping Norton began active discussions with the OW & W to build a railway into their town, and the point at which the road to Bledington crossed the railway was to be its junction – an unassuming starting point for what eventually became the Banbury & Cheltenham Railway.

## THE NEED FOR A BRANCH

News could travel with surprising speed in Victorian England. When the report confirming the Oxford, Worcester & Wolverhampton Railway's Enactment of 4th August 1845 reached the people of Chipping Norton, they wasted no time in responding to it. Two weeks later, on 20th August, they made the first approach to the company in the form of a Memorial through Abram Rawlinson, the mayor of the town. The script has not been discovered, but the response by the OW & W directors was cool, and read: 'Subject will be duly considered at proper time'.

Of those who were interested in a railway connecting with the OW & W, William Bliss had the most to gain by it, being the largest employer in the district. The strong case – which he prepared – in support of a proposed railway was put before the OW & W Directors in a draft letter dated December 1845, stating:

'That he carries on business as a woollen manufacturer at Chipping Norton [where] the manufactory has existed … for quarter of a century.

'The principal article of manufactory is horse clothing, horse blanks, tilting for wagons, shaws and tweeds. (sic)

'He has two mills and in his works he uses both water and steam power. Until within the last five or six years he has been deterred from using steam power in consequence of the high price of coals.

'On some occasions his water mill has been stopped for months at a time for want of water.

'The Inconveniences experienced from this cause in the interruption of trade – and the opportunities of increasing this trade at length make the use of steam power absolutely necessary.

'The present high price of coal prevents him using coal to a greater extent than absolutely necessary to keep pace with his demand. If he could procure coal at a lower rate, he should greatly increase his consumption – and in all probability to the extent of putting up another or a larger engine.'

Bliss went on to discuss his existing coal suppliers:

'The Derbyshire Moira coal, the Wedgbury from near Dudley, and the Bedworth from Coventry, all…conveyed to Banbury by canal – and thence by wagon. The cost of conveyance, a distance of 12 miles, is 6s 8d per ton.

'This great cost compels him to purchase the most expensive coal in order thereby to get the greatest amount of strength out of the same weight of coal… The gross price paid by him including carriage is 26s 8d per ton for the best and 20s to 23s for the inferior qualities.

'By… the proposed Railway which will pass within about four miles of his manufactory… he would be enabled to get the Staffordshire coal at a price of about 15s.

'He is of opinion that he should at once progressively increase his consumption of coal from 250 to 350 tons per annum.

'The Railway would be the means of introducing a superior description of coal for general consumption at a price ⅓rd lower than that now – and would lead in his opinion to a greatly increased consumption.'

Bliss demonstrated that the goods manufactured at Chipping Norton were supplied to places as far afield as London, Oxford, Bristol, Exeter & the West, Evesham, Worcester, Wolverhampton, Birmingham, Liverpool, Manchester, Scotland and Ireland. He conveyed by road to Oxford, Worcester, Wolverhampton and Birmingham, and to London and Liverpool by train from the stations at Oxford and Birmingham respectively, the cost of conveyance to Birmingham being 2s per cwt.

'The proposed Railway will give him a Railway communication with all the places he has named.

'He calculates the saving he should thereby effect at about ⅓rd of the present cost.'

Another advantage was accessibility 'to the places from which he obtains his raw materials…London, Oxford, Wellington, Bristol, Kidderminster, Stoke Prior near Droitwich, Birmingham and the North.'

He then referred to an alternative proposal relating to the London & Birmingham Railway, and objected to the fact that

'his nearest point would be Banbury, a distance of 13 miles by a road without any public conveyance. This line would give him no communication with the important markets of Bristol, Exeter and the West, Worcester & Wolverhampton.'

In defending the OW & WR proposal he opined that 'the wool grown in his neighbourhood would command a better price upon the opening of the railway.'

'He was heard at a Public Meeting at Chipping Norton held in the month of April when resolutions in favour of this line were passed without a dissentient voice – and the opinion then expressed is, as far as his knowledge extends, still the general sentiment of the town.'

Sometime during the next twelve months, support for the proposed OW & W route was modified into a resolve to establish a branch link from that line into Chipping Norton itself.

In the Minute Book of the OW & W dated 26th January 1847, there is a reference to a 'Memorial from the inhabitants of Chipping Norton and Neighbourhood recommending a Branch Line to that Town'. The OW & W dismissed the Memorial with a politely worded and thoroughly evasive reply:

'The Board are aware of the importance such a Branch would be of; (sic) and it should receive due consideration.'

There is no further reference to the matter in subsequent minutes, so it is reasonable to infer that the Directors thought that little consideration was due to such a scheme. The ambivalence of the OW & W must have been irritating to the people of Chipping Norton, but they did not give up. On 23rd September 1847, William Bliss wrote to William Lewis, one of the Directors of the OW & WR.

Dear Sir,

On my return today I hoped to have found a line or two from you informing me what decision (if any) was come to at your meeting last Tuesday respecting the result of the survey which you made of this part of the line last Monday week.

I now trouble you with this to enquire how we had better proceed to bring the matter fairly before your Board – it appears to [me] that as we have already addressed two Memorials (signed by very respectable Inhabitants of this Town and Neighbourhood) as well as [a] letter to your Chairman and a letter to Mr. Brunel it now only remains for us to appoint a deputation to wait upon and press our interests upon your notice and I shall be glad if you will let me know what will be the best way and fittest time to do so.

We are determined if possible to have Railway communication with the Town and if you are not willing to give it us the sooner we know it the better as we shall then at once proceed to open a negotiation with the London and North Western Interest at Banbury who have already made some overtures to us.

Seeing that Chipping Norton is the most important place you will have on your line between Evesham and Oxford (a distance of 36 to 38 miles) our tonnage being about 3,500 Tons annually I cannot think that you will consult your own Interest by letting this Town and Neighbourhood fall into the hands of your opponents which it most certainly will if you do not give us a Passenger's Station at Bleddington Mill. A Station at Addlestrop Gate and Shipton Bridge will be of little or no service to us and instead of leaving our interest in the hands of Local Directors I wish you and a few others of the Directors would visit this Town and see what interest we have to offer, or if you can make an appointment with your Chairman to receive a deputation we shall be glad to wait upon you at any place or at any time.

Waiting the favor of a reply to this,
I am,
Dear Sir,

Yours truly

W. Bliss

P.S. You must bear in mind that we are the connecting link between your line and Banbury and that there is only 17 miles of rail wanted to connect the Wash with the Bristol Channel or the East and West Coast of this island which I think may ultimately be of great importance.

W. Lewis Esq.

Although the directors of the OW & W had not recorded receiving the second Memorial from Chipping Norton, and had clearly not discussed the request from the respectable inhabitants of the area at their previous meeting, it might be expected that they would take William Bliss's letter seriously, if only because of an explicit threat that Chipping Norton might enter the London & North Western Railway's network. William Bliss's interest in developing a railway link is made clear by his reference to the tonnage (presumably coal) that Chipping Norton was consuming, and his implied criticism of 'Local Directors' must have referred to Robert Beman at Broadwell, who alone had a personal knowledge of the district. Bliss's letter was read and discussed on 5th October 1847, and duly transcribed into the company's Minute Book, but the official reply was still unhelpful:

> 'The subject of the Site for the Station on the Line in the neighbourhood of Chipping Norton has been carefully considered, and....after personal inspection by the Chairman and Officials of the Company the opinion of the Board is that the sites fixed upon are the most eligible and proper to meet the wants and the convenience of the district generally.'

The opinion of the Board was almost certainly ill-founded, as the directors could have had little idea of the determination and pertinacity of William Bliss. They had enough problems of their own with the local aristocracy, and even for them they were not prepared to make any particular concessions. Lord Northwick and Lord Leigh of Adlestrop were putting pressure on the company to make special provisions for their respective estates; Lord Northwick and Lord Redesdale were demanding a station on the Paxford Road, with a promise that one train each way every day would stop there; Lord Leigh of Adlestrop Park insisted that, on a signal, first class trains should stop at Adlestrop and take up and set down passengers for Adlestrop House. By March 1848, the company was not to be pressurized into making such provisions: they recorded that Lord Leigh's 'proposal is so objectionable that it cannot be conceded.'

However, by 1848 the OW & W was no longer in a position to consider expansion; the company was finding itself hard pressed to maintain even the nominal construction work that still continued.

For the next 3½ years, from 1848 to 1852, there is no record of any petition being made from Chipping Norton.

William Bliss, however, was discovering success in a different direction; at the Great Exhibition of 1851 he showed various tweeds, kerseys, trouserings, shawls etc. One shawl especially made and shown, was presented to Queen Victoria herself. At this Exhibition, his firm was awarded medals for its tweeds and shawls, the award being couched in these terms:

Hyde Park, London 17th Oct 1851
Exhibition of Works of all Nations
Bliss – William, Chipping Norton, Oxon (270 Class 12 and 15)
Shawls made from different materials and of Great Merit for the adaption of new articles of tissue, such especially as the Viouna, which is here shown to great advantage. He is an enterprising manufacturer of Great Merit.'

These shawls were 'beautifully soft and withal [at the same time] durable'. The best known were 'the Himalayan Shawls and rugs, with a hand raised ripple effect on the surface'.

At the same time, Bliss was expanding his business. He was reported as 'building a power loom shed and carding room with machinery driven by a steam engine of the old beam type' in the Upper Mill, and he filled it 'with carding engines and looms to turn out 100 pieces of Tweed and 100 pieces 6/4 Military Serges for soldiers' trousers and also tweed making a return of about £100,000 a year.'

In April 1852, construction of the line in the Evenlode valley to the west of Chipping Norton was probably showing signs of rejuvenation, and the town was prompted to approach the company with a third Memorial, also in April, though the reply – that the company had neither the power nor the funds – was inevitable. This was countered by a letter from the mayor of Chipping Norton, who proposed the construction of a tramroad from the town, south-westwards to a junction on the OW & W near Bledington. The company's response is not on record.

Towards the end of that year, yet another approach was made to the OW & W from Chipping Norton, and this further Memorial was read to the Traffic Committee, consisting of Directors of the Company. The Committee responded that it was still not in a position to entertain a branch, but that it would consider a station at Bledington Bridge, five miles south-west of the town. This Memorial appears also to have been referred to the Land & Works Committee, for in its Minutes, it is recorded that the company was fully sensible of the need for a branch to Chipping Norton, but was not in a position to proceed.

By the end of 1852, construction work was well advanced on the section between Evesham and Wolvercot Junction, doubtless watched with some frustration by the townspeople.

On 2nd June 1853, the Inspector made his first official journey between Evesham and Wolvercot and back with his broad gauge engine and carriage, and sanctioned the opening of the line to the public.

At around the time of the opening of the line through to Oxford, the people of Chipping Norton made their last formal approach to the company. William Bliss and Henry Field Wilkins led a deputation to the OW & W Board to request a station at Bledington Mill. This, like all previous approaches, was rejected. The company sent representatives to Chipping Norton to explain the reasons for their decision.

Meanwhile, the townspeople made the best of their situation. The much-needed supply of coal for the Bliss manufactory was now available, being carried from the new station at Shipton-under-Wychwood, six miles distant. Adlestrop and Charlbury stations were approximately the same distance, but Shipton was preferred. For passengers, Shipton also became the main station for the locality, and an omnibus service ran twice daily in each direction between the station and Chipping Norton. This certainly improved the transport situation considerably, but was far from ideal as the journey involved horse-drawn haulage over an unsurfaced turnpike road, and included the steep climb up Shipton Hill.

## TURNING POINT

Bliss knew that the only lasting solution lay in the provision of a station at Bledington Mill, just to the south of Kingham village, and beside the River Evenlode. From that location, a shallow valley led directly to Chipping Norton, which made possible a branch railway into the town, four-and-a-half miles away.

The turning point came in 1853, about two months after the opening of the main line. Having discussed the situation, William Bliss and William Simpkins Hitchman, a brewer with a business in the town, concluded that all obvious means to secure a branch had been attempted and exhausted. Bliss could not see a way forward, but Hitchman suggested the possibility of the townspeople funding and building the railway independently. Bliss was cautious; he had built up his cloth manufactory on tried and tested principles, and was not convinced that the line would pay. However, he did not dismiss Hitchman's suggestion. Bliss then met John Fowler, the OW & W engineer, who gave him precise instructions on how to approach the business of branch railway construction. Bliss and Hitchman then began to persuade other tradesmen and professional people of the town to support the project, whilst Fowler made preparations.

In a letter dated 22nd August 1853, John Fowler wrote to the OW & W Solicitor, James Burchell, of Burchell & Parson, and enclosed a letter from William Bliss. Fowler asked the solicitor 'to draw up a sort of Subscription Contract that he may get the signatures of his friends to it…', adding 'I think we should give them all the encouragement we can.'

He then referred to the present situation for the people of the town using Shipton Station: 'I discussed with him [Bliss] the best means of having Chipping Norton recognized on the line, and we agreed that 'Shipton and Chipping Norton Road Station' at the Shipton station would be the best mode of accomplishing it… Recognition will have some effect in attaching them to us.'

From these tentative beginnings, the Chipping Norton branch was born. At a public meeting in Chipping Norton town hall in August, a Railway Committee was appointed to make all requisite arrangements to obtain permission and rights, and to carry out the construction of the branch railway. It was resolved that the subscription list referred to the Directors by John Fowler on William Bliss's behalf be opened to raise that proportion of the capital required from public sources. The estimated cost for constructing the railway was £8,000 to £10,000, but this more than doubled after detailed discussions with the OW & W. William Bliss was Chairman of the Committee, Abram Rawlinson represented their legal interests, and William Rolls, secretary, was to prove invaluable to the project. Amongst those involved were:

Abram Rawlinson, attorney
Weston Aplin, attorney
Tilsley (& Wilkins), attorney
Henry Field Wilkins, attorney
Thomas Keck, rope and sack manufacturer
Thomas Hopgood, chemist and druggist
Rolls & Kimber, drapers and tailors
Samuel Guy, farmer
Jacob Loveland, grocer and tea dealer
Thomas Hopgood, surgeon
John Henry Kingdon, wine and spirit merchant
John Ward, carrier

Other people quickly started to show an interest in the project, and three days after the meeting was held, various parties had subscribed a quarter of the required amount. One of the subscribers was James Haughton Langston of Sarsden House, about four miles from Chipping Norton, who owned some three miles of the land through which the railway was to pass. Langston was MP for Oxford City between 1841 and 1865, and was therefore able to exert considerable influence. 'Squire' Langston had been negotiating for a setting down and pick up point on the OW & W main line, but given the company's responses to previous concessions requested by local landowners, his chance of success was remote. However it is worth noting the minutes of the meeting of the OW & W Traffic Committee held at Worcester on 20th November 1852:

'A letter was read from Mr. Varden relative to a siding near Sarsden. Resolved that Mr. Lewis and Mr. Busby with the Superintendent call upon Mr. Langston and ascertain the amount of traffic likely to be put upon the line to and from the point where the siding is required.'

This facility on the OW & W main line was never built. However, some time after the opening of the Chipping Norton branch, a siding named Sarsden was provided on that line, and because Langston had requested a private setting down and pick up point, the origin of Sarsden Siding has popularly, but not conclusively, been attributed to him.

By the end of October 1853, the *Oxford Journal* was able to report that all the shares had been taken, and that various landowners had come forward 'very handsomely' in offering the required lend at a cheap rate. William Bliss reported this success to the company, only to find his spirits dampened by the news that a further £2,000 was required. However, this sum was quickly raised.

As the year drew to a close, the relevant parties, in great earnest, got down to the serious business of building a railway. At five minutes past ten on the morning of 30th November, the plan and section of the Chipping Norton branch was deposited for public inspection by John M. Davenport, Clerk of the Peace for Oxfordshire.

In representing the subscribers at Chipping Norton, Abram Rawlinson wrote on 7th November to Messrs Burchell & Parson, the OW and W solicitors:

Dear sirs,

In reply to yours of the 4th inst I have to inform you that the Parishes of Chipping Norton and Churchill are the only two thro' which it is intended that the branch shall pass, but it will run very near the Parishes of Kingham, Cornwell and Salford which should therefore also be inserted – all in the County of Oxford. I have been hoping to receive a copy of the resolution of your Directors.

On 12th December, Abram Rawlinson received the notices from the OW & W solicitor, Burchell and Parson, and replied:

'The notices arrived this afternoon and are now in course of being served. In examining them with the Book of Reference I found one or two omitted which I thought would have been enclosed and I have therefore thought it expedient to make a list of all the parties named in the Book of Reference for whom I have not received notices in order that you may compare it with your list of notices posted. The notices to which I particularly refer as not having been sent are for J. H. Langston, Esq, whose country seat (Sarsden House) is only 4 miles distant and for Stephen Clark, who commonly resides in this town, although he has another residence at Batsford, near Moreton in Marsh. I should like to know what has been done about these. If they have not been served, I will do the needful on your sending the notices.'

The notices were listed:

John Barford
Thomas Beesley
Thomas Carpenter
James Coling
John Evans
John Gillam
John Goddard
Anna Theodoria Heynes
John Matthews
Henry Hall
John Taylor
Stephen Clark, Chipping Norton
William Arkell
Charlotte Goodman
The Rector of Witney (Patron)
Willoughby Richard Crofts
The Dean & Chapter of Gloucester
J.H. Langston Esq., Sarsden House
Mary Minchins
Revd. George Crabbe Rolfe

## On 23rd December, William Bliss wrote:

My dear sir,

You will be pleased to hear that I have succeeded in getting the Parliamentary Contract signed for the whole £10,000, with the exception of [?your] £1000 to Mr. J. Lawrence Grisewood's £500.

This Contract will be sent on Monday next to Messrs Burchell & Parsons for the signatures of Mr. Peto, yourself to Mr. Grisewood, whose signature can be obtained any day at the Stock Exchange. You promised to see that Mr. Peto's signature should be obtained in due time.

I am disappointed to find that Mr. J. Langston has not settled the point about taking the extra traffic… and has not got the Company's Seals – Be so good as to see to this at the next Committee meeting to get it finally settled.

I shall also be glad to hear that Mr. Peto signed the Contract to make the Branch and forgo all expenses for £24,000.

Hoping to hear from you soon – that the agreement is finally settled and Sealed.

The official estimated cost of constructing the railway was £24,000, valued by John Fowler, the OW & W Engineer, which included land purchase and contingencies as stated in William Bliss's letter. The OW & W was authorised to issue 2,400 additional shares of £10 each, called 'Chipping Norton Branch Shares'. The shareholders were nominated on attachment to the Act.

On 20th December 1853, John Fowler and Samuel Morton Peto both signed separate Branch Subscription Contracts for the construction of the Chipping Norton Railway. John Fowler subscribed shares to the value of £1,000, and Sir Morton Peto, with far-sighted optimism, subscribed the astonishing sum of £14,000.

Other main supporters were James Haughton Langston and William Bliss, who had agreed to subscribe £1,000 and £1,200 respectively. The other 43 subscribers made up the balance with sums of between £600 and £20, mostly of £100 or less. These people represented a considerable number of trades and professions, many of which would be expecting to benefit directly from the proposed railway.

Also on 20th December, Abram Rawlinson wrote to the OW & W solicitors, Burchell & Parson, requesting clarification of the essential legal processes:

Dear sirs,

Chipping Norton Branch

When must you have the Parliamentary Contract back, bearing in mind that you will have to obtain the signatures of W. Peto and W. Fowler?

By what time must the 10 percent Deposit be collected and when must it be paid?

Can you send me a copy of the draft proposed agreement between the Company and Messrs Peto and Betts? And what has been the result of the question raised by W. Thorpe as to the mode of calculating the ⅓rd of extra profit as proposed by Mr. Peto?

PS. The Parliamentary Contract arrived yesterday.

Obtaining all the subscription signatures was not an easy task. In returning the Parliamentary Contract, Abram Rawlinson wrote to the solicitors, Burchell & Parson, on 27th December:

'with 3 signatures only for me to obtain, namely Mr. Peto, Mr. Fowler, Mr. Grisewood - the two former are well known – the latter has recently purchased an estate near this place called Daylesford, but he is a member of the Stock Exchange and is to be found there and you will not, I expect, find any difficulty in obtaining his signature.'

The notice of the Bill was published in November, and its preparation took place during the early part of 1854.

In a letter dated 19th January, from an unidentified source representing the OW & W Chipping Norton Branch subscribers, Messrs Burchell and Parson were asked the following:

Oxford Worcester and Wolv'tn Ry (Stratford)
do     do     (Chipping Norton)

Before the meeting of Parliament on the 31st instant it will be necessary that we should have the names of two Members who will take charge of each of these Bills. Application should be made for their consent to the printing of their names on the back of the Bills – the Speaker requiring that in no case shall a Member's name be used without his permission.

On 24th January, Abram Rawlinson was able to report to Messrs Burchell and Parson:

Mr. Langston is quite willing to have his name placed on the back of this Bill in conjunction with that of either of the gentlemen you have named.

I return you one of the copies of the Bill with some observations we send back. The most important alteration that the Subscribers desire is that which I have made in the 29th December and which is in accordance with the arrangement. Perhaps my wording may not be quite correct but it will acquaint you with my object and ought to be carried out, as it has been sanctioned by your Board.

The Bill was amended accordingly. The most important alteration was that of Clause 25, defining the profits for the branch. Elaborate accounting requirements were set out, the purpose of which was to identify the receipts arising solely in consequence of the construction of the branch in the three years following its opening; and to ensure that no doubts should enter into the figures, the clause stated the requirement that the 'traffic manager for the time being of the Great Northern Railway Company' was to determine the amount of the receipts.

James Haughton Langston was responsible for guiding the Bill through Parliament, but details of working arrangements still continued to be finalised.

The line was to be constructed in the standard ('narrow') gauge, the OW and W's proposed mode, a matter which would not endear the company to the Great Western Railway.

In a letter dated 24th January 1854 to John Fowler, Abram Rawlinson raised the sensitive issue of the proposed rate of working expenses for the construction work, writing:

> Are you aware that by the Bill it is proposed to fix 50 per cent as the amount of working expenses? You know that it has been twice agreed by the Directors that it should be cost price – not exceeding 50 per cent, and it might therefore to be so by the act – Does Mr. Peto sanction the proposed variation from those times?
>
> It is also proposed to limit the calls to £4 a share at not shorter intervals than 8 months – and not more than ⅔ths of the whole in one year. Will not Mr. Peto want the money quicker than this in making the line?

It is not clear how these matters were resolved. However, on 3rd February 1854, Abram Rawlinson wrote once again to the OW & W solicitors to enclose the affidavit of a Mr. Hartley 'in proof of the execution of Contract'.

On 11th March he sent 'copies of statements of traffic as furnished … by Mr. Bliss the manufacturer, which is expected to pass over the branch, and then follows the evidence of different Witnesses in support … of this statement'. Unfortunately the statements have not been discovered.

The Bill was going through the usual Parliamentary processes and all was looking well. At this point the Great Western Railway entered the scene in an attempt to thwart the outcome for the Chipping Norton branch, lodging a petition against the Bill. With barely disguised bitterness, the Great Western launched into a fierce attack against the OW & W, beginning with their failed obligations towards the Great Western. Not surprisingly, the focus of the issue was the question of gauge.

In a draft version, they reminded the honourable House

> 'That it was not only the intention of the parties who promoted the Oxford Worcester and Wolverhampton Railway but also of Parliament in sanctioning the line that it should be worked upon the said Gauge as and in connection with your Petitioner's Railway as a through line of communication between London and Wolverhampton.
>
> 'That contrary to the intention of the legislators in passing the Oxford Worcester and Wolverhampton Railway Bill the Oxford Worcester and Wolverhampton Railway Company have constructed and opened and worked their Railway on the narrow gauge so far as the same is completed and opened for public traffic while they have only complied with the requirements of the said Act in laying down a single line of rails on the broad gauge upon which single line of rails it is impossible with safety to carry on any portion of your Petitioner's Traffic.'

Now the Great Western turned their attention to the Chipping Norton branch. The point of their objection was

Clause 13, which stated that the 'Railway may be constructed on broad gauge if Company think fit'. The petition went on:

> 'That it is desirable that further provision should be made for enforcing the due fulfilment of the intentions of Parliament in passing the said Act of 1845 and further that the branch Railway to Chipping Norton by the said Bill sought to be authorised as well as the main line and branches now authorised should be constructed and completed with a double line of rails on such gauge so as to admit of their being worked continuously with your Petitioner's Railway.
>
> 'That unless provision is made for enforcing such objects the Oxford Worcester and Wolverhampton Railway Company will construct the branch railway to Chipping Norton on the narrow gauge instead of on the broad gauge to the great injury and detriment of your Petitioners and the public'.

With this last paragraph the Great Western neatly summarised the problem with its competitor, the OW & W: they did not want the Chipping Norton branch to be constructed in standard ('narrow') gauge, because they wouldn't be able to work or earn revenue from it. By now, it must have been clear to the Great Western that the OW & W had no intention of revising this arrangement; they had determined to work with the standard gauge.

In its petition, the GWR continued:

> 'That there are various clauses in the said Bill prejudicial to your Petitioner's interests and that if the said Bill be allowed to pass other provisions ought to be inserted for the protection of your Petitioner's rights.
>
> 'That your Petitioners are informed and believe that the said line is open to many objections in an engineering point of view – that the line is badly selected and that the estimate is insufficient and cannot be supported by evidence.
>
> 'That the Preambles of the said Bill is incapable of proof.
>
> 'Your Petitioners therefore humbly pray your Honourable House that the said Bill may not pass into a Law as it now stands …'

The paragraph referring to clauses 'prejudicial to your Petitioner's interests' does not clarify the nature of the 'other provisions', which, it was suggested, should be inserted for the protection of the GWR's rights, so unfortunately it is not possible to be certain what the Great Western had in mind. However, it is likely that they were looking for concessions from the OW & W.

What is clear is that the Great Western Railway had lost this particular 'Battle of the Gauges' to the OW & W. The petition may well have been their last serious attempt to overturn it.

Any remaining doubts over gauge or the viability of the proposed railway or the resolve of the people of Chipping Norton were finally and decisively laid to rest when the Bill passed into law and duly received Royal Assent on 31st July 1854. The resultant Enactment was entitled 'The Oxford, Worcester and Wolverhampton Railway (Chipping Norton Branch) Act, 1854' (17 & 18 VICT – SESS.1854).

After nine years of persistent determination, the railway had at last become a reality. The people of Chipping Norton could consider themselves very privileged not only to have the services of one of the eminent engineers of the day, namely John Fowler, but also one of the most successful contracting partnerships in the form of Messrs Peto & Betts. However, it was the single-minded and expansive vision of

William Bliss which brought together the 'respectable inhabitants' of Chipping Norton to make it happen.

William Bliss and Sir Samuel Morton Peto had much in common. They were both of the same age and social class, they both achieved success and prosperity in the expanding industrial world, and both were devout Christians closely associated with the Baptist denomination. In addition, they shared a path, along with other similarly-enlightened individuals of their generation who promoted the advancement of their society.

Sir Morton Peto had many projects to his credit, including the building of Nelson's Column in Trafalgar Square, London, to constructing the first public toilet in 1852. Peto built and founded the Bloomsbury Central Baptist Church, which opened in December 1848. He had a reputation for being a very good employer, and was especially concerned for the moral and spiritual welfare of his workforce, providing, as far as it was possible, lodgings in the towns and villages close to the construction workings. Where Peto's workforce was employed, a significant expansion of nonconformist church buildings quickly followed.

At the time the Chipping Norton branch project was beginning, Peto was engaged in the construction of the Balaclava Railway, a military line serving the war effort in the Crimean Peninsula. Indeed, many of the wagons used on the construction of the Chipping Norton Railway went on to be used there. In addition, he refused to take remuneration for building the Balaclava Railway, an action which earned him a baronetcy in 1854.

Like William Bliss, Peto was generous in character, and a businessman whose practice was motivated by an 'enlightened self interest': that which was of benefit to him would also benefit others. He was prepared to risk an investment in anticipation of a return; during the construction of the Oxford, Worcester & Wolverhampton Railway, he invested much of his own money in order to see it completed. As has been revealed, in a remarkably brave gesture, he offered to subscribe shares to the value of £14,000 to construct the railway to Chipping Norton; had he not done so, it is difficult to imagine how the railway could have been built.

John Fowler was born at Wadsley Hall, Sheffield, in 1817, and was only 36 when he surveyed the route of the proposed Chipping Norton branch in 1853. Later, he went on to design docks and works associated with river improvements. He acted as Consulting Engineer in Egypt and was knighted for his services (KCMG) in 1885. His last and most famous achievement was in the design and construction of the Forth Bridge (1882–1890) jointly with Sir Benjamin Baker, for which Fowler received a baronetcy. He died In 1898.

With the combined contracting abilities of Peto & Betts and the guiding hand of John Fowler, work began in an excellent spirit on the construction process.

The Describing Works in the Act referred to it as:

'A Branch Railway from and out of the Oxford, Worcester and Wolverhampton Railway, at or near the point in the parish of Churchill, in the County of Oxford, where the said main line is crossed by the public carriage road from the village of Churchill, in the said county of Oxford, to the village of Bleddington, and terminating on the Great Common in the parish of Chipping Norton, in the county of Oxford, at or near the turnpike road leading from Chipping Norton aforesaid to Moreton-in-the-Marsh.'

By the time the Royal Assent had been given on 31st July 1854, constructional plant had already been delivered to the point of the junction with the main line, and work was started three weeks later. As with the construction of the OW & W main line two years earlier, an influx of 'navvies' arrived at the town, numbering some three to four hundred, and all seeking accommodation. Married quarters were provided at Chipping Norton by the contractor in the form of substantial huts on Elmsfield, north-west of the proposed station site. The foundations of these remained visible for many years after their eventual disuse. The name of the tavern in New Street known as 'The Three Goats' was changed to 'The Railway Inn'.

To speed the construction of the line, work was carried out day and night, during the latter with the aid of huge fires to illuminate the works.

The whole process of arranging to construct a railway line was much simplified if landowners along the proposed route were agreeable to the sale of their land for the purpose. One such offer to the 'Committee appointed by the subscribers for promoting a Branch Railway from the Town of Chipping Norton to the Oxford, Worcester and Wolverhampton Railway' read thus:

'I beg to state that I am willing to sell for the purposes of the proposed Branch Railway such portions of land of which I am owner as may be required at the rate of £100 per acre in full satisfaction of every claim in respect of severance, compulsory sale or otherwise. And that I shall be satisfied with level crossings over the said Railway to connect any land of mine which may be severed.'

Contrary to the Great Western's petition stating that the line was 'open to many objections in an engineering point of view', the works were extremely light, with just one substantial cutting at the point where the line was to terminate in the area later known as Hawkyard's Common, and the diversion of several watercourses which accumulated in marshy ground at the proposed station site.

Owing to the unchallenging nature of the formation, progress was rapid.

It was all the more unfortunate, therefore, that while events were going so well for the OW & W, a problem occurred at one of the three level crossings. This drew considerable unwelcome public attention, to a degree that the company did not anticipate, and that actually threatened the very opening of the line.

The clauses relating to the proposed level crossings in the Act were stringent, and necessarily so, as level crossings were (and are) a potential danger to all users, and the occasionally fallible human element plays an important role in their use, a situation which does not equally apply to bridges. The company were clearly aware of the importance of the methods by which the proposed roads were to be crossed, because a late change in the Bill was the substitution of the proposed level crossing over Road No. 37 for a bridge; this was the Kingham to Bledington road, which crossed the railway at Trigmoor, close to Kingham Mill. This change may well have been necessitated by the sharp curve from the junction station onto the line of the proposed branch. This bridge was known as 'New Line Bridge', to differentiate it from the recently-constructed 'old' bridge, which took the Churchill to Bledington road over the OW & W line immediately to the south of the proposed Junction station site.

Clause 12 of the Act defined the crux of the matter. It stated:

> 'Provided always, That it shall be lawful for the Board of Trade, if it shall appear to them necessary for the Public Safety, at any Time either before or after the Works hereby authorized to be made, or any of them, shall be completed and opened for public Traffic, to require the Company, within such Time as the said Board shall direct, and at the Expense of the Company, to carry any of the herein-before mentioned Roads either under or over the railway by means of a Bridge or Arch instead of crossing the same on a Level, or to execute such other Works as under the Circumstances of the Case shall appear to the said Board the best adapted for removing or diminishing the Danger arising from any such level Crossing.'

The problem occurred on Road No.5, at Swailsford, which went from Chipping Norton to Stow-on-the-Wold via the village of Cornwell, and was known locally as the 'Old London Road'. At this time, the road was an operating turnpike with its own turnpike Trustees. Difficulties over the proposed crossing had been simmering for some time. During the period of the Bill's readings, attention had been drawn to it by 'The Dean and Chapter of Gloucester (who have one small field that is crossed).' They were the corporate Rector of Chipping Norton, and patrons of the benefice.

In a letter dated 11th July, sent by Abram Rawlinson to Messrs Burchell and Parson, the OW & W stated that the landowners concerned were in 'active opposition' of the level crossing. He continued: 'The subscribers have informed them that the Bill contains a Clause enabling the Board of Trade to compel the erection of bridges where it appears necessary.'

The subscribers then sought clarification as to what the clause implied:

> 'What is proposed as to the Clause that I pointed out as not being in conformity with our agreement with the Company? This the subscribers are anxious about, and also that we should be furnished with a copy of the terms of agreement.'

Opposition among local people continued to mount, and they alerted the OW & W. Included in the Minutes of OW & WR Traffic Committee for 1st September 1854 was:

> 'Read Mr. Rawlinson's letter 2842 with observations in reply to the memorial to the Board of Trade of parties objecting to a level crossing of the Chipping Norton and Stow Road by the Chipping Norton Branch Line. A copy of the observations was directed to be sent to the Board of Trade.'

The nature of the objection is not clear, but may have related to sighting difficulties around the curve in the direction of Chipping Norton Junction.

Nevertheless, the OW & W did not take their protagonists' views seriously and continued to build the crossing,

whilst the foundations for the crossing lodge were already in place. On 11th May 1855 the Board of Trade ordered the company to substitute the crossing with a bridge; work on the lodge was duly suspended, but the company were reluctant to comply with the directive. After all, the construction process of a bridge would be a serious obstruction to existing road traffic! Thus, in time-honoured fashion, the OW & W stalled, but the problem did not go away.

Local people rallied to support the company, and eighty people signed a protest to the Board, claiming that the small amount of traffic on the road would not warrant a bridge. The problem generated considerable argument, running to fifteen pages of correspondence; arguments and counter-arguments flowed back and forth between the two sides, all faithfully recorded in the reports of the Railway Department of the Board of Trade. The OW & W found themselves under increasing pressure from Chipping Norton Borough Council to build the bridge.

After Lt. Col. Yolland of the Board of Trade had inspected the site and considered the situation, he concluded that until the requirement for a bridge was met or guaranteed, the opening of the line for passenger traffic could not be sanctioned without danger to the public.

The situation at Swailsford continued in gridlock, with neither side giving way, and an opening date looming on the horizon. Meanwhile, the construction of the remaining sections of line continued, and were completed.

The line was ready enough to allow goods trains to run from 1st June 1855. However, in July, the morning branch goods train failed to stop, and crashed into some trucks at Chipping Norton Station.

On 26th July, the Board of Trade inspection took place, and Lt. Col. Yolland observed that sufficient land had been purchased and the works constructed to allow for doubling later.

The single track was laid to the 'narrow' gauge, using 65lb (some sources say 60lb) double-flanged edge rail in lengths of 21 and 24 feet, secured with standard cast iron chairs to larch sleepers measuring 8ft 6in x 9in x 4½in spaced 3 feet apart and ballasted with gravel.

The dispute over the bridge at Swailsford by now had reached the eleventh hour. Finally, on 8th August, just two days before the official opening, the OW & W gave way to the Board of Trade, issuing an undertaking that the bridge would be built.

How the crossing operated while goods trains were running is not known, but there must have been a railway policeman employed to guard the approach, and this arrangement would have held true for passenger/mixed trains once the line was opened until such time as the bridge was built.

The day before the railway officially opened for passenger traffic, the *Banbury Guardian* issued this report:

> 'Chipping Norton: The Railway
> '9th August 1855
>
> 'The opening of the branch railway for passenger traffic is to be celebrated by a public dinner in the Town Hall tomorrow. Sir S. M. Peto, Mr.

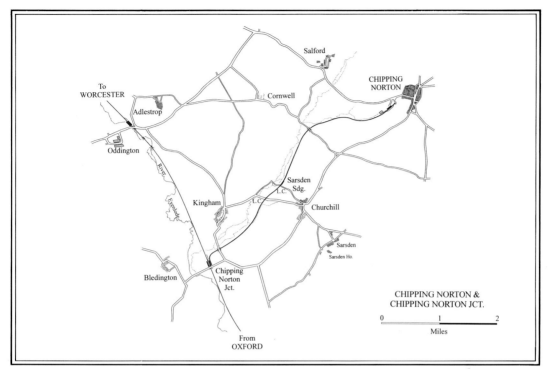

Salford
To WORCESTER
Adlestrop
Cornwell
Oddington
CHIPPING NORTON
River Evenlode
Sarsden Sdg.
L.C.
Kingham
L.C.
Churchill
Sarsden
Sarsden Ho.
Bledington
Chipping Norton Jct.

CHIPPING NORTON &
CHIPPING NORTON JCT.

0        1        2
Miles

From OXFORD

Fowler (the engineer of the company) and the Directors of the Oxford, Worcester & Wolverhampton Railway are expected to be present. A handsome piece of plate will be presented to W. Bliss Esq., Mayor, for his indefatigable exertions in promoting the interests of the Town. The tradesmen have consented to close their shops at noon. Arches of evergreens will be erected from the Station to the Town Hall. The workmen who have been connected with the formation of the rail will be supplied with a dinner, and a varied programme of amusements will be provided for the evening.'

## A GRAND OPENING

The opening of the Chipping Norton branch of the Oxford, Worcester & Wolverhampton Railway took place on Friday 10th August 1855, and the occasion was celebrated with exuberance in a truly grand style that only the Victorians could accomplish.

Ten years almost to the day had passed since Abram Rawlinson delivered the first Memorial to a deeply-troubled and seemingly ambivalent Oxford, Worcester & Wolverhampton Railway. Now, with the branch railway completed, the people of Chipping Norton were in jubilant mood.

The dawning of the day was greeted with the loud pealing of the bells of St. Mary's Church. Initially, most of the attention was focused on Chipping Norton Junction where, as Lt. Col. Yolland reported, 'a house has been erected for the issue of tickets to passengers'. The junction, as described by the *Oxford Chronicle and Berks and Bucks Gazette*, 'was gaily decorated with evergreens and banners, besides other indications of pleasure appropriate to the occasion. A few yards from the platform was erected a triumphal arch, in evergreens and flowers, surmounted with the arms of England, France and Turkey, indicative of the firm alliance that now

subsists between these countries.' The latter referred to the Crimean War, 1854–56.

The report continued: 'A considerable number of the inhabitants of the locality were congregated at the station.' Among them were almost certainly those resident at the Workhouse and 'poorer' classes who received 500 free tickets from the OW & W.

Shortly after twelve o'clock, a special train arrived at the junction, and the names of the dignitaries on board made an impressive list. These included Sir Samuel Morton and Lady Peto; Miss Peto; a Mrs. Kemp; a Miss Broadbent; Noel T Smith and John Parson (secretary and Deputy or Vice Chairman respectively of the OW & W), Richard Johnson (Director of the OW & W) and John Fowler.

A band played 'See the Conquering Hero Comes' as the train arrived, and there to meet the party were William Bliss, William Lewis, Alderman of Worcester, and G. H. Busby, these latter also Directors of the company.

The assembled group remained at the junction for forty-five minutes. As they greeted one another 'a small tank locomotive, named Eugenie', in honour of the French Empress, and 'gaily decorated with banners', was made ready to take the special train to Chipping Norton.

At 12.45, the train departed for the fifteen minute journey to Chipping Norton, where it arrived shortly before 1.0 'amid the cheers of a large assemblage of the inhabitants. The station house and its vicinity presented a very gay and animated appearance', the *Oxford Chronicle & Berks and Bucks Gazette* reported. A fairground had been set out complete with booths and stalls.

'The feeling of the whole town was of a very enthusiastic character. The whole of the shops were closed; flags were pendant from various parts of the Borough; the church bells rang a merry peal; a really very good brass band from Blockley played some inspiriting march or national melody during the day; and, altogether, the example set by this "independent" little place is one that not only does it infinite credit, but will we trust be followed by hundreds of towns situated within short distances from through lines of railway.'

The visitors left the station and proceeded to the residence of William Bliss, attached to the front of his Upper Mill in New Street. Here, in the sumptuous surroundings, was prepared the elegant luncheon, which was laid on for upwards of twenty guests.

WILLIAM BLISS

It was reported that after lunch the visitors were given a tour of inspection of the Upper Mill to see the steam engine, before returning to the railway again with a visit to see 'Mr. Bliss's new factory in course of erection near the railway station, where about two hundred and fifty men, women and children in his employ were provided by him with a substantial dinner, furnished by Mrs. Bishop of the Crown and Cushion Inn.'

A toast was enthusiastically proposed for the health of Sir Morton (he chose to be called 'Sir Morton') and Lady Peto after which the Baronet gave a heartfelt speech. He began by praising the good working relations 'which appeared to subsist between the employer and the employed in Chipping Norton', particularly those at Bliss's factory. He added that what he had been told about the contrasting 'healthiness of appearance and general character' of Bliss's employees, 'who presented such a healthy, smiling and good humoured appearance', compared to their counterparts in the north of England, was found to be true. Peto finally turned his attention to the railway, congratulating the employees on the success of the opening event, and ended by expressing 'a hope and confident belief that all classes, from the highest to the lowest, would be benefited by it, either in a greater or lesser degree'.

Sir Morton Peto received hearty adulation on the conclusion of his address.

Several further toasts were proposed, and following a kind word of appreciation from William Bliss, the visiting party of

dignitaries was whisked away amid loud cheering from the factory workers.

The highlight of the day's events was the public dinner in the town hall, which, according to the local press, 'was neatly decorated for the occasion.'

Various banners were suspended. *The Oxford Chronicle* reported that the banner at the head of the room bore the inscription 'Unrestricted Commerce, the People's friend.' Confusingly, a separate account describes two banners and transposes the inscription, one of the banners reading 'Unrestricted Commerce' while the second flatteringly states: 'William Bliss, the People's Friend'.

After the dinner, which was served at 3.0 p.m., Henry Field Wilkins, the Deputy Mayor, 'presented a very handsome silver salver and bread basket to the Mayor', as William Bliss had become, 'as a testimonial from his fellow townsmen, neighbours and friends, of their estimation of his... character and particularly with respect to the invaluable services he had rendered in carrying the Chipping Norton Branch line to a successful completion.'

William Bliss responded with a confirmation of 'his love of his native place, that during the seventeen years in which he has resided in it, everything had tended to strengthen his love and attachment, not only to the town, but also to the people.'

There followed the customary duty of presenting speeches and toasting the people who had made the railway possible.

John Parson, Deputy Chairman of the Oxford, Worcester & Wolverhampton Railway spoke first:

> 'The branch line in itself was not a very large work, or a very important undertaking to the public in general, but it was a sample, a pattern, a beginning of a very important undertaking; for if branch railways were to be formed all over England to places near main lines, then they must be made on the same principle as this branch, to be more fairly remunerative to the shareholders and the promoters, than railways in years past have been.'

Sir Morton Peto followed, explaining the circumstances by which he came to be involved, and the precedent now set for other branch lines to follow. As the *Banbury Guardian* reported, he explained that:

> 'The days were past when landowners could obtain extortionate prices from railways for land ... and when the promoters of lines were content to buy off the opposition of landholders by giving them any amount or accommodation works they required.
> 'Branch lines in this country were considered what was termed "suckers" and not "feeders" to main lines ...'

because, he said, they had been designed to protect traffic and annoy neighbours 'rather than ... developing the traffic of the districts through which they were constructed.'

He expressed his appreciation at the 'liberal-mindedness' of the landowners, saying:

> '... And here I must express my conviction that if Mr. Langston and the landowners in this district had not met you in good spirit, in a willing old English spirit and given their land for little more than an agricultural price, the line would have cost from £12,000 to £15,000 per mile.'

He concluded that branch lines like this would benefit the country through which [they] passed, give profit to the promoters and to the parent lines with which they were connected, 'and…would very largely…increase the commerce of our common country.'

John Fowler then launched into his inspirational speech:

'The commencement and carrying out to its present state of completion of the Chipping Norton Branch would be a little history in itself. It had

many phases. It sometimes looked promising and sometimes gloomy, and I am convinced that it would be a very interesting history, and perhaps a profitable and useful one to trace out in its various stages…'

He then made a comment at the expense of the Great Western, recalling their devotion to the broad gauge: 'There had been some talk about the GWR compelling us to lay

*The extent of the Bliss Manufactory, with Chipping Norton station in the centre. The scene is presented with false perspective to emphasise the prominence of the business in this c.1860 lithograph. A private horse-drawn tramway is reputed to have existed between Bliss's residence at top left and the terminus.*                    COLLECTION ALAN BRAIN

*Bliss's residence in New Street was built by his father c.1815. Typically, the mill owner's residence was attached to the factory. The house had no name, the letterhead simply stating 'New Street, Chipping Norton'. Bliss spent large sums of money improving the property. At the height of the firm's prosperity, it contained the finest features available, including a breathtaking inverted painted glass dish, set into the roof above the main stairway.*

AUTHOR'S COLLECTION

*The Bliss Tweed Manufactory Lower Mill, shortly after its completion in 1856. This view from the south features the railway in the foreground, with the cottages Bliss built for his workforce behind.* CHIPPING NORTON MUSEUM

down a broad gauge to Chipping Norton. They [the OW & W] did not see much harm in it, because they did not mean to do it.' He went on to mention some 'useless expenses which had been thrust on them', probably referring to the difficulties at Swailsford, and 'hoped that shareholders might be spared' any more 'useless expenditure in future.'

Fowler concluded by honouring James Haughton Langston, MP, who 'had taken great interest in the line and had spared no pains or labour, even when suffering from illness and could not leave his carriage, to further it in every way he could.'

William Rolls recalled 'the difficulties encountered concerning the branch line – legal, pecuniary, open and concealed – but they had triumphed over all of them.' He referred to objections made in relation to Swailsford bridge, and had 'not been prepared for the opposition which had long delayed the opening of the railway ... and from the high position in the State of the gentleman who had been the cause of it, they could not have anticipated his throwing difficulties in the way of a spirited little town.'

Why had they succeeded? 'The determination and the assistance of the professional gentlemen who had been connected with them and the unity of those concerned'.

At 5.30 p.m., Sir Morton Peto and the 'chief guests' left the town hall and travelled down to Chipping Norton station to board the 6.0 special train for London.

Congratulations continued to be expressed all round at the public dinner. Among the recipients were James Langston, the Mayor and Corporations of Banbury and Stratford, the landowners of the line and the Press, not forgetting 'the health of Mr. Wheeler, the stationmaster, and may he be speedily restored from the effects of his late accident'.

After the dinner, celebrations continued elsewhere. At the Unicorn, William Bliss entertained fifty masons employed

on the construction of the Lower Mill on the Common, railwaymen and porters dined at the Blue Boar, and the band and constables were at the Fox Inn. William Simpkins Hitchman's and Mr. Bickerstaff's men were treated to a supper at the Blue Lion, while the bellringers were at the King's Arms.

After the great opening day, the railway began to settle into its normal operating routine.

At the General Meeting of the Proprietors of the OW & WR company on 28th August 1855, the report of the Directors read:

'...the short branch line to the town of Chipping Norton was opened for passenger traffic on the 10th instant.
  'The shares created and issued, or to be issued, under the powers of the Oxford, Worcester and Wolverhampton Railway (Chipping Norton Branch) Act of 1854, which shall be existing at the time of such conversion, and in respect of which the whole money subscribed shall have been paid up, shall, when and as the same respectively shall have been fully paid up, be converted and consolidated into a Chipping Norton Branch Railway stock.'

There were inevitable teething problems, and a number of items remained to be completed, including building the bridge at Swailsford. The Engineer's report of 18th August 1855, signed by John Fowler, referred to:

'... sidings at ... Chipping Norton Junction have been finished and are available for the various purposes for which they have been designed.'

On 30th August 1855, the *Banbury Guardian* published this report:

'The Chipping Norton Railway, as far as the experience of the past warrants us to judge, the traffic on this line will be quite equal to, if it does not exceed the expectations of its projectors. Some slight inconveniences have been felt, but, on the whole, the arrangements of the trains (three up and two down per day) have been made with a view to afford the greatest accommodation to the public, and we doubt not that such modifications will be adopted as experience may suggest as best calculated to promote that end.'

Clearly the line was a great benefit to the people of Chipping Norton, particularly the tradesmen and industrial concerns such as Hitchman's Brewery, allowing the easy conveyance of freight, and for passengers there was now a direct rail link to Oxford and London.

By far the greatest advantages were felt by William Bliss, whose new 'Lower Mill', completed around 1856, was provided with access to the railway by means of a private siding from Chipping Norton station. Not only was Bliss able to obtain his much-needed supply of good quality, but cheap, coal to generate steam power, he also had a suitable means of distributing his finished cloth products.

The Chipping Norton line was provided with an early service of just three passenger trains in each direction. By January 1856, six branch trains each way were running, with the first and last running through to Shipton for main-line connections with trains that did not call at the Junction station. The first train of the day left Chipping Norton at 8.30 a.m. for Shipton, where it connected with the 7.0 a.m. express from Dudley, which conveyed through coaches to Euston (due 11.30 a.m., via Yarnton), and provided a connection at Oxford for Paddington (due 11.25 a.m.). The branch train made its way back at 9.15 a.m. from Shipton to Chipping Norton, having collected passengers from the 8.10 a.m. train from Oxford (with a connection from the 6.15 a.m. Paddington). The final train of the day left Chipping Norton at 6.55 p.m. for Shipton (7.15), returning at 7.40 p.m. with connecting passengers from the 6.45 p.m. Oxford (4.50 p.m. Paddington and 5.0 p.m. Euston through coaches) to Wolverhampton service. Branch trains were mixed from the outset. Trains operated from their own bay platform on the east side of Chipping Norton Jct. station.

From the opening, it is almost certain that the line was worked by one of the two small 0–4–2ST locomotives built by E.B. Wilson & Co. for the OW & W in 1853/5. These were Nos.35 and 36 (later GWR Nos.221 and 222), having 3ft 5in driving wheels and 3ft 0in trailing, and a weight of 13 tons 16cwt.

In January 1856, there were just four goods trains running on the main line in each direction, with the six mixed branch trains feeding and connecting with them. In the down direction ran three mixed goods and empties, with one dedicated coal empties as far as Round Oak. Two coal trains ran in the up direction, from Dudley and Fearnall Heath (Droitwich), and two mixed goods and coal. With the exception of one up train, all of these called at Chipping Norton Jct. to pick up or detach traffic. The calls were mostly brief, but one train in each direction called for longer: the 3.0 a.m. Dudley to Shipton coal was scheduled to work at the junction from 11.55 a.m. to 12.30 p.m., whilst its return trip, the 1.35 p.m. Shipton to Worcester goods and empties, called between 1.45 and 2.20 p.m. These two services probably handled most of Chipping Norton's coal and return empties, and goods to and from the north, attached as required to the branch's mixed trains. In the London direction, two of the main-line goods trains each

## CHIPPING NORTON BRANCH.

| STATIONS. | DOWN. | | | | | |
|---|---|---|---|---|---|---|
| | A.M. | A.M. | P.M. | P.M. | P.M. | P.M. |
| Chipping Norton ..........................dep. | 8 30 | 11 10 | 12 5 | 3 40 | 6 10 | 6 55 |
| Chipping Norton Junction ..................,, | 8 45 | 11 20 | 12 20 | 3 55 | 6 25 | 7 5 |
| Shipton................................arr. | 9 0 | ... | ... | ... | ... | 7 15 |

| STATIONS. | UP. | | | | | |
|---|---|---|---|---|---|---|
| | A.M. | A.M. | P.M. | P.M. | P.M. | P.M. |
| Shipton................................dep. | 9 15 | ... | ... | ... | ... | 7 40 |
| Chipping Norton Junction ..................,, | 9 25 | 11 25 | 12 25 | 4 0 | 6 35 | 7 50 |
| Chipping Norton ..........................arr. | 9 35 | 11 40 | 12 40 | 4 15 | 6 45 | 8 10 |

*Taken from OW&W timetable for January 1856.*

way ran to or from Handborough, for Yarnton and the L & NW route, whilst the remaining trip in each direction ran though to Oxford.

Although no goods services as such were shown in the timetables, it is possible that specials did run over the branch at times of exceptionally heavy traffic, where the regular trains would otherwise not have been able to handle the amounts to be moved.

The year 1859 marked the end of the special financial arrangements concerning the shareholders, when the OW & W entered into a guarantee to pay 4% per annum to the holders of branch shares. The separate accounts were then closed. Construction had cost £32,232, including purchase of the land, compensation and engineering work.

## THE LAST DECADE OF THE OW & WR

As for the Oxford, Worcester & Wolverhampton Railway, the opening of its main line in June 1853 was not the end of its story, but a beginning of sorts. At this point, it was a very incomplete railway. The southern section between Wolvercot Jct. and Evesham comprised long sections of single track in mixed gauge, with nine intermediate stations. 'Narrow' gauge passing places were provided at seven of these, but broad gauge at only four. Given the great lengths of single track, the line was insubstantial and difficult to operate.

Daily traffic over the line through the Evenlode Valley during the first summer amounted to a return goods train between Dudley and Handborough, the junction for the L & NW connection, and five passenger trains. Two passenger trains each way were run on Sundays.

Once opened, the company proceeded to extend the broad gauge as required by the 1845 Act, beginning in the summer of 1853 with the line between Dudley and Evesham. However, in true OW & W style, this was added only to the down line, with no passing places or sidings.

During that summer, the lines were also doubled over the four miles between Wolvercot and Handborough; this was mixed gauge, duly passed for traffic by Galton, and opened in November 1853.

Doubling was also carried out at this time on the five-mile section between Honeybourne and Evesham, but the second line was to the narrow gauge only, and its opening was refused on grounds of operational safety; with its usual contempt for Acts of Parliament, the OW & W nevertheless operated it. The OW & W's statement that the broad gauge on that section would be completed when additional capital was available made a nonsense of a previous assurance to Chancery that they had more than sufficient funds to complete the whole line to mixed gauge. The Board of Trade became suspicious of the OW & W when a timetable submitted to them for approval showed two trains passing on this unauthorised section, and took action to stop the illegal running; they now seemed to have the measure of the OW & W's underhanded behaviour, and kept pressure on the company until it eventually caved in and added the missing broad gauge rail, the section being opened as double track between Evesham and Campden in March 1855.

Meanwhile, further doubling of various sections occurred throughout the 1850s. Although the company's selection of gauge appears random, doubtless the OW & W applied its own logic to the process of deciding whichever gauge would be laid down for the second line of rails. The section between Charlbury and Handborough was completed in mixed gauge during August 1854, and was approved without conditions by the Board of Trade.

The determination of gauge on the OW & W was financially motivated, as indicated by the company's complaints to the Board of Trade of 'inadequacy of funds for further works'. The situation became so desperate that the company begged the BoT to sanction completion of the 'narrow' gauge line, following which the increased credit raised by operating it would enable them to raise the remaining capital to complete the broad gauge rails.

In April 1854, the connecting line between the L & NW's Buckinghamshire Railway and the OW & W at Yarnton was opened to traffic. As agreed with the L & NW, through passenger traffic between London (Euston) and Wolverhampton (L & NW) via Bletchley and the OW & W commenced, whilst that to and from Paddington ceased. This agreement was to be current for 21 years, though circumstances would change considerably before that time had elapsed. The GWR connection was maintained by traffic between Handborough and Oxford, and it was still possible to travel to and from Paddington by re-booking at Oxford.

A much-needed change of direction in June 1856 brought about a new Board, which included a Mr. Fenton as Chairman and Sir Morton Peto as his deputy; their attitude towards the Great Western was in great contrast to their predecessors, and the company now looked towards a more friendly relationship with its neighbour.

With OW & W finances showing signs of recovery due to an increased traffic income, the directors approached the Great Western in a spirit of settlement, though with the traffic agreement with the L & NW still current, they were not able to move far down the road to reconciliation. Nevertheless, a start had been made.

A long-running dispute over the charges levied for the use of the Great Western's Oxford to Wolvercot section by the OW & W was resolved in February 1858, and amongst a number of other mutually-approved changes, the Great Western for its part agreed to the removal of the broad gauge over the OW & W. Thus, the years of conflict came to an end.

Also significant for the traffic using Chipping Norton Junction was the doubling of the single line between Chipping Campden and Charlbury in August 1858. It was the last section of the OW & W to be so completed.

More friendly relations, this time with the Newport, Abergavenny & Hereford Railway, brought about an agreement to amalgamate, and also to purchase the Worcester & Hereford Railway; this became an Act in June 1860, whereby the two other companies were amalgamated in the Oxford, Worcester & Wolverhampton Railway, and the name for the three then changed to the West Midland Railway.

The West Midland Railway was now a company of some considerable size and standing, and from this time it appears that the new company began to have ideas of reaching London. During late 1860, it came to light that an old scheme to build a railway between London and Yarnton had been resurrected, backed not only by the promoters involved in the previous attempts, but also by the West Midland. When challenged by the Great Western, the West Midland denied any knowledge of or involvement in it, given that it would breach a recent agreement whereby neither the West Midland nor the Great Western would support a competing railway against the other.

Shortly afterwards, the West Midland complained to the Great Western that, as the Great Western was assisting the Wycombe Railway Company in a similar route via Thame and Oxford, which occupied the district through which the proposed Yarnton and London route would pass, they were also in breach of the agreement (though how this proposed rural branch was deemed to compete against the West Midland was unspecified). Fenton, the West Midland Chairman, wrote to the Great Western with an offer to withdraw the proposed Yarnton scheme if the Great Western did the same in respect of the Thame line, thereby admitting involvement. The Great Western declined, then demanded to know how the West Midland could abandon a scheme they had purported to know nothing about.

All was at last revealed. The West Midland was indeed heavily involved in this scheme to compete directly with the Great Western and the London & North Western in a bid to reach London, and made preparations to take the matter forward. The bill was duly prepared, but on the day it was to appear before the House of Commons, news came out of the blue that the Great Western and West Midland had agreed on terms for an amalgamation. The Yarnton & London bill was immediately withdrawn, and an agreement between the two rapidly effected. The original OW & W section was immediately leased to the Great Western, and running powers were granted over the rest of the West Midland. The West Midland was granted similar powers on the Great Western line between Oxford and Paddington, though the two effectively operated as one company.

With this, the agreement with the L & NW was abandoned, as it could not in any event be enforced by law. Trains continued to run to Euston until September 1861, and from then to Paddington.

This arrangement held until 1863, when the Bill for the full amalgamation was submitted; it took effect from 1st August that year.

During the nineteen years since the tentative beginnings of the Oxford, Worcester & Wolverhampton Railway, the entire face of the railway network across the British Isles had changed beyond recognition. Major centres of population were now linked – it was possible to travel between London and Bristol, Birmingham, Liverpool, Manchester, Glasgow,

Newcastle, Edinburgh and Aberdeen. Nevertheless, a large gap remained in the railway map in connections between the north-east and south-west of the country.

There had been moves to correct this: William Bliss had been in active discussion with the London & North Western Railway during 1855 about a possible branch link between Chipping Norton and the Buckinghamshire Railway at Banbury, which apparently the OW & WR would not sanction without a westerly connection to Cheltenham. The task was difficult; there was a considerable range of hills and deep valleys to cross before those places could be reached. Although the connection between Banbury and Cheltenham would not be made for another twenty-four years, by 1862 a move towards Cheltenham had already begun; an independent and determined company, following on from the success of the Chipping Norton branch, and called the Bourton-on-the-Water Railway Company, had taken up the challenge.

*Based on contemporary information, a speculative view, to the south-east, of Chipping Norton station in its final years as a terminus, after the addition of a wooden train shed in the mid-1860s.*
SEAN BOLAN

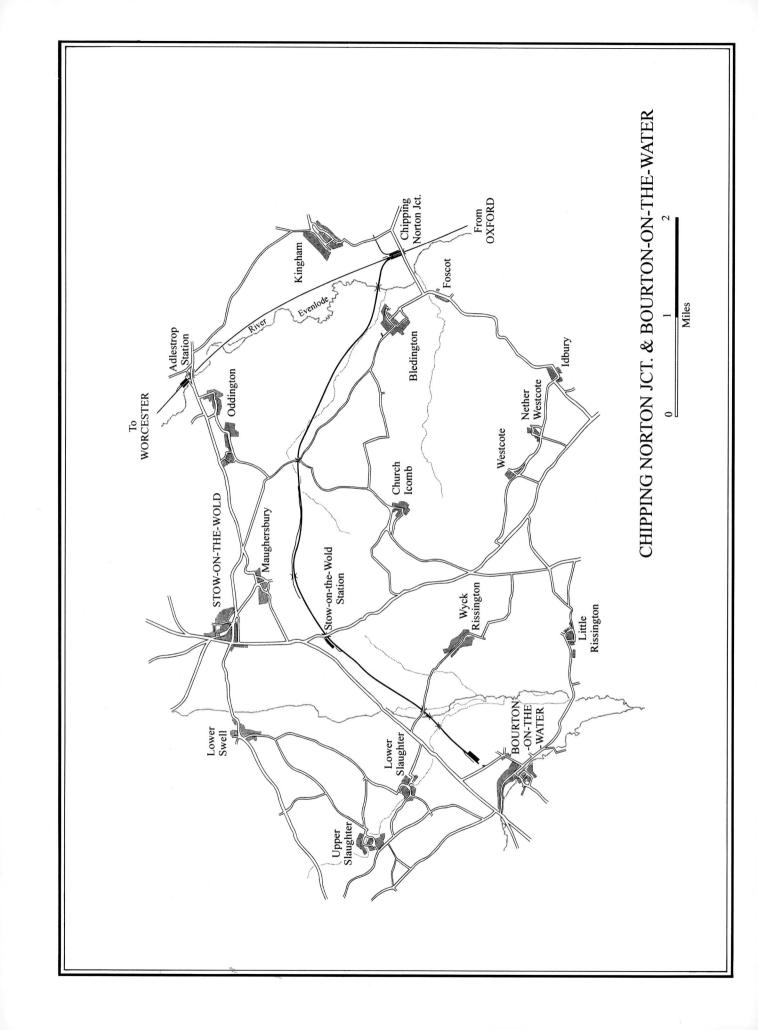

CHIPPING NORTON JCT. & BOURTON-ON-THE-WATER

# CHAPTER THREE

# THE BOURTON-ON-THE-WATER RAILWAY
## 1859–1874

THE Oxford, Worcester & Wolverhampton Railway's successfully-completed branch to Chipping Norton, along with its services and connections to Oxford, London, Worcester, the West Midlands and South Wales, had caught the imagination of the inhabitants of other small Cotswold settlements.

Chipping Norton's hard-won campaign to become connected to the railway system must have generated considerable interest throughout the local communities, and encouraged many to seek their own link to this revolutionary mode of transport. One such place was Bourton-on-the-Water, in Gloucestershire.

Bourton-on-the-Water is a village situated in the heart of the Cotswolds, twelve miles south-west of Chipping Norton, in the valley of the River Windrush, close to the ancient frontier line and Roman road, the Fosse Way. Today, Bourton is one of the most popular places on the Cotswold tourist trail, but in the 1860s it was a relatively isolated community of around 950 people, its charms still waiting to be discovered. *Pigot's Directory* described Bourton as a 'neat and genteel little village ... the clothing trade was at one period possessed by this place to a considerable extent; it is now nearly extinct. Here are two very large flour mills, which, in the business transacted in corn and malt, forms the principal trace here.'

As with most of the towns and larger villages in the district, Bourton possessed a full complement of trades and services, including two schools, two surgeons, an attorney, three taverns, two millers, two maltsters, and over forty other shopkeepers and specialist tradesmen covering an amazing variety of food, clothes, shoes, and household goods supplies, as well as farm and domestic services.

Situated partway between Bourton and Chipping Norton, and also alongside the Fosse Way, is the small town of Stow-on-the-Wold. Occupying a commanding position on a hill, some 300 ft above the valleys close to it, and with a population in the 1840s of around 2,000 people, Stow had grown up around the intersection of several roads, all branching out into the surrounding Cotswold region.

As with many small market towns, Stow traditionally held 'fairs' in addition to the regular market days. In the earlier part of the 19th century, Stow held its fairs in March, May and October for horses, sheep, cattle, cheese, cloth and blankets, in July for wool, and in December for cattle. The regular market was held on Thursdays.

Contemporary journalists visiting the small Cotswold towns had little good to say about them, or their prospects. A decade or so before the proposals for the branch lines appeared, *Pigot's Directories* for Gloucestershire had this to say of Stow-on-the-Wold:

'In respect to trade, it is a place of trifling importance; a little is done in the woollen business, and at one time it possessed some celebrity for the quality and number of shoes manufactured; but in this branch it is no longer noted.

'The general business is reciprocally maintained by its own inhabitants.'

This picture of an 'inward-looking' town was quite common in the period, when many traditional rural industries were fading from the scene in the face of increasing 'mass production' elsewhere.

Stow was not blessed with the same lines of communication as Chipping Norton, and no through coaches of any note served the town. However, there were local carriers with routes to London, Banbury, Birmingham, Burford, Cheltenham, Chipping Norton and Cirencester, though these wagons were considerably slower and rather less comfortable than coaches, being mainly for the conveyance of goods.

The railways were, in the 1840s, still rather distant. Pigot's presented the options available to the townspeople:

'The nearest stations are Cheltenham, 18 miles from Stow, on the Gloucester and Birmingham line, and Faringdon, about 23 miles distant on the Great Western line. From the former station passengers may proceed to Birmingham, and from thence to various parts of England; and from the Faringdon station to London and intermediate places; and westwards to Bath, Bristol and parts further west.'

'Faringdon' was the station at Faringdon Road, later renamed Challow, on the Great Western Railway's main line between Reading and Swindon. The branch to the town of Faringdon from Uffington was not opened until June 1864. A connection to the station from Stow was provided by the 'Little Wonder road coach', which left Moreton at 6.45 a.m., and called at the Unicorn 'every morning (Sunday excepted)'; it subsequently ran via Burford, Bampton and Buckland on its way to Faringdon Road.

In the late 1830s, a gaping hole in the railway network still existed between the major centres of the Midlands and the North, and the west and south-western parts of the country, though there were moves in hand to plug the gap. In November 1840, the Birmingham & Gloucester company opened their line between those cities, connecting Cheltenham with Gloucester in the process. A connection from Gloucester to Bristol was effected in July 1844, whilst Great Western traffic between Cheltenham and Gloucester commenced at the same time. The Great Western arrived in Gloucester from Swindon in May 1845.

The proposal for the Cheltenham and Oxford Railway of 1845 was the first major scheme to confront the topographic challenge of the Cotswold Hills. This railway was to branch westward from the Oxford, Worcester & Wolverhampton

Railway near Shipton-under-Wychwood, and follow a route across the Cotswolds to Cheltenham similar to that eventually constructed. There was no denying the advantage to the OW & W in giving a direct connection between the London & North-Western Railway on the northern out-skirts of Oxford and the Midland Railway's Bristol & Birmingham line at Cheltenham; the benefits to the commercial interests of tradesmen across the district would be considerable.

One of these tradesmen was George Mathews of Chipping Norton who, in his letter of support for the railway, described himself as a 'Grocer, Chandler and Provision Dealer'. His particular concern was the plentiful supply of good quality cheese. With a turnover of 'about twelve tons in the course of a year', George Mathews was hoping for a better means of communication with the national cheese markets. He explained:

> 'The Stow market is supplied from Gloucester, and the quantity sent has been for some time falling off. The quality of the cheese is also much deteriorated of late...[but] if the proposed railway were constructed it would open to witness the markets of Rugby, Leicester, Reading and Gloucestershire where the best description of cheese is sold...He is aware of the proposed Cheltenham and Oxford line, [and] that if that line were constructed in the connection with the present line it would open the Bristol market for groceries...'

However, the advantages offered by the railway were not only for traders like George Mathews – providing for the rapid and efficient conveyance of groceries such as eggs, milk, butter and flour – but for the whole of society, from the agricultural dealerships transporting livestock, to the recipient of a humble letter. The most important single advantage was probably in the conveyance of coal, which had been a slow and costly process by canal and road.

The inhabitants of those market centres which did not have access to railways began to make plans for them, whilst those that were already at the end of a new branch line, such as Chipping Norton and, following closely behind, Witney with its newly-authorised Witney Railway, were looking to extend to further markets.

William Bliss was interested in a potential connection with Cheltenham because it would give him a more direct route to another, new source of coal – South Wales – and importantly, increased accessibility and reduced journey times (and therefore costs of conveyance) both from the sources of his raw materials and to the outlets for his finished cloth products.

## A MODEST SCHEME

It is not clear how the proposal for a Bourton-on-the-Water railway came into being, but in the absence of recorded information, the likelihood is that the idea was discussed during casual and business conversation among similar-minded individuals. Of these, William Bliss, with his vision and experience, had the necessary leadership abilities to bring the project to fruition. The resultant proposal was to construct a branch line of six-and-a-half-miles from Chipping Norton Junction to terminate at Bourton, with an intermediate station at Stow. From the outset, this modest scheme was simply the first stage of a proposal to construct a railway that would reach Cheltenham, and give access to markets beyond it.

Towards the end of 1859, the proposals were sufficiently advanced to enable the Parliamentary Bills for this first stage to be prepared, and they were then advertised in the local press. On 26th November, Jackson's *Oxford Journal* placed this advertisement:

> 'BOURTON-ON-THE-WATER RAILWAY
> 'Notice is hereby given, that application is intended to be made to Parliament, in the ensuing session, for an Act to incorporate a Company for making and maintaining the railway following, with all necessary stations, works and conveniences (that is to say) A railway, commencing by a junction with the Oxford, Worcester and Wolverhampton Railway, in the parish of Churchill, County of Oxford, at the Chipping Norton Junction Station on that Railway... and terminating in the parish of Bourton-on-the-Water, in the County of Gloucester, in or near a field called "The Lower Coach Ground", in the parish and county last aforesaid, and in the occupation of Henry Wilkins...'

In the same journal, alongside this advertisement, was another, promoting two other railways: The Cheltenham and Northleach Railway, and by virtue of its extension, The Northleach and Witney Railway, the latter making an end-on connection with the Witney Railway, soon to be constructed, and providing a through route to its junction at Yarnton on the OW & WR. This railway was essentially a reworking of the Cheltenham and Oxford Union Railway, whose plans were deposited by the OW & WR in the Parliamentary session of 1853.

Also in hand were proposals by the Bourton interests for an extension to Cheltenham. The challenge facing the company was considerable; the railway would cross the expanse of the Cotswold Hills, rising to some eight hundred feet above sea level, and dropping down by two great steps into Cheltenham, six hundred feet below.

Anyone looking at a contemporary map of the region would have had no difficulty in realising the implications of these proposals. Were they to be constructed, the Northleach and Witney railways would provide a direct link between Oxford and Cheltenham, closely following the route of what is now the A40 trunk road, with a distance of some thirty miles between the two. The Bourton Company's proposal, including the extension to Cheltenham and utilising the existing section of the OW & W to Chipping Norton Junction, was some ten miles further. In a direct contest between the two railways linking these major centres, there was no doubt that the Northleach route was the clear winner.

How those involved in the Bourton Railway responded to these proposals is not known, but they would have felt uncomfortable had they read this letter from Lord Redesdale of Batsford, near Moreton-in-Marsh, which he appended to his copy of the Bills:

> 'I do not see how this line can pay. I understand that the Promoters avow it to be their intention, if the Bills, papers, so apply for an extension to Cheltenham, if this therefore is intended as the commencement of a line from the O.W.W to Cheltenham it ought never to go to Bourton on the Water and lose the elevation it has attained at the foot of Stow Hill, and make an angle by so doing. I would however advise the promoters to consider the whole question very carefully as to this line to Cheltenham.

'Do what they will, they cannot make as direct a line between that place and Oxford as can be made by Witney and Northleach, and when they have gone to the expense of going down the hills into Cheltenham and into the town and making a station there at a cost which I very much question whether the traffic they could get from the place would repay, the Witney and Northleach line by an extension of a few miles at a comparatively small outlay might join them at the foot of the Cotswold and take away the whole of the Cheltenham, Oxford and London traffic which the Company hope to secure. Such a result would be ruin to this company and also be materially injurious to the O.W.W. That Company has made mistakes enough already and I should be sorry to see them add another to the list. As I know this country pretty well, I have given my opinion on the subject thus openly, and am anxious that at all events the promoters of this line should not for want of proper consideration and taking a wider view of the possible contingencies than those who have not seen much of railway matters are apt to be contented with. I may of course be wrong, but I am afraid there is money to be thrown away here.'

Naturally, the promoters of the Bourton Railway didn't see the situation that way, and continued to develop their scheme. However, alternative proposals to reach Cheltenham across the Cotswolds did not go away, and indeed were to become extremely significant to the Bourton Railway Company, as will be seen.

The OW & W were also involved in the financial arrangements of the Bourton Railway. At the OW & W Board meeting on 19th January 1860, it was recorded that, 'the sum of £2,400 was authorised to be deposited in the names of Mr. W Bliss and two others in this matter by this company and an arrangement to be made for raising the money.' The two others concerned were Charles Barton and William Dolly Sylvester.

During the following meeting, in February 1860, it was resolved 'that a subscription of not exceeding £3,500 be made to this scheme'. The OW & W were at the time heavily involved in the final stages of discussions over the formation of the West Midland Railway, but still found time to consider the little company. This may have been a situation where the OW & W were manoeuvring so as to be able to exert some power over the smaller concern, in order to influence decisions.

The Bill was brought in by Sir Morton Peto and James Haughton Langston MP, it being stated that: 'Charles Barton, William Dolly Sylvester, William Bliss and all other persons and corporations who have already subscribed, shall be united into a company called the Bourton on the Water Railway Company.'

Several minor changes were made to the Bill (some of which had been hand-noted by Lord Redesdale), which generally tightened up the clauses relating to contractual and company matters. For example, clause XIX: 'The quorum of a meeting of Directors is three.' was amended to read 'The quorum of a meeting of Directors shall be three where there are six Directors and two when they are reduced to less than six directors.' Clause XXVII, whereby 'The Company may purchase by agreement, and hold any quantity of land for the extraordinary purposes mentioned in "The Railway Clause Consolidation Act 1845" not exceeding in the whole sixty acres', was reduced to just two acres. Clause XVIII stated that 'The powers for the compulsory purchase of lands

by this Act conferred the company shall not be exercised after the expiration of three years from the passing of this Act.', but the timescale was amended to two years. Originally, the railway was to be completed within five years from the passing of this Act, but this was reduced to four years.

Interestingly, Clause XXXI, relating to powers to cross certain roads on the level, was deleted entirely. Further, the trustees of the Stow and Moreton United Trust of Turnpike Roads, signed by their Chairman, Lord Redesdale, lodged an objection against the Bourton company's proposal to provide approach gradients of 1 in 20 at the bridge where it was to cross the railway at Stow, raising the Burford road by eight feet. They 'Resolved that the Trustees dissent from the proposed crossing unless the gradients be made 1 in 30. Clerk to communicate this resolution to the Company. If not that a petition be presented to the House of Commons praying that the power to adopt a gradient of 1 in 20 be struck out of the Bill and if necessary that a similar petition be presented to the House of Lords.' The clause was not inserted into the Enactment.

The Bourton-on-the-Water Railway Company was incorporated by its Act (23 Vic. cap. 82) of 14th June 1860. From the beginning, the company was closely associated with the OW & W, the Worcester company being authorised £3,000 towards its share capital, and to appoint two directors. The OW & W's General Manager, A. T. Adcock, and its Engineer, Edward Wilson, became Secretary and Engineer respectively of the Bourton-on-the-Water Railway Company.

In Bradshaw's *Shareholder's Manual* of 1861, capital was given as £30,000 in £10 shares, with loans of £10,000.

'Bourton on the Water Railway Company.

'Notice is hereby given that the first Ordinary Meeting of the Company will be held on Tuesday December 11th ... for the election of Directors and auditors and for the [?] transaction of the general business of the Company. At the termination of the Ordinary meeting of the Company an extraordinary general meeting of the Company will be held at the same place, at which an agreement with the West Midland Railway Company under the powers and provisions of the Bourton-on-the-Water Railway Act 1860 will be submitted to the proprietors then present personally or by proxy for their sanction.'

On 6th December 1860, in preparation for that meeting, William Bliss drafted the report of the Directors 'for perusal of Mr. Sherrif'. On 11th December, at that meeting, the secretary, A.T. Adcock, summed up the situation:

'Bourton Railway Company.

'The Directors in meeting the shareholders of the Company for the first time have great pleasure in being able to congratulate them on the success which has attended the past efforts of the Company (more especially on the unopposed passage of the Bill through Parliament and the consequent avoidance of the expense and delay attending even unsuccessful oppositions) and also on the prospects which the undertaking holds out with reference to the future. Within two months from the Bill receiving the Royal Assent sixty two shareholders had subscribed the share list for the portion of the capital required to be raised in the locality and the remainder having since been subscribed for by the West Midland Railway Company and Sir Morton Peto the share list is now complete.

*The Unicorn Hotel, Stow, venue for the first Ordinary Meeting of the new Bourton on the Water Railway Company held on Tuesday, 11th December 1860. The cart on the left is seen in several photos of the hotel and regularly plied between there and Stow station.*

COLLECTION R. SHARP

'The Directors have entered into a Contract with Sir Morton Peto for the purchase of the land, the construction of the line and of the stations, sidings and other necessaries including the payment of all expenses for the sum of forty thousand pounds to be raised out of the Capital of the Company and by the exercise of their borrowing powers in favour of the Contractor or his nominee to the extent of ten thousand pounds, the works to be at once commenced and continued with vigour until they are completed.

'The Directors have further entered into a Contract with the West Midland Railway Company which will be submitted for the sanction of this Company at the Extraordinary General Meeting whereby the West Midland Company undertake to work the Bourton Railway when constructed and maintain the line in repair on the terms and conditions which will be submitted to the meeting.

'The Engineer reports that the centre line of the Railway from the junction with the West Midland line to Bourton on the Water has been laid out and that negotiations have for some time been in progress with the landowners along the line but he is sorry to state that in two or three cases the demands are so exorbitant as to prevent an amicable arrangement being arrived at. Further, that the Working Drawings for the construction of the works by the Contractor are quite ready and nothing is now required for proceeding with the operations but the conclusion of arrangements with the various landowners.

'The Directors cannot conclude without referring in grateful terms to the liberal conduct of Charles van Notten Pole Esquire who in addition to becoming a Subscriber for a large number of shares has offered to present free to the Company the portion of his estate of the length of nearly a mile and a quarter required for the purpose of the Railway.'

The company's report reflected its buoyant mood, summing up the general satisfaction as to the way events were unfolding. However, the optimism expressed in the last paragraph did not bring about quite as favourable an outcome as the report suggested. Sometime between the

First Ordinary Meeting and the possession of the land by the contractor, Mr Pole changed his mind about the terms concerning conveyance of the land at Wyck Hill and Oddington to the Company, and sold it, albeit at a generously low price.

The draft/deed of conveyance dated 3rd February 1860 to Messrs Kendall, the Bourton Railway Company's solicitor, read as follows:

'To the Provisional Directors of the Bourton on the Water Railway.

Gentlemen,
On and ... that this railway be constructed so far as relates to my property in the parishes of Wick Rissington and Oddington on the deviation line and upon the terms stipulated and agreed upon between my surveyor ... and Mr Wilson on the part of the Company ... I offer to sell to the above Company the land required by them from me containing 67.2 acres or thereabouts for the sum of £700 including all drainage. On the completion of the land upon the above conditions without receiving any ... for the same, and I further propose and agree on this being completed with the line and the hedges over the same at Wick Rissington and Oddington being completed ... to become a subscriber ... to the Capital of the Railway for 70 shares at the original price of £10 each dated ... day of February 1860.'

Charles van Notten Pole was a notable local resident who had risen to prominence whilst engaged in attempts to help the people of Stow obtain an efficient and clean water supply. Stow-on-the-Wold, being in an elevated position on a layer of limestone rock, was subject to a notorious lack of water, the only supply up to the late eighteenth century being a series of badly-deteriorated, unsafe wells. In 1836, Mr Pole, who was described as 'the most public-spirited man in the neighbourhood', formed a company to enable Stow to obtain its water from the nearby village of Upper Swell. Here, he set up a water wheel to produce power to pump supplies, though this attempt was abandoned, as had previous experiments, due largely to the great expense involved and the frequent failure in times of drought. The supply of water reverted to being conveyed by cart or on foot. It was not until 1867 that Stow obtained a reliable supply. Notten Pole was also Trustee of St. Edward's Hall, a grand building erected in 1878 in Stow market square for use by the local community.

Mr Pole occupied Wyck Hill House, a large property situated on the slopes of Rissington Hill, south of Stow-on-the-Wold. The property overlooked the proposed line of the railway, and a large portion of the estate was to be crossed by it. Evidently a man determined not to allow technological inadequacies to stand in the way of advancing the needs of local society, Mr Pole also became involved in the Bourton-on-the-Water Railway Company, and was soon to become one of its Directors.

It appears that William Bliss and the other Directors had not confirmed Mr Pole's legal responsibilities regarding the ownership of the land he occupied on the Wyck Hill Estate.

Charles van Notten Pole did not own the estate, but was only a tenant for life of the larger portion of land taken for the railway, and in such capacity, had no power to convey it to the company. None of the directors was aware that the land he had willingly sold was not actually theirs for the taking, and, typical of legal problems dealing with the conveying of property, eventually it would come to light, with disastrous consequences for the Company.

Unaware of the legal implications regarding the Wyck Hill Estate, the company took possession of the land and began to prepare for the construction work. A contract was entered into with Sir Morton Peto for the construction of the single line, with Peto taking shares to the value of £15,680 in part payment. The Indenture signed by Peto and Betts was a duplicate of the contract which was made for the construction of the Chipping Norton Branch, with those elements relating to that railway simply lined through and replaced with the clauses relating to the Bourton-on-the-Water Railway Company.

William Bliss wrote on 4th February 1861, assumedly referring to the Bourton Railway, and probably addressed to its Shareholders:

*Market Square, Stow. St. Edward's Hall on the left was erected in 1878 at the direction of one of its trustees, Charles Van Notten Pole, who was a director of the Bourton Railway Company.*    COLLECTION R. SHARP

'We think the first sod of your line shall be turned towards the end of this month. This will be done without any demonstration but...proposed that you should have a public dinner...'

Details of the turning of the first turf are not known.

The Board of Directors was as follows:

The Hon. R. H. Dutton MP. Timsbury Manor, Romsey, Hants
C. V. N. Pole Esq. Wyck Hill House, Stow-on-the-Wold.
W. Bliss Esq. Chipping Norton, Oxon
W. Lewis Esq. Rainbow Hill, Worcester
H. G. Busby Esq. Moreton-in-the-Marsh
J. Bennett Esq. Rissington, near Stow-on-the-Wold.

The Engineer was Edward Wilson, whose experience ranged from contracts with the Great Western, Metropolitan and Great Eastern Railway companies. Work on the construction began, but was hampered by problems in obtaining possession of certain sections of the lands through which the railway was to pass.

In March 1861, Edward Wilson reported that works had commenced at Chipping Norton Junction. However, the landowners holding out for greater remuneration had still prevented an 'amicable arrangement' being effected.

The Report of the Directors for 14th August 1861 explained that

'the attention of your Directors and Engineer has been directed to the obtaining, as quickly as possible, possession of the land required ... and it will be seen that some difficulties still exist, which will render it necessary...that compulsory possession should be taken of the land required for the Contractor, as soon as possible.

'It is a source of gratification to your Directors to be able to report progress of so promising a character in the execution of the works on land in possession up to this time.'

The Engineer's Report added:

'Since my last Report considerable progress has been made in the construction of the Line, and I have now the honour to inform you that the works are in active operation on all the land which the Contractor has obtained possession of, being about four and a half miles.

'The Cuttings and Embankments are finished for about the distance of three and a half miles.

'The Bridges are all in hand, the stonework of two of them being nearly completed.

'I am sorry to say that the demands of some few of the Landowners are still so very unreasonable that I see no prospect of settling with them amicably.

'Provided we can give the Contractor possession of the remaining portion of the land (about two miles one furlong) and the weather is at all suitable, the line shall be completed by the end of October.'

Construction continued, and the compulsory purchases were made. Captain J. H. Rich arrived on 14th February 1862 to inspect the line, and submitted his report the following day. It stated that the line:

'... extends from Chipping Norton (Junction) to Bourton on Water.

'The new line of Railway is 6 miles and 53½ chains long – Single throughout with sidings at Stow station and at Bourton – the land has been purchased and the overbridges have been constructed for a double line.

'The width of the line at formation level is 16 feet.

'The gauge is 4 ft 8½ ins. The interval between the thro' lines of rails where there are sidings is 6 feet.

'The rail used is double-headed, in lengths of 27 feet, and weighs 65 lbs per cubic yard – the joints are fished.

'The chairs weigh 25lbs each – they are spiked to larch sleepers, laid at 3 feet intervals.

'The sleepers are semicircular, 9 feet long, 9 in by 4½ in average scantling – the flat side is laid on the ballast, which is gravel 12 ins thick under the sleepers.

'There are three overbridges – two with masonry piers and brick arches, the third has wrought iron girders.

'The under bridge which has wt. iron girders & masonry abutments – besides several culverts...conveying brooks under the Railway. Two of these are of timber with brick piers.

'The whole of the above are well built and of sufficient strength.

'There are no level crossings and no Engine turntables, as it is contemplated to extend the line.'

An undertaking was supplied by the Bourton company with regard to working of the line, and to engine turntables, which Captain Rich assessed as 'satisfactory'. He continued:

'The state of the line is good, but two of the approaches to the overbridges are not yet completed. The company undertakes to keep a man at the gates till they are finished, which will probably be in a week or ten days.

'The stations at Stow and Bourton are not yet built, but there are good platforms provided, with semaphores and distant signals, and a wooden ticket box.

'I beg therefore to report that I consider that the portion of the Bourton on Water Railway between Chipping Norton & Bourton may be opened for passenger traffic without danger to the public using the same.'

The undertakings referred to from the Secretary of the Bourton company gave an assurance that the line would be worked by 'Train Staff and Ticket systems in accordance with Section C Article III laid down in the printed Regulations of the Board of Trade for working single lines.' He also assured the BoT that an engine turntable would be erected at Chipping Norton Junction and at either the projected terminus of the line (Cheltenham), or at Bourton-on-the-Water 'in case it shall remain as the Terminal Station of the Branch.' He undertook to use only tank engines 'til such Turntables are fixed.'

Captain Rich did determine that the line was carried outside the agreed Parliamentary boundaries for a few chains some two miles from the junction station, though this was stated to be at the request of the landowner. The Board of Trade therefore approved the opening of the line, although much work remained to be done at the stations. Nevertheless, passenger traffic commenced on 1st March 1862, with goods and mineral traffic following a few days later, when the accommodation for it was completed.

The Bourton branch opened with a daily service of four return trains; the first left Bourton at 9.0 a.m., and the last arrived back there at 8.50 p.m.; like the Chipping Norton branch, the trains were mixed, with passenger and goods vehicles attached. As the branch was operated from the Bourton end, it must have possessed engine servicing or stabling facilities; although no positive details of a shed have been discovered, an unidentified building does appear on the plan at the termination of the line against the road leading to the Fosse Way. At Chipping Norton Jct., the Bourton trains are believed to have operated into and out of the main-line platforms.

A working agreement for the branch was finalised on 14th April 1862 between the Bourton and West Midland companies, and Sir Morton Peto. This took the common format of

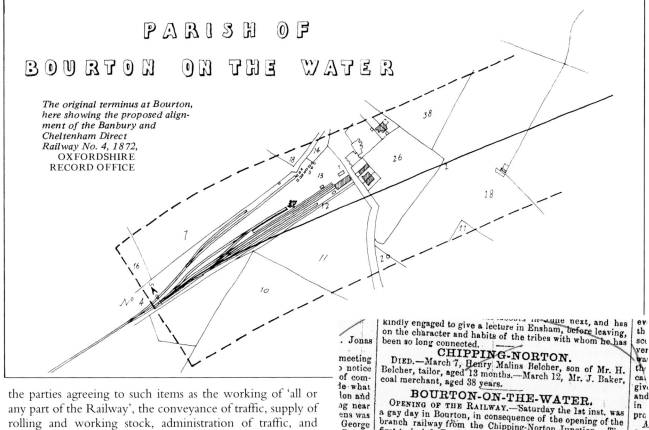

PARISH OF
BOURTON ON THE WATER

The original terminus at Bourton,
here showing the proposed align-
ment of the Banbury and
Cheltenham Direct
Railway No. 4, 1872,
OXFORDSHIRE
RECORD OFFICE

the parties agreeing to such items as the working of 'all or
any part of the Railway', the conveyance of traffic, supply of
rolling and working stock, administration of traffic, and
management and repair of the railway. Financial aspects
were also agreed upon.

The Report of the Directors for 28th March 1863 stated:

'The Directors have now the pleasure to report to the Shareholders that,
since the opening of the line, the Traffic in both Goods and Passengers
has been gradually developing itself, and considering the length of time
that has elapsed, the results may be looked upon as favourable for the
present, and promising for the future.

'The balance sheet annexed will show that the Profits on the line, after
payment of Debenture Interest and Working Expenses, amount to
£434 11s 2d., and that after bringing forward £66 6s 7d. balance from
last account, and deducting the charges applicable to Revenue, the
balance available for Dividend will be £150 2s 11d., and your Directors
recommend a Dividend after the rate of £1 per Cent. Per Annum, to be
paid from this sum.'

R H Dutton, Chairman

The completion of the stations was taking much longer
than anticipated, as admitted in the Engineer's report.

'Since my last Report the Trains have continued to work with regularity
over your Railway, and the whole of the Permanent Way and Works are
in excellent condition.

'The Station at the Junction is in progress, and also those at Bourton
and Stow: and the Contractor has promised to have the whole finished
by the beginning of June.'

The Director's Report for the following half-yearly
meeting, 29th September 1863, gave this optimistic appraisal:

'Although it is not in the power of the Directors to report to the
Shareholders that the Traffic of the line has very considerably increased,

kindly engaged to give a lecture in Ensham, before leaving,
on the character and habits of the tribes with whom he has
been so long connected.

**CHIPPING-NORTON.**
DIED.—March 7, Henry Malins Belcher, son of Mr. H.
Belcher, tailor, aged 13 months.—March 12, Mr. J. Baker,
coal merchant, aged 38 years.

**BOURTON-ON-THE-WATER.**
OPENING OF THE RAILWAY.—Saturday the 1st inst. was
a gay day in Bourton, in consequence of the opening of the
branch railway from the Chipping-Norton Junction. The
first train left Bourton at nine o'clock, amid the cheers of
a large crowd of persons, who had assembled at the station,
and a merry peal of the church bells. The Wyck brass
band were in the train, and much enlivened the scene by
their exhilarating strains. The opening was celebrated by
a dinner at the New Inn, where about 50 sat down, under
the presidency of the Rev. C. W. Payne Crawford, Curate
of Bourton, and a very pleasant afternoon was spent. [The
above paragraph was accidentally omitted to be sent last
week.]

**MORETON-IN-MARSH.**
LECTURE.—On Monday evening last a highly interesting
and instructive lecture "On the Introduction of Christianity
into the British Isles" was delivered at the National School
by the Rev. Henry Uh......

*Jackson's Oxford Journal, 15th March 1862.*

yet it is satisfactory to be able to state that the Receipts for the Half-year
ended 30th June are somewhat in excess of those for the Half-year ended
31st December 1862; and also that the number of passengers and weight
of Goods has considerably increased since the 1st July last. The Directors
have every reason to believe that the Receipts for the present Half-year
will far exceed those of previous periods.

'The Net Revenue, as is shown by the accounts annexed hereto,
enables the Directors to recommend the payment of a Dividend at the
rate of 1 per cent. per annum, after liquidating Debenture Interest and
other expenses.

'It will be seen by the Engineer's Report that the stations are now
nearly completed, and that the Way and Works are in good condition.'

At the same time, Edward Wilson, the Engineer, reported:

'I have much pleasure in reporting that during the past Half-year, the
Trains have worked with perfect regularity over your line of Railway.

'The Permanent Way and Works are in good condition.

'The Stations are all but complete, only a little painting and finishing-
off being required.'

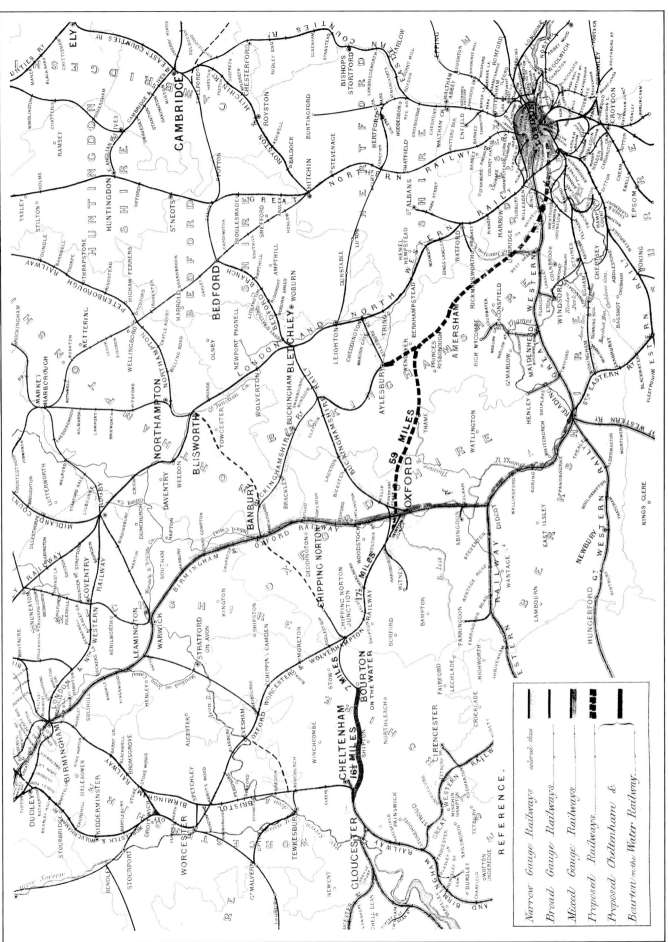

A map of c.1861 showing the original Bourton and Chipping Norton railways, with a possible extension to Banbury and the Bourton Company's proposed Cheltenham extension.

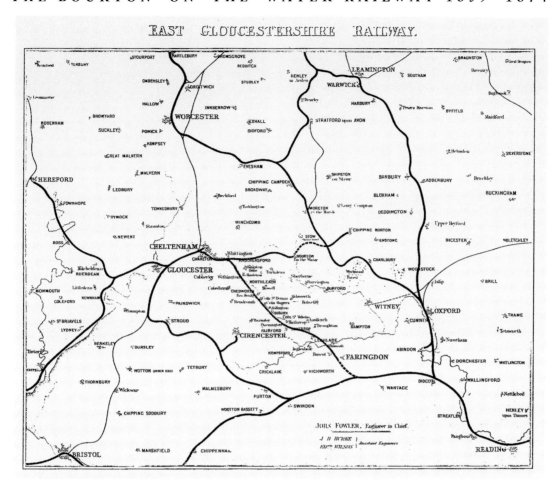

EAST GLOUCESTERSHIRE RAILWAY.

## A PROSPECT OF CHELTENHAM

Meanwhile, negotiations were continuing over the proposed extension to Cheltenham. These had developed considerably since the Bourton Railway Company was first formed in January 1861 and also included tentative plans for an extension from Chipping Norton to Banbury. According to *The Worcester Herald*, at the opening of the Bourton-on-the-Water Railway, William Bliss had explained the origin of the line. 'He said that he suggested to Sir Morton Peto that a branch from Chipping Norton would be the most feasible way of getting another link towards extending a railway to Faringdon and Banbury and Sir Morton had immediately taken up the scheme, and guaranteed the shareholders 4 per cent on their outlay for seven years.'

In February 1861 William Bliss noted that he was glad to 'receive the prospectus of the line from Banbury, Blisworth and Cheltenham' which he hoped would be carried out some day. This line was clearly intended to produce a through route linking the centres, which must have involved a connection with the London & North-Western network at Banbury. Although Bliss warmed to the idea, his vague response to its prospectus indicates that he did not wish to become personally involved in it; his most important priority was the Bourton extension.

The Bourton company's Cheltenham extension proposed a route westwards over the Cotswold Hills, with a single narrow (standard) gauge line 15¾ miles long, with substantial engineering and earthworks, steep gradients, and a 1,474 yard tunnel under residential areas of Cheltenham.

Also being developed were proposals for railways connecting Cheltenham from the south, which took the original Cheltenham, Northleach and Witney railways a stage further. This project in its revised form was now known as the East Gloucestershire Railway, and was born at a meeting held at Hatherop Castle, near Fairford, in 1861. The meeting was attended by many influential people who had, for some years, been attempting to extend a railway through the area. The proposal was similar to the original Cheltenham, Northleach and Witney Railways, with a line leaving Cheltenham and rising eastwards through the Chelt valley to Andoversford, where it turned south-eastwards and descended to Fairford, Lechlade and Witney, joining the existing Witney Railway. A junction at Lechlade would be constructed with a line running south to join the Faringdon Railway. There were also to be short connecting lines to the Midland Railway at Cheltenham, and a direct connection at Yarnton between the London & North-Western and the existing branch to Witney, which was to pass under the OW

& W main line. Two through routes would provide a direct service to London, via the Faringdon Railway's junction with the Great Western at Uffington, and at Yarnton Junction, near Oxford.

The primary focus of interest for the two companies was, of course, Cheltenham, the easiest route out of which required the railway to climb the side of the short valley of the River Chelt, rising up the Cotswold escarpment to Andoversford, whence the two railways would diverge. The selection of this route was not arrived at easily for the Bourton company, and it appears there were plans to avoid it. On 23rd June 1860, with reference to the original Northleach & Cheltenham Railway, a letter addressed to Edward Wilson (who was also the Engineer of this proposed railway) suggested the possibility of an alternative route for the Cheltenham extension via Winchcombe. The letter gives an interesting insight into how problematic the route's descent into Cheltenham was perceived to be, and of the ways that the railway engineers·sought to develop their alternative proposals.

'We called on Mr. Waddingham of Guyting Grange yesterday to obtain signatures to the Bourton Railway Contract and he then entered very fully into the question of the continuation of this line towards Cheltenham … He ridiculed the idea of following the intended course of the Northleach and Cheltenham line into Cheltenham and said that the gradients would be steep. The expense of cutting through Cheltenham enormous, the difficulties to be thrown in our way by public Bodies in the town very considerable. Also, very little aid will be obtained from Cheltenham people … and lastly that a junction with the Midland line beyond Cheltenham is absolutely necessary if the line is to be a paying one.'

The alternative proposal was

'to follow up the course of a stream which flows from the hills by Winchcombe and by which means we may skirt the hills and run down into the valley of the Midland line three or four miles north of Cheltenham. We should run chiefly through or near the estates of Lord Sudely, Lord Ellinborough and Mr Deat, who are very anxious for a line to be brought that way and as Mr. Waddingham is informed, will support it handsomely and take a moderate price for their land.

Mr Waddingham said he had reason to believe that the Midland Company would not oppose this project and that eventually we might aid them in forming a loop line into Cheltenham and which would obviate the inconvenience of their present station.

Now what we propose is this … If you can come on Tuesday bringing with you if possible a large Ordnance map and could meet at Guyting Grange and you could go into the matter with Mr. Waddingham and get some better idea of the practicality of his proposal, you could then go back by the Ashchurch Station viewing the ground by the way. Please let us have a line by return of post if possible.'

Perhaps this was merely a paper exercise, and certainly nothing came of it; the Bourton and East Gloucestershire companies both opted for the steep descent through the narrow valley of the River Chelt to obtain the vital foothold into Cheltenham.

This shared interest in Cheltenham, via the all-important Chelt valley, coupled with the powerful influence of Sir Morton Peto (who was promoting both railways) must have produced an interesting dynamic between the two companies. After all, the East Gloucestershire, in much the same way as the Cheltenham, Northleach and Witney Railways

had done before it, was promoting a direct rail link with the L & NW at Oxford. There is evidence that the Bourton Railway Company were not completely comfortable about the arrangements, and sought clarification as to the viability of their proposal when developed in conjunction with the East Gloucestershire scheme.

William Bliss wrote, probably addressing the company's shareholders, dated 20th May 1861, not being able to offer any guarantees of success, but still characteristically optimistic:

'I feel it is to be my duty to make you acquainted with all that has transpired in respect to our railway affairs since we met … Failing in meeting with Sir Morton Peto again that afternoon I accepted an invitation from him to breakfast … at Kensington Palace Gardens … when he told me that he felt sure that if the Faringdon Scheme was carried out our connection from Bourton on the Water would form part of it.'

But it was not only the Cheltenham extension to receive attention. In the letter, William Bliss described how he was actively pushing ahead with plans for an extension north-eastwards from Chipping Norton to Banbury, and also apparently for an interconnecting line between the two branches at Chipping Norton Junction. He closed by confidently affirming:

'For if these two schemes are carried out next year … we will have this built railway accomplished.'

Doubtless as a result of the promises of support from Peto, the Bourton company went to Parliament in 1863 for powers to build their extension to Cheltenham.

On 13th May 1864, Messrs Burchells, Peto's solicitor, wrote to Kendall and Son, the Bourton Company's solicitor, the following letter:

'This Bill is appointed for Thursday 26th instant. We shall rely upon you for getting up some good Evidence from the neighbourhood of Bourton from gentlemen such as Mr Waddingham, Mr Hipsley and others in favour of the Bill.'

On 24th May Burchells wrote again, hoping to see the gentlemen the Bourton solicitor mentioned, a Mr Whitmore and Mr Dutton already having been contacted, but still awaiting their replies. They then requested that Messrs Kendall and Son 'Please send us up your Draft Proofs by tomorrow's post that we may have them briefed and delivered to Counsel on Thursday morning.'

John Waddingham replied, indicating that he 'will go to town to give evidence in favour of the proposed railway.'

Among those giving written evidence in support of the proposed Cheltenham extension were the Reverend Edward Witts of Upper Slaughter, Thomas Barton, a mealman and farmer from Bourton, Arthur Acock, an auctioneer and Robert Cornely, also a farmer. The Rev Witts wrote on 24th May 1864, to Kendall and Son, to be sent forward to Burchells:

'I should have preferred going up to town on Thursday morning, but if you cannot we'll arrange otherwise, and will go up by the 11.20 train tomorrow. I wish to add to the evidence … as Chairman of the Bench of Guardians …'

His Evidence followed:
'Bourton on the Water Railway
'Proposed Extension to Cheltenham

'To Prove

'That Witness who is the Rector of Upper Slaughter Gloucestershire is also a magistrate and Deputy Lieutenant for the county and has lived in the neighbourhood all his life.

'Considers that the district stands greatly in need of Railway communication with Cheltenham and the County town and knows that the population in the neighbourhood are very anxious for such communication. The proposed extension line would meet this want.

'Well aware that when the Bourton Branch line was first proposed a great deal of the support that was given to it, especially by the country gentlemen was upon the hope that it would very shortly be extended to Cheltenham. The neighbourhood of Stow and Bourton is situated on the extreme eastern boundary of the County and magistrates and witnesses who have to attend the assizes and sessions are put to great expense and loss of time in [?] performing the journey and in preference to a tedious journey along bad roads over the hills they frequently prefer to go by rail round by Worcester, a distance of between 70 and 80 miles.

'Believe that the proposed line if made would be largely used … for the transaction of agricultural produce and manure and especially coal, which is cheap at Cheltenham but very dear in the district of Bourton and Stow.

'Witness knows the inconvenience and expense of sending patients to Gloucester and the County Infirmary as also to the lunatic asylum which inconvenience would be greatly removed by rail communication direct.

'As a Clergyman, Witness knows and has heard his brother Clergymen complain of the difficulty of access to the Bishop. In addition to coal there will in Witness' opinion be considerable traffic in timber, especially deal and laths as he knows from experience when building that they come from Gloucester, the best port for their transportation. By waggon, 22 miles, or by water carriage to Tewkesbury and Evesham and thence by rail to Bourton. Also farmers and cattle dealers attend the monthly markets at Stow from Witness's parish and the neighbourhood.

'Call,
Revd. E. Witts'

The Reverend Witts had compiled his evidence thoughtfully, but he was surely mistaken about the possibility that the railway would afford his 'brother Clergymen' greater 'access to the Bishop'!

Robert Cornely gave his evidence, offering another perspective on the social and economic forces acting upon the district through which the railway was to pass.

'To Prove

'That Witness is a farmer, feed and manure merchant carrying on business at four farms, at Notgrove, Condicote, Bourton on the Water and Maugersbury, about 1100 acres, all in the County of Gloucester, distance respectively about 16 miles from Cheltenham…

'Corn from Gloucester into the neighbourhood would be largely increased [as would] the consumption if the cost of transit could be lessened, which Witness calculates by more than one half. Witness considers that this district cannot at present compete with many others in its powers of agricultural production … on account of the costs of carriage of heavy goods … to the conveyance of grain from this district to the markets, Cheltenham is the principal market in the neighbourhood and a great deal of grain and farming produce being at first sent there from these parts at a cost in carriage of at least 10/- a ton. Witness calculates that the costs would be about 4/- a ton if the line were made.

'The cost of Staffordshire coal at Cheltenham is 12/- per ton and at Bourton 15/- being the same distance from the coal fields, consequently a large part of the district between the two places is already supplied by land carriage from Cheltenham, though at heavy cost. If this proposed line were carried out the coal from Cheltenham would supply nearly the entire district.

'The consumption is very considerable owing to the increased use of steam power for the purposes of threshing and still more in connection with the water in the corn mills. Witness believes that if the cost of coal

were diminished, as it would be by the construction of this line, almost every corn mill in this neighbourhood, and they are very numerous, would use steam power.

'Call,
Robert Cornely'

In his evidence, Arthur Acock added:

'That Witness is a licensed auctioneer and a farmer at Cold Aston in the County of Gloucester, about three miles from Bourton and has been in business for 20 years, can confirm the evidence … especially the prices of coal in the neighbourhood and the depreciating effects of the costs of land carriage.

'The sales of stock and agricultural produce are very large in this neighbourhood. During the present spring season … Witness sold … by auction at the Bourton Railway Station … between 5000 and 6000 sheep …

'The construction of the proposed line would afford much greater facilities than at present exist for the attendance of dealers and others at these sales and consequently would produce a greater competition and enhance the value of the stock.'

'Call,
Arthur Acock'

The statement of Thomas Barton of Bourton, who 'has two mills there, one worked by water alone and the other by water with steam power affixed, [and] could send out 700 sacks of flour a week', concurred with the others.

On 25th May Burchells acknowledged receipt of the statements, writing to Kendall and Son, the Bourton Company solicitor:

'We have to acknowledge the receipt of the draft Proofs of Messrs Witts, Cornely, Acock and Barton, and also the Petition signed by the chairman of the meeting.

'We have got an outline of Mr Waddingham's Proof from him which we will put into proper shape'.

At a special general meeting on 11th June, the proprietors approved a 'Bill to extend the Bourton on the Water Railway to Cheltenham, and amend the Act relating to the Bourton on the Water Railway Company.'

The Bill was prepared and duly submitted to the House of Lords, proposing:

'A railway commencing in the parish of Cheltenham, in the County of Gloucester, by a junction with the Great Western Railway, and terminating in the same parish at or near a field at the north-east end of Sandford Terrace, and known as Sandford Mead.

'A railway commencing in the parish of Cheltenham, in the County of Gloucester, at the hereinbefore described point of termination of the last mentioned intended railway, in the aforesaid field known as Sandford Mead and by a junction there with the last mentioned intended railway, and terminating in the said parish of Bourton on the Water in the County of Gloucester, by a junction there with the Bourton on the Water Railway, at or near termination thereof at Bourton on the Water.

Various clauses had been revised, including:

15. The required capital to be raised was reduced from £400,000 to £220,000.
16. Instructions to make them performance shares.
20. That the Company may raise by borrowing the sum of £133,000, was amended to read £73,000.

This was the proposal from which the Bourton on the Water Railway Company expected to build their extension. They had made a financial arrangement with the East Gloucestershire which had been left open-ended, as a handwritten footnote to the Bill instructed the Bourton Company to pay half the expense of the railway between Cheltenham and Andoversford within nine months after completion unless they wished to have running powers only, and give five months notice to that effect.

In the event, it was the East Gloucestershire Railway Company who obtained the powers to build a line to Cheltenham, and the Bourton Company's interest was restricted to the section between its existing line and that of the East Gloucestershire near Andoversford. How the Bourton company responded to this development is not known, but they would not have been aware that this decision was going to give rise to serious difficulties for them in the years to follow.

It can be assumed that the Bourton Railway Company had probably been quite happy to let Peto take the lead in all these developments. After all, had they come to fruition, and the original branch became part of a through route, then the holders of the original shares must benefit.

Nevertheless, there is evidence that Peto was using the company to serve his own interests, as illustrated by the following undertaking, which he signed in March 1864, addressed to and set out in the minute book of the Bourton company.

'In consideration of your affixing at my request the seal of the Bourton-on-the-Water Railway Company to conditional agreements with the landowners on the proposed extension to Cheltenham, I hereby agree before the Bill to authorise that railway shall be read a third time in the House of Lords to pay into a bank to be agreed by you, a sum of money equal to the aggregate amount of the liabilities incurred in respect of such contracts in your names and I moreover agree to indemnify you from all costs and expenses in respect of that Bill.'

The Bourton-on-the-Water company's Cheltenham extension received the Royal Assent on 25th July 1864, officially titled 27 and 28 Vict. Sess 1864. Extension to Cheltenham Act 1864.

Clause 5 of the Act described:

'A railway commencing at or near Whittington Lane, in or near the field numbered on the deposited plans 24, in the parish of Whittington, in the County of Gloucester, and terminating in the parish of Bourton on the Water, in the County of Gloucester, by a junction there with the Bourton on the Water Railway, at or near the termination thereof at Bourton on the Water.'

Thus it came to be that the Bourton Railway did not achieve the Parliamentary powers to build its desired link to Cheltenham, but only secured running rights over the East Gloucestershire's metals into Cheltenham.

The Act stated that the compulsory purchase of lands required should be carried out within three years. Also, that if the extension railway were not completed within five years, the powers of the Act would cease to be exercised, and the Bourton Company would be liable to a penalty of £50 per day. Penalties would not be charged in circumstances where the 'Company was prevented from completing or opening such Extension Railway by unforeseen accident or circumstances beyond their control, but the want of sufficient funds shall not be deemed a circumstance beyond their control.'

The Great Western Railway were enabled powers to enter into working arrangements. The company were authorised to raise £220,000 for the sole purpose of completing the railway, 'and for laying down a second line of rails on the Bourton on the Water Railway.' They were enabled to divide the capital to be raised into new shares, not less than £10 to be called Extension Shares.

On 29th August 1864, Messrs Burchells wrote to Kendall and Son, in Bourton, informing the solicitor that by breakfast they had 'forwarded a copy of the Extension Act of last session' and reported that 'Our Mr Burchell who attended the Chipping Norton and Banbury Railway is absent from town during this week.'

The Bourton Company had authorisation to build their line, albeit four years after the idea was first mooted, and not quite as they had first expected. Also, plans were progressing well for the extension from Chipping Norton to Banbury. All these positive developments might have given reason to rejoice; but the storm clouds were gathering over the Bourton Company. The legal problems resulting from the 'sale' of the land at Wyck Hill all came to light when Charles van Notten Pole died. He ceased to become a director after 1864. The estate was being offered for sale under an order of the Court of Chancery, and the solicitors advised that the company would have to pay for the land, suggesting that a local land agent be asked to state a fair price. The Directors had no alternative but to comply. Unfortunately, the company had no reserves, the whole of the surplus having been paid out in dividends; further dividends had therefore to be suspended until sufficient funds had accumulated to make a payment.

For the next year (1865) Mr. Pole's former position was not filled, though in 1866, A.C. Sherriff, MP for Worcester, stepped in. Sherriff was a railway entrepreneur of the first order, holding directorships in no less than six other railway companies, stretching from the Metropolitan Railway to the Bala & Dolgelly company, together with other related concerns.

Meanwhile, the East Gloucestershire Company began to construct the earthworks for its proposed railway between Cheltenham and Andoversford, building the necessary cuttings and embankments, including the approaches to a tunnel at Dowdeswell. From the East Gloucestershire's point of view, this was a wise decision in that were the Cheltenham to Andoversford section completed first, the running rights given to the Bourton Company over that section would earn revenue for the East Gloucestershire, enabling them to complete their line. Of course, this depended on the Bourton Company completing their own line.

Unfortunately, events did not unfold as planned. A financial disaster took place in 1866 with the failure of the finance house of Overend & Gurney, and this in turn led to the bankruptcy of Sir Morton Peto. Plans for the railways to Banbury and Cheltenham collapsed, and work on the East Gloucestershire Railway between Andoversford and Cheltenham came to a halt.

This alerted the OW & W, who then panicked. Without a guarantee to complete the line, there was a risk that the penalty of £50 per day would be enforced upon the Bourton Company. With no forewarning, the OW & W instructed their solicitor, Messrs Burchell, to apply for abandonment of the line, and the Notice was duly published. Unfortunately for the Bourton Railway Company and its shareholders, this was the first they had heard of it, and not all of them at that. The first official information which Kendall and Son, the Bourton solicitor, received was from Burchells, in a letter dated 16th November:

'Re Bourton-on-the-Water Railway extension to Cheltenham.

'We have no doubt that you are surprised at seeing the Notice for the abandonment of the above Bill. We quite concur in the importance of a line to connect Bourton-on-the-Water with Cheltenham, and shall very much regret if it becomes necessary to carry the Bill of which we have given notice, but it must be manifest that the Bourton-on-the-Water Company are unaided and in the present times are not strong enough to spend a very large sum of money in extending their line, not to Cheltenham but to Andoversford, especially when the East Gloucestershire Company who are to meet them there, and over whose line they were to proceed into Cheltenham, are not constructing the intermediate link.

'When the Bill was passed, the Bourton-on-the-Water Company relied upon the power of Sir Morton Peto and his firm to find the necessary Capital. You can yourself appreciate the value of that reliance under present circumstances. Should however either Sir Morton Peto be able to carry out his engagements in this matter, or should other arrangements be made we should with great pleasure receive instructions to withdraw the Bill of which we have given notice. The question of the abandonment of the line depends entirely upon the pecuniary support which the Bourton-on-the-Water Railway can obtain.'

Mr Kendall immediately informed William Bliss, who wrote back, on the 18th November:

'Under the weight of your favour of 17th I was not aware of Burchells' notice for Bill to abandon the Bourton on the Water and Andoversford line. I shall much regret if this action is allowed to be carried out and shall be glad to write … with any plan to avoid it.

'Hoping to hear again from you as to what the "local magnates" intend doing under the circumstances.

'I have written Burchells for further information which you shall have when I get it.'

Many of the Bourton Railway shareholders were uncertain about what the implications might be for the Cheltenham extension. A Mr W Nash Skillicorne wrote on 20th November to William Bliss, desperately hoping that abandonment meant merely a route alteration.

'I should feel obliged if you would have the kindness to inform me as to the state of the Bourton on the Water Railway. The advertisement here rather puzzled all the parties interested in it. They are doubtful as to whether the line is to be given up or only to be deviated.

'I am unable to give them the information they require and as the East Gloucestershire is in anything but good repute I should wish to have some authority for stating my opinion, which is that the Bourton have found out a better line, that therefore they have abandoned the old route and are going for the new one. I hope this is the real state of affairs. I hope you and all your family are quite well.'

Correspondence passed rapidly between all the relevant parties involved in the project as they attempted to clarify the situation. On 20th November, James Burchell wrote directly to William Bliss, and explained in grave tones:

'Your favour of the 18th only reached me by this morning's post. The Notice for the abandonment of the Extension to Cheltenham was inserted by me at the express direction of Mr. Sherriff. You will recollect that the line was promoted by the Company under a guarantee from Sir Morton Peto. The Company is liable to a penalty of £50 a day if the line be not constructed by the stipulated time. You will be able yourself to appreciate under existing circumstances the importance of the liability and the value of the guarantee. At the same time I do not think that the Bill for its abandonment will ever be passed. The Extension to Cheltenham is in my opinion too important to the Great Western for them to allow the Company to drop the line. I wrote to you according to my promise requesting you to summon a meeting in London but no meeting ever was summoned and is now far too late to insert any Notice for an Extension of time – none in fact is necessary as there are yet 6 or 8 months in which Notices to treat can be served, and having been served in time it would be easy to apply to Parliament in the ensuing session for an Extension of time for the construction of the works. Probably the best thing you can do now is to summon a Board to take the state of the Company into consideration.'

William Bliss responded immediately by post on the 21st November, sending his letter through Messrs Kendall and Son in the usual way, and his tone was most unhappy.

'I have received your favour of the 20th with explanation but I am not all satisfied with it for I think Mr. Sherriff has been very premature and inconsiderate in the matter. I think he might have called a meeting and taken the sense of the Directors, Promoters and local magnates about it before he took on himself the responsibility of giving you orders without even consulting one of the individuals who have had to do with it from the past.

'I look upon the connections between Banbury and Cheltenham as one of the most important schemes afloat and after the trouble [and] expense attending the getting of these two Bills it seems to me folly to give them up without the slightest effort to carry them out. I am sure you must agree with me and I wish you would get Adcock to call a meeting of all the shareholders in London or at Bourton to fully consider the matter at once for the step which has been taken if carried out will destroy the Bourton Branch which cost about £50,000 and will rob our branch of one half its importance.

'I shall depend upon you taking up this matter at once doing your best to setting it all going again on a new footing with an independent extension from Andoversford to Cheltenham.

'PS … Money is now cheap and contractors will soon come to life again.'

Messrs Kendall started to look at the practicalities of the situation, and gathered the support of the various shareholders. They wrote to William Bliss on 23rd November:

'We have posted your letter to Mr. Burchell, the contents of which we cordially approve of, and send you herewith the letters of Messrs. Burchell and Skillicorne to yourself of which we have taken copies for further reference if necessary. We have been in communication with Mr. Whitmore, Mr. Witts and Mr. Waddingham upon the subject – Mr. Whitmore though taking a deep interest in the matter does not know what to suggest but will aid us in anything that may be determined to stop the present application. Mr. Waddingham says that we should obtain the signatures of landowners and others to a Memorial to Messrs. Burchell or the promoters of the abandonment scheme to postpone their application until the fate of the East Gloucestershire can be ascertained and Mr. Witts called on us to back up that suggestion but on our intimating that the powers to purchase the land next July and that Burchell's might probably decline allowing their Client to be placed in the position of being under a penalty to make a line, the powers of which had expired, Mr. Witts admitted the difficulty.

'In fact this land question appears to us to be at the bottom of the difficulty just now. Messrs. Burchell suggest that we can give Notices to treat during the 6 or 8 months yet remaining and that so our power to purchase the land may be kept alive. Possibly so, but these notices to treat, if given, are irrevocable without the consent of the parties receiving them – in fact they bind us to buy unless the landowners will let us off and who is the party who will, as the business stands now, authorize the giving these notices. In truth the whole matter wants looking into and we think a meeting should be held for the purpose as you suggest. Mr. Sherriff should if possible be induced to attend and the question raised: Can any other Contractor and Capitalist be induced to take up the project with a view to make the line and if so upon what terms? You may rely upon the Gentlemen about here lending their aid for any step that may be resolved on but the question they ask is "What are we to do?"'

John Waddingham also responded to the situation, and very shortly would occupy the unenviable position of one of the Bourton Railway Company directors during its troubled times. He was well qualified, being described as 'a man very well acquainted with railway matters having had great experience in lines in the north of England. Also that he is a resident landowner of considerable property and fortune at Guyting – that he knows the nature of the country thereabouts and is well acquainted with the society at Cheltenham and his own neighbourhood.'

He wrote to Messrs. Kendall from his home at Guyting Grange on 20th November:

'I think Messrs. Burchell may very fairly be asked to defer their application to Parliament for power to abandon the Bourton extension scheme, until we see what will be the fate of the East Gloucestershire. I am quite willing to join in an application to them for that purpose. If the East Gloucester be made, some local support might probably be got towards continuing the link between Bourton and Andoversford, but a line from Bourton to Cheltenham, if made at all must be the work of one of the great Railway Companies.

'My advice therefore is that you should get the signatures of landowners and others to an application for postponement, unless Messrs Burchell will consent to do this on your recommendation.'

Ten days later, Messrs Burchell wrote to William Bliss, enclosing a copy of a letter he had received from Frederick Saunders, Secretary of the Great Western Railway, dated 29th November 1866:

'Dear sirs,

'My attention has been drawn to a notice of intended application to Parliament for power to abandon the Bourton on the Water Extension line.

'Considering the relations which have existed between us I am a little surprised that such a notice should have been given by the Bourton-on the Water Co. without any previous communication with us.

'Will you be good enough to let me know for the information of my Board under what circumstances this notice has been given and what steps are proposed to be taken upon it.'

James Burchell added his own comments:

'I thought that they would wake up to the fact of such a Bill being proceeded with very shortly. I can only repeat to you my conviction that the very best thing you can do is as early as possible to have a Board meeting, and if possible in London for facilitating communication with the Gt. Western and other parties.

'I hope you are not suffering as you were when I saw you last.'

William Bliss was suffering, and had been for some time; it is tempting to speculate that the circumstances surrounding the Bourton Company were taking their toll on his health. In a letter to John Waddingham on 1st December, he wrote: 'I went to London last Monday to see Burchells, about your line. I had caught a severe chill which has confined me to my room ever since …'

In the letter, which is written in an almost indecipherable freehand, William Bliss informs that Mr. Adcock had been appointed to call a Board meeting of the Bourton Company on the following Thursday in the hope that Mr. Sherriff (who was also going to be in London that day) might be in attendance. Without any real knowledge of the motivation behind Mr. Sherriff's actions, the impression among the Bourton Company was that the 'hasty insertion of the Abandonment Notice' was carried out 'with the hope of driving the Great Western to give some material assistance'.

Evidently, neither the representatives of the GWR nor Mr. Sherriff was able to attend a meeting. Following the meeting of the Board, at which only Mr. Bennett and Mr. A T Adcock attended, the latter was compelled to write to William Bliss, who had been absent due to suffering from a 'congested liver':

'Mr Bennett wished you to be informed that there are some of the Directors who do not approve of the abandonment of the extension line to Cheltenham.

'I am afraid, however, that necessity has no law, and that the Company have no alternative but to take the course they have done.

'I shall be glad to hear when and where you can attend a meeting, and whether you can come here, as it is absolutely necessary a meeting of the Directors should be held before the end of the year, to enable me to comply with requirements of the Act of Parliament as to returns which have to be made regarding the issue of Debentures.'

When William Bliss responded, on 18th December, he was too unwell to write himself, and he dictated the letter through his son:

'From the enclosed you will see that Mr. Adcock now proposes a meeting at Worcester before the end of the year, but unless a better attendance of those really interested can be secured, my Father thinks it would be only time thrown away for him to be there.'

William Bliss went on to make a full recovery. The Cheltenham extension did not.

As the hopes of securing a positive outcome for the line faded, an air of resignation gradually fell upon the Bourton Company. The scheme which had promised so much was reluctantly laid to rest, along with William Bliss's cherished hopes of providing a through route between Banbury and Cheltenham via Chipping Norton.

Mr. E. Kendall's letter, dated 9th May 1867, some five months later and probably addressed to William Bliss personally, gives an intimate portrayal of the circumstances. He writes:

'I have done all I can to keep the poor Bourton extension from going under the water but see no hope for it, weighted as it is by Mr. Sherriff. On receipt of yours notifying a monthly respite I wrote to Mr Waddingham, Mr Whitmore and others to see if they would join in anything with a view to move the GWR and afterwards had a long interview with Mr Whitmore but I cannot move them.

'They all consider the fate of the scheme settled by the omission to go in for further time and though Mr Whitmore would subscribe £1000 or so and perhaps a few thousands might be raised among the other gentry, the aid so obtained would be a "flea bite" towards the preposterous sum named in the Act (£220,000 with power to raise £73,000 or more).

'Under these circumstances I see no possible object to be gained by attending the board meeting, the scheme must go and we must wait for better times and a fairer prospect. Thanking you very sincerely for all your exertion.
I am yours very truly, E [?] Ominid Kendall'

Despite the efforts to avoid it, formal authorisation for the abandonment of the Cheltenham extension took place by an

Act of 12th August 1867 (30 and 31 Vic. Cap.210), with a proviso 'to refrain from raising the capital so required'. The company was also required by the Act to pay the compensation in respect of the abandonment, and to pay the outstanding debts.

The Bourton Company's assets were already under some strain, and they resolved to 'claim against the Estate of Sir Morton Peto for costs incurred in the abandonment Bill', although it was probably recognised that trying to obtain recompense from a bankrupt source was generally a futile exercise.

In 1869, along with John Waddingham, C.S. Whitmore's name was now added to the Board of Directors. Of the five, only William Bliss and Mr. J. Bennett began with the originally-formed Bourton Company in 1860.

More problems developed, this time in renewing debentures, and so proposals from the Great Western for absorption must have come as a welcome relief to the company. Powers were obtained in an Act of June 1870, which authorised the GWR, with the consent of their shareholders, to issue 5% consolidated preference stock up to a maximum of £55 for every £100 of Bourton shares.

In September 1871, an advertisement was placed to officially inform the Bourton shareholders of the proposals, and of a general meeting to discuss the situation,

'...for the purpose of considering, and if so determined, approving an arrangement made with the Great Western Railway Company for the Amalgamation of the two Companies in accordance with their respective Parliamentary powers, upon the terms of an Allotment of Fifty-five Pounds of Great Western Railway Consolidated Stock in exchange for every One-hundred Pounds of Bourton-on-the-water Railway Ordinary Shares.'

However, a quorum of shareholders was not present, and the meeting did not take place. Neither did the Great Western rush to exercise these powers. The solicitor's costs in the case of the late Charles van Notten Pole had still to be settled, and the GWR insisted on protection against possible liabilities arising under the abandonment of the Cheltenham extension.

At a special meeting of the Bourton Company on 7th September 1872, with Sherriff in the Chair, it was resolved that 'the arrangement made with the Great Western Railway Company for a Transfer to that Company the Undertaking of the Bourton-on-the-Water Railway Company' for the £55 for £100 share terms previously mentioned, and 'the adoption of Great Western Company of the Debenture Debt of the Bourton-on-the-Water Railway Company' be approved and confirmed.

However, it was not until early 1874 that outstanding matters could be satisfactorily resolved, and absorption became a reality on 1st February of that year.

As for the East Gloucestershire Railway, they had the effects of Peto's bankruptcy to contend with. Further, the application to Parliament by the Midland Railway for powers to subscribe had been successfully opposed by the Great Western on the grounds that such powers would have been contrary to an existing agreement between them. At the same time, a proposed working agreement with the Midland was overruled by an arbitrator for the same reason. The East Gloucestershire was forced to reduce its share capital, content itself with building only the first fourteen miles of its line, between Witney and Fairford (opened in 1873), and arrange with the Great Western to work the line. The East Gloucestershire Railway was finally absorbed by the GWR in 1890.

The Bourton Company's Cheltenham extension had been a brave and ultimately unsuccessful initiative, and its abandonment was a sad end for a proposal that had promised so much. Nevertheless, due to the vision and enterprise of William Bliss and the people of the scattered communities of the north-east Cotswold region, the seeds were already sown for a railway which would replicate the course of the original scheme.

Even as the final arrangements for absorption of the Bourton Company were taking place – on 1st February 1874 – and the door finally closed on its existence, another was opening for a company that would see the project through.

The Banbury & Cheltenham Direct Railway had received its Enactment, and land acquisitions were steadily proceeding. One year later, almost to the day, the first sod of the new railway was cut in a field twenty-three miles from that 'genteel little village', from which the Bourton Railway Company had taken its name. The long hoped-for extension to Cheltenham moved forwards once more.

# BOURTON-ON-THE-WATER RAILWAY.

*No Train or Engine must be allowed to run on the Bourton-on-the-Water Railway*

*without the Train Pilot Ticket or Staff.*

| Miles from Bourton-on-the-Water. | STATIONS. | WEEK DAYS. | | | | | | SUNDAYS. | |
|---|---|---|---|---|---|---|---|---|---|
| | | 1 | 2 | 3 | 4 | 5 | 6 | | |
| | | a.m. | a.m. | a.m. | p.m. | p.m. | p.m. | | |
| — | Bourton-on-the-Water dep. | 7 15 | 8 50 | 11 20 | 3 10 | 7 0 | | | |
| 2¼ | Stow-on-the-Wold ... „ | 7 22 | 8 57 | 11 27 | 3 17 | 7 7 | | | |
| 6¼ | Chipping Norton Junc. arr. | 7 35 | 9 10 | 11 40 | 3 30 | 7 20 | | | |

No. 1 runs on the first Wednesday in the month only.

| Miles from Chipping Norton Junc. | STATIONS. | WEEK DAYS. | | | | | | SUNDAYS. | |
|---|---|---|---|---|---|---|---|---|---|
| | | 1 | 2 | 3 | 4 | 5 | 6 | | |
| | | a.m. | a.m. | p.m. | p.m. | p.m. | p.m. | | |
| — | Chipping Norton Junc. dep. | 8 17 | 9 42 | 12 20 | 4 20 | 7 40 | | | |
| 4½ | Stow-on-the-Wold ...... „ | ... | 9 55 | 12 33 | 4 33 | 7 53 | | | |
| 6¼ | Bourton-on-the-Water... arr. | 8 37 | 10 5 | 12 40 | 4 40 | 8 0 | | | |

No. 1 runs on the first Wednesday in the month only.

## 20    CHIPPING NORTON BRANCH.

| STATIONS. | 1 | 2 | 3 | 4 | 5 | | | |
|---|---|---|---|---|---|---|---|---|
| | A.M. | A.M. | A.M. | P.M. | P.M. | | | |
| Chipping Norton...........dep. | 7 25 | 8 5 | 11 35 | 3 20 | 7 15 | | | |
| Chipping Norton Junction ... | 7 40 | 8 15 | 11 47 | 3 32 | 7 27 | | | |
| Shipton ... ... ... | 7 50 | ... | ... | ... | ... | | | |
| Charlbury ... ... ... | 8 5 | ... | ... | ... | ... | | | |
| Handborough ... ... | 8 20 | ... | ... | ... | ... | | | |
| Yarnton Junction ... ... | 8 30 | ... | ... | ... | ... | | | |

No. 2 runs on the first Wednesday in the month only.

| STATIONS. | 1 | 2 | 3 | 4 | 5 | | | |
|---|---|---|---|---|---|---|---|---|
| | A.M. | A.M. | P.M. | P.M. | P.M. | | | |
| Yarnton Junction ... ... | ... | 8 50 | ... | ... | ... | | | |
| Handborough ... ... | ... | 9 0 | ... | ... | ... | | | |
| Charlbury ... ... ... | ... | 9 15 | ... | ... | ... | | | |
| Shipton ... ... ... | ... | 9 28 | ... | ... | ... | | | |
| Chipping Norton Junc. dep. | 7 42 | 9 35 | 12 25 | 4 20 | 7 40 | | | |
| Chipping Norton ... arr. | 7 55 | 10 0 | 12 40 | 4 35 | 8 0 | | | |

No. 1 runs on the first Wednesday in the month only.
### ALL TRAINS WORK GOODS WAGONS.

*West Midland Railway Timetable, July 1863.*

# CHAPTER FOUR
# THE EARLY YEARS
## 1862–1881

IN June 1860, the month in which the Bourton-on-the-Water Railway Company received the Enactment to build its 6½-mile branch from Chipping Norton Junction, the Oxford, Worcester & Wolverhampton Railway amalgamated with the Worcester & Hereford and Newport, Abergavenny & Hereford Railways to form the West Midland Railway. The routes of the new company included the OW & W main line and the Chipping Norton branch. In August 1863, the West Midland was absorbed into the Great Western Railway.

When the Bourton Railway opened to traffic on 1st March 1862 the company entered into a working arrangement with the West Midland, but continued to trade as a separate company. However, public timetables referred to both branches under the new title of the West Midland and continued to do so for many years.

It was in this 'independent' fashion that the line to Bourton-on-the-Water, along with its West Midland/Great Western neighbour, the Chipping Norton branch, functioned side by side for twelve years. Then, in February 1874, the Bourton Company was also absorbed into the Great Western. Despite these considerable changes, the two railways presented much the same appearance for some twenty years, operating in an easy-going fashion until the first stage of the Banbury & Cheltenham Direct Railway, to Cheltenham, was opened in 1881.

The companies did not operate in isolation; the timetables of both branches were arranged around the timetable of the Oxford & Worcester main line, connecting with both the local and express services calling at Chipping Norton Junction.

During 1861, the London & North Western Railway ceased to operate its through passenger services onto the OW & W via Yarnton. Later in the same year, the Great Western completed the addition of 'narrow' gauge rails into Paddington, and through coaches duly commenced, via Oxford, for and from the OW & W.

At the opening of the Bourton line, both the Chipping Norton and Bourton branches were operated by two of R. Stephenson & Co's 2–2–2WTs Nos.52 and 53, built for the OW & W in 1859. No 52 had worked the first passenger train from Honeybourne to Stratford-on-Avon in July 1859, for which event it had been named *Ben Jonson*, whilst No.53 had been the original locomotive on the isolated section of the Worcester & Hereford Railway between Henwick and Malvern Link, opened later in the same month. In its days on the two branches from Chipping Norton Junction, No.53 came to be familiarly known as 'Mrs Jonson'. As built, they had 5ft 6in driving and 3ft 6in carrying wheels, and had a distinctly foreign look about them; unusually, a full cab with side windows was provided, whilst the design included inside frames, outside cylinders, and some rather

ornamental features. The two engines became GWR Nos.223 and 224 respectively, and seem to have worked the branches almost continuously until they were withdrawn in March 1878 and October 1877 respectively.

The first train out of Chipping Norton continued to provide a connecting service for London at Shipton, though by 1861 this had been extended to Charlbury, and by February 1863 to Handborough, then, by July of that year, to Yarnton (this was also the junction for the Witney branch, opened in 1861), connecting for Oxford. In July 1863, the first branch train left Chipping Norton at 7.25 a.m., and was due into Yarnton 8.30 a.m.; from Yarnton, the 8.15 a.m. Witney train gave the connection into Oxford (due 8.45 a.m., five minutes before the Dudley express). This up express, 6.15 a.m. from Dudley, was speeded up in this period, and now called daily only at Evesham and Moreton en route between Worcester and Oxford (though with three other conditional stops), with a Paddington arrival of 10.25 a.m.; this gave passengers from Chipping Norton a three-hour journey to Paddington.

On its return, the branch train left Yarnton at 8.50 a.m., following the 8.30 a.m. Oxford (6.0 a.m. Paddington) to Chipping Norton Junction. Through running from the branch towards Oxford ceased in the late 1860s, when better connections were provided at Chipping Norton Junction.

In that final West Midland timetable of July 1863, four trains were running on each branch daily. On the first Wednesday of each month, these were joined by a through service from the Bourton line to serve Chipping Norton market; this left Bourton at 7.15 a.m., and was due into Chipping Norton at 7.55 a.m., departing again at 8.5 a.m. with a Bourton arrival of 8.37 a.m., in time to commence its usual working day. Main-line passenger trains calling at Chipping Norton Junction amounted to a meagre four down and three up, the fourth up service being provided by the 7.25 a.m. Chipping Norton and Yarnton connection for Oxford. One of the enginemen based at Chipping Norton in 1864 was Thomas Tompkins, who was from Chalford, in Gloucestershire.

During the OW & W and West Midland era, services over both the Chipping Norton and Bourton-on-the-Water branches were operated with mixed trains. However, as has been mentioned previously, for a short time before the full opening of the Chipping Norton line, goods-only trains were operating between the town and the main line.

The Bourton traffic was probably lighter than on the Chipping Norton branch, with no heavy industry being served, although agricultural traffic was probably significant at times, particularly the movement of stock into and out of Stow Fair. Grain was a principal incoming commodity, serving the two flour mills in Bourton, with coal also being a regular supply.

The main focus of attention during the early 1860s was the reconstruction of Chipping Norton Junction station. Without any existing plans showing the layout of the junction as it was in 1855, it is difficult to be precise about the scale of the alterations that took place during 1861–3. What is clear is that, after the opening of the Bourton branch, the original station building was replaced with a new structure along with identical buildings at Bourton and Stow, all three stations projecting a clear and distinct visual identity to travellers along the branch. These buildings were executed in masonry and timber, in the Carpenter Gothic style, a popular development of the fashionable Arts and Crafts movement. The buildings were charming, but not practical for passengers waiting on the platforms in adverse weather conditions; only Bourton was fitted with a canopy, and its contrived appearance suggests it may have been added at a later date.

In its rebuilt form, there was an assortment of buildings providing for goods operations at Chipping Norton Junction, including a weighbridge, although a through road goods shed was never provided. On the up side was a signal box, giving a clear view through the single-arch road bridge round a shallow bend towards Shipton. Also on the up side was an island platform with two separate waiting rooms (generally one for each gender was provided) connected by a long, broad canopy. No footbridge existed and access between the platforms was via a simple barrow crossing.

Presiding over these alterations at the junction was Edward Jackson Cuff, stationmaster from c.1861–1865. He was born in 1839, at Brighton, his railway career taking him from Dursley Green in Shropshire in 1859 to Wolverhampton in 1860 before his posting to Chipping Norton Junction. He was not living at the junction, although a station house may have existed then, but travelled to work from his home in Kingham village, one mile north-west of the junction.

On 13th August 1863, Charles Seabury Nairn, a locomotive driver, was accidentally killed by falling from the engine and crushed under the wheels of passing carriages at the junction.

Both termini were equipped to deal with their motive power. Chipping Norton was provided with an engine shed from the outset, and it is likely that Bourton was similarly provided with the necessary facilities.

This period marked a peak in the great Victorian boom years before the financial bubble burst in 1866. William Bliss took the opportunity to expand his manufactory at the Lower Mill, spending a massive £35,000 on improvements.

In addition to his involvement in the Bourton Company, and particularly its proposed Cheltenham extension, William Bliss was showing interest in the need for a railway connection between Chipping Norton and Banbury. A plethora of schemes sprang up during the first half of the 1860s, and depending on the advantages or otherwise for the town, Bliss took up a position of positive support or decisive opposition.

There were two objectives. The first was a westward drive from Banbury to the West Midland line near Blockley, running through the Stour Valley. Various proposals had been put forward since 1851 (or earlier) to develop the route, which attracted great support from the people of Banbury. It would be cheap, direct, relatively easy to construct, and most importantly, it gave Banbury good access to the West Midland markets.

The people of Chipping Norton were uncomfortable with these developments, and backed a series of alternative schemes which all linked Chipping Norton with Banbury, giving access to the markets beyond. For three years, the two towns battled it out.

The weight of favour lay with the people of Banbury, a town of around 8,000 inhabitants, as opposed to Chipping Norton with only 3,000 people. Banburyans voted with their feet against the Chipping Norton proposals, though Bliss was always prepared to meet the challenge. The problem for Chipping Norton was made clear during one highly-charged meeting at Banbury town hall, to which William Bliss made a special visit in order to win support for a proposed Chipping Norton route (probably the Northampton & Banbury Junction extensions). The agent for the opposing scheme, Mr W. Champion, told the people of Banbury: 'You will have made greengages of yourselves with a vengeance if you support a line which ends in landing you in Chipping Norton and takes you nowhere else.'

Besides the opposition from Banbury, two other peculiarities adversely affected Chipping Norton's attempts to extend their existing line to Banbury. The town's position on the north-eastern edge of the Cotswolds was not ideally suited to railway expansion. Chipping Norton occupied the north-west facing slope of a shallow valley, with the railway station lying at its bottom, some 200 ft below, at around 480 ft above sea level. Upstream of the terminus, the valley quickly became narrower and steeper until it reached the high ground north of the town, which attained a height of 750 ft. In railway terms, the valley effectively went nowhere, although this topographic challenge might have been overcome with some expensive engineering. However, it was made impossible by the location of Lt. Col. Dawkins' estate at Over Norton Park, which straddled the valley one mile north of the town; understandably, Captain Dawkins did not want a railway near his estate.

There was to be no easy engineering solution for the railway promoters at Chipping Norton. The proposed railway would need to be taken through the hillside into the adjacent valley to the north to permit it to resume its north-easterly course. Tunnelling would thus be obligatory from the existing station site, and in order to reduce the length of bore to the minimum, the railway would be required to enter the hillside perpendicular to its existing alignment, performing a tight left-hand curve as it did so, and all on a substantial rising gradient. One can picture the scene at Chipping Norton in the early 1860s: the railway surveyors gathered on the slopes of the Great Common, with their

*Chipping Norton, viewed from the 'Great Common' c.1860.*          CTY. MAYOR & CLERK TO CHIPPING NORTON TOWN COUNCIL

vernier theodolites, the most advanced optical instruments of the day, set up to measure the landforms to chart the ideal course for an extension of the Chipping Norton branch to Banbury.

The first proposal to connect the two towns was called the Chipping Norton & Banbury Railway, put forward by John Fowler and Edward Wilson in 1863, and deposited on 30th November of that year. This route had an advantage of directness, hugging the high ground east of the Swere valley, passing south of Swerford and east of Wigginton, parallel to the Chipping Norton and Banbury road. This proposal took a course north of Twyford and swung round in a broad curve to drop into the Cherwell valley one mile south-east of Banbury. A later route alteration took the railway south of Twyford to join the Oxford & Birmingham line at Twyford Mill.

The Banburyans' attention was taken by an alternative proposal by John Collister called the Northampton & Banbury Junction Extension Railway, put forward in 1864. This scheme, whose agents were Gregory, Champion and Eady, connected Blissworth in Northamptonshire with Banbury, and included two extensions, one westward to Blockley and a second to Chipping Norton, the latter similar to that eventually constructed. The people of Chipping Norton backed this scheme enthusiastically, though Banbury typically opposed the Chipping Norton route, but its most important objection came from a source much closer to home: Lt. Col. Dawkins of Over Norton Park. The nature of his objection to the railway is not clear, but in what was

almost certainly an attempt to keep the proposed railway as far from his estate as possible, he deflected attention away by promoting another, whose route passed at a more tolerable distance.

On 11th April 1865 he wrote:

> 'It is proposed next year to bring in a railway similar…(to the Chipping Norton route) but having a branch from near Tadmarton or Stours Well to Blockley. Thus it is most desirable for the villages (of the Stour valley) that the Northampton and Banbury extension should be thrown out this year; for it gives them no communication to the south without going first to Banbury.'

The alternative proposal was the Chipping Norton, Banbury and East & West Junction Railway. Its north-south connections were no better, but Lt. Col. Dawkins was probably looking for an excuse to dismiss the original scheme. The railway was similar to the Northampton & Banbury with its two extensions, but connected Banbury with the East & West Junction Railway near Moreton Pinkney.

It had come to the notice of the people of Chipping Norton that Lt. Col. Dawkins was lodging an objection to the Northampton & Banbury, and they took decisive action. They had every reason to oppose the new railway; the proposed route of the East & West Junction Railway did not actually pass through Chipping Norton, but effectively bypassed the town, joining the Chipping Norton branch around three-quarters-of-a-mile west of the existing terminus. Were this railway to be constructed, the status of Chipping Norton station would not be improved, the junction too far from the town to be of use.

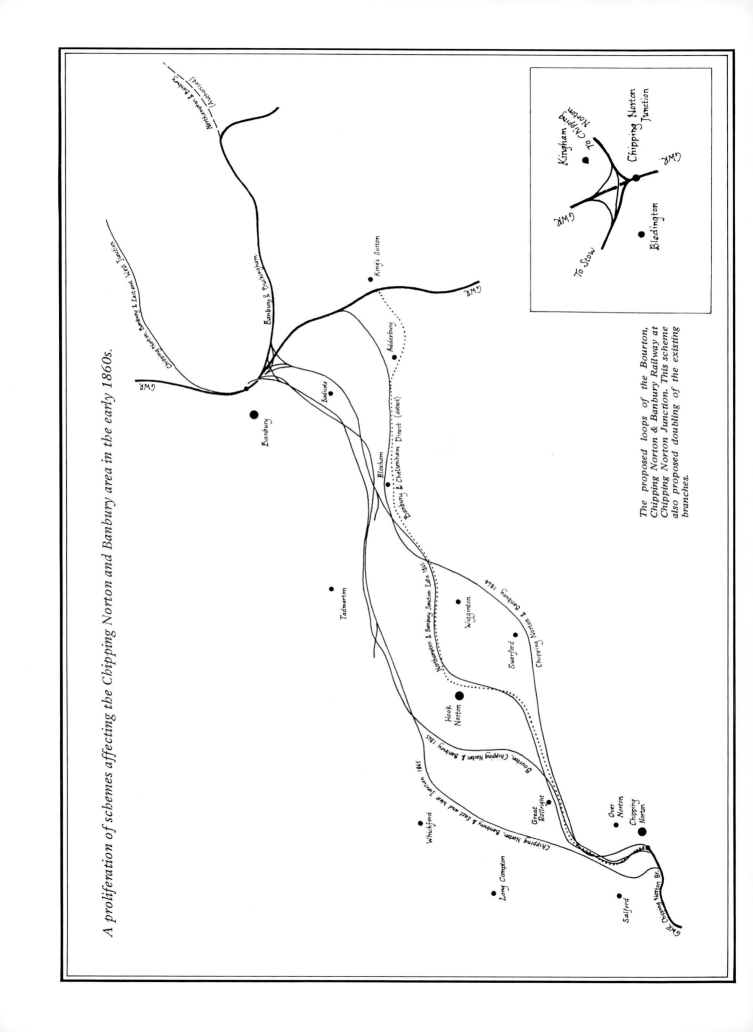

*A proliferation of schemes affecting the Chipping Norton and Banbury area in the early 1860s.*

The proposed loops of the Bourton, Chipping Norton & Banbury Railway at Chipping Norton Junction. This scheme also proposed doubling of the existing branches.

Kingham

To Chipping Norton

Chipping Norton Junction

GWR

GWR

To Stow

Bladington

Northampton & Banbury [Authorised]

Chipping Norton, Banbury & East and West Junction

GWR

Banbury & Buckingham

King's Sutton

Banbury

Bodicote

Adderbury

Blexham

Banbury & Cheltenham Direct (dotted)

Tadmarton

Whichford

Long Compton

Salford

Over Norton

Chipping Norton

Great Rollright

Northampton & Banbury Junction Extn 1865

Wigginton

Swerford

Chipping Norton & Banbury 1864

Hook Norton

Bourton, Chipping Norton & Banbury 1865

Chipping Norton, Banbury & East and West Junction 1865

GWR Chipping Norton Br.

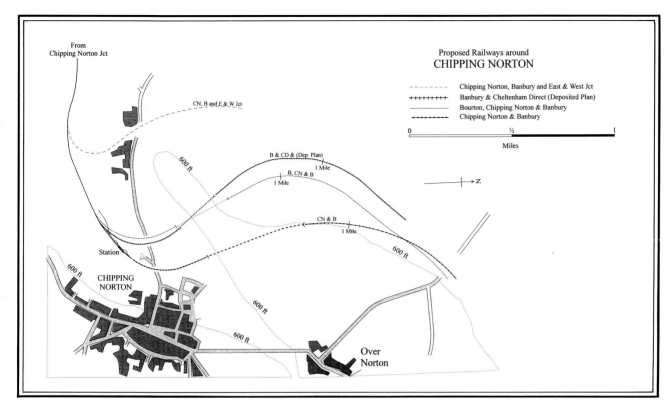

Proposed Railways around
**CHIPPING NORTON**

- – – – – – – Chipping Norton, Banbury and East & West Jct
- +++++++ Banbury & Cheltenham Direct (Deposited Plan)
- ·············· Bourton, Chipping Norton & Banbury
- ·—·—·—· Chipping Norton & Banbury

The Borough Councillors hurriedly met on 20th March to discuss the situation. The mayor, George Tilsley, William Bliss, Abram Rawlinson and Mr Wilkins were present, and the following was recorded:

'MINUTES OF CHIPPING NORTON BOROUGH COUNCIL, 1865, TO DISCUSS RAILWAY PLANS

'Special Council Meeting to consider what steps shall be taken in consequence of Colonel Dawkins having lodged a petition against the Northampton and Banbury Extension Railway.

'Resolved: that the following Memorial be sent to Colonel Dawkins by the Town Clerk.

'To Lieutenant Colonel Dawkins

'The mayor and Corporation of Chipping Norton having heard that Colonel Dawkins has lodged a Petition against the Proposed Northampton and Banbury Junction Railway Extension beg respectfully to address him on this subject.

'The Corporation as representing the Inhabitants of the Town of Chipping Norton are strongly convinced that the proposed Line which effects a railway communication between Chipping Norton and Banbury and thence to the north of England would be a great benefit and convenience to the inhabitants of Chipping Norton and the Neighbourhood and believe it is laid out with as great advantage and as little inconvenience to the Country through which it passes as is practicable.

'The Corporation believe that the competing Line of the East and West Junction Extension so far from being any benefit to the Town of Chipping Norton would be a very serious injury thereto, removing as it would their Station considerably further from the Town than it is at present and leaving Chipping Norton on a branch instead of placing it on the Main Line.

'They therefore most respectfully submit the above considerations to Colonel Dawkins, earnestly entreating him to withdraw his opposition to the Northampton and Banbury Junction Railway Extension and not to give his support to the competing scheme.

Geo. F. Tilsley

'This meeting was adjourned to 10 o'clock tomorrow 21st instant.'

Then:

A joint Memorial to be presented to Parliament by the Corporations of Banbury and of Chipping Norton ... sheweth

'That a Bill is now pending in your Honourable House entitled 'A Bill for making a Railway from the East and West Junction Railway in the parish of Canons Ashby and County of Northampton to Chipping Norton in the County of Oxford to be called the Chipping Norton, Banbury and East and West Junction Railway ...

'No.2 A Railway commencing in the said parish of Warkworth by a junction with the Great Western Railway about 10 chains southward of the passenger booking office of the Banbury Station of that Railway and terminating in the parish of Chipping Norton in the County of Oxford by a Junction with the Chipping Norton Branch of the Great Western Railway at a point about 40 chains Westward of the Chipping Norton Station of that Railway ...

'They believe that the proposed Railway to have been laid out without due regard to the requirements of that district and that a far preferable line could with ordinary care and skill have been selected ...

'That the junction of the proposed Railway No 2 with the Chipping Norton Branch of the Great Western Railway is about 52 chains westward of the present Station at Chipping Norton.

'That the trains running on to the proposed Railway from the Eastward would have to be backed into the said station and in like manner trains leaving the said station and going eastward would have to be backed out of the said station along the existing railway before they could enter the proposed Railway involving great loss of time and inconvenience to the public using the Railway.

'That the Curve into the said Chipping Norton Branch Railway is objectionable and dangerous the radius being only one furlong upon a

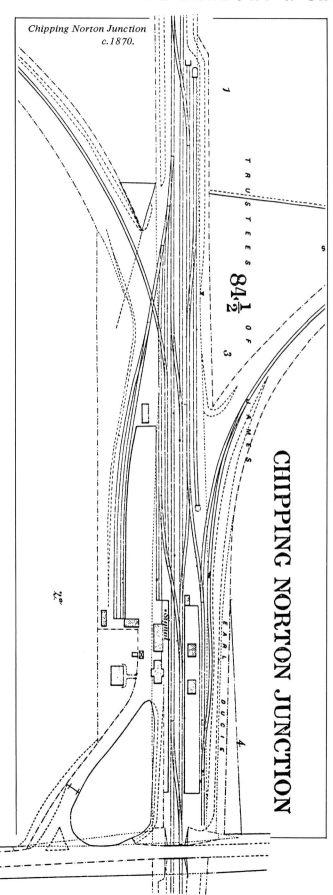

*Chipping Norton Junction c.1870.*

CHIPPING NORTON JUNCTION

descending gradient in one place 1 in 63 and in other part of it 1 in 165…

'Your Petitioners therefore humbly pray your Honourable House that the said Bill may not pass into a Law and that they may be heard by their Counsel Agents and Witnesses against the Preamble thereof…

'Done at a Meeting of the Council of the Borough of Chipping Norton held this twenty-first day of March 1865.

'George F. Tilsley, Mayor'

The minutes then authorised a body who would take the matter forward.

'Committee appointed in the event of the Town Council of Banbury agreeing to Co-operate with this town:

The Mayor
Mr Bliss
Mr Rawlinson
Mr Wilkins'

Fortunately for the people of Chipping Norton, the Chipping Norton, Banbury and East & West Junction Railway did not pass into law. The Northampton & Banbury Junction Extension and a new proposal by Edward Wilson and John Fowler, called the Bourton, Chipping Norton & Banbury Railway did not pass into law either. This latter scheme threw caution to the winds by slicing into the undulating uplands to the west of Hook Norton, and incorporated a complex pattern of loops at Chipping Norton Junction to allow through running in every direction.

The great stock market crash of 1866 put an immediate stop to these developments, and the focus of Chipping Norton once again reverted to its purely local role as a country branch line terminus.

In the late 1860s, the stationmasters at Bourton and Stow were Samuel P. Hunt and Thomas Tibbs respectively. Towards the end of the decade, George Adams took over the stationmaster's post at the Junction, replacing Edward Jackson Cuff, remaining there until 1870. He had previously served on the Witney Railway, at South Leigh station, and whilst there he married Emma Pearce.

Also serving at Chipping Norton Junction were signalman William Slade, who had progressed from porter during his time there, and a booking clerk by the name of Thomas Bye. This young man was born in the nearby village of Bledington and was probably no more than twelve years old when he began at the Junction. Sadly, his railway career was to be very short-lived; in an unfortunate set of circumstances on 2nd November 1869 he 'died of injuries received by a locomotive engine accidentally passing over him…'

During July 1867, there were six daily trains each way over the Chipping Norton branch, the first leaving the terminus at 7.25 a.m. (for Yarnton) and the last arriving back at 8.48 p.m. On Saturdays, a seventh train ran in the late afternoon. From around this time, Sarsden Siding featured in the service timetable, with an instruction that trains would stop there if required. It also stated that 'all trains work goods wagons'.

The Bourton branch service started at 7.15 a.m. from the town (to Chipping Norton, now daily), whilst the fifth return train arrived back at 8.48 p.m. The through Bourton & Chipping Norton train had ceased by 1870.

*The earliest known photograph of Chipping Norton Junction. Aden Eaton, at far left on the down platform, was station master at the junction from 1870 to 1879, after George Adams. He relinquished the post to take over the grocery and drapery business in Kingham from John Phillips, who had held the business for the previous fourteen years. George Brecknell replaced Aden Eaton as station master.*
COLLECTION MICHAEL LAINCHBURY

Aden Eaton became stationmaster at Chipping Norton Junction in 1870. Born in Church Handborough in 1843, he worked at Witney Station until 1867, followed by a short posting to Fladbury in Worcestershire before moving to the junction.

Among the staff in 1871 were two porters, Charles Faulks and William Widdows, aged 18 and 19 respectively, who lodged with Thomas Bridge in Brook Cottage, Kingham.

Excursions were soon established for branch patrons. On Thursday, 17th August 1871, an excursion left Handborough at 7.40 a.m. for Birmingham, calling at Chipping Norton Jct. at 8.10 a.m. Running empty from Oxford, the train was formed with two First class coaches, twelve 'covered', two 'break' coaches and a 'break van'. Those excursionists wishing to travel on this train from Chipping Norton were enjoined to leave the town on the 7.55 a.m. ordinary service to the junction, although those from Bourton were afforded a special train, which left at 7.45 a.m., calling at Stow ten minutes later. At Chipping Norton Jct., two additional 'covered' coaches, previously positioned there, were attached to the excursion for those passengers from Chipping Norton, whilst those from Bourton and Stow had three. Suitably strengthened and filled, the 22-coach train departed at 8.15 a.m. for Birmingham.

The return was at 8.0 p.m. from Birmingham, travelling along the same route as outbound, via Hatton, Bearley, Stratford, Honeybourne and Moreton. The train reached Chipping Norton Jct. at 10.18 p.m., to be met by a special train for Chipping Norton, which departed the junction at 10.25 p.m., and another for Bourton, which left at the same time.

Chipping Norton station was a compact affair, with the passenger platform and building on the north side of the line, a goods shed on its west side, and a cattle dock to its east, at the extreme limit of the line. A single-road engine shed was located to the south of the passenger platform, with a water tank and coaling stage at its eastern end. The station approach led north-eastwards from the site, joining with the turnpike on the western outskirts of the town. The approach was lined with horse-chestnut trees, planted by Bliss, some of which survive to this day.

Following complaints made to the GWR of the 'exposed state of the Chipping Norton station', an overall roof was provided. In November 1865, a plan laid before the Traffic Committee showed a platform covering supported by iron pillars at a cost of about £200; however, this was deemed too costly, and the matter was referred to the expenditure committee with the recommendation that a less-expensive covering in wood should be provided at a cost not exceeding £100. This was duly supplied.

Among the staff at Chipping Norton in the early 1870s were firemen Henry Dixon and James Simms, and engine cleaner William Gardiner.

In 1872, a siding to serve the new Chipping Norton Gas Company was provided; this was situated alongside the railway to the west of the Bliss mill. The Inspecting Officer for the Board of Trade pointed out that the 'sharp curve' between the station and siding prevented it being seen from the lever frame from which it was worked. The outcome of the inspection was that the company was required to protect the new siding by a signal in each direction, interlocked with the points and safety points independently of the station distant signal. The report reveals that the siding was served from the station rather than by an arriving train, the branch locomotive servicing it while in possession of the single-line train staff.

Freight into Chipping Norton included bricks and coal, the bulk of the latter destined for the industrial concerns of Hitchman's Brewery and the Bliss mills. The tweed manufactory continued to supply a large quantity of incoming and outgoing goods from the town. By 1870, the business had reached the height of its prosperity, employing 700 people at the two mills, and producing an annual turnover of £260,000, a far cry from its humble origins in the old flour mill sixty years earlier.

At 5.0 a.m. on a February morning in 1872, disaster struck the Bliss company. A boiler exploded in the Lower Mill, setting the building ablaze and killing three people. A Mr

*The burnt-out remains of Bliss's 'Lower Mill' following the fire in February 1872. The caption mistakenly has misplaced the date by two years.*
AUTHOR'S COLLECTION

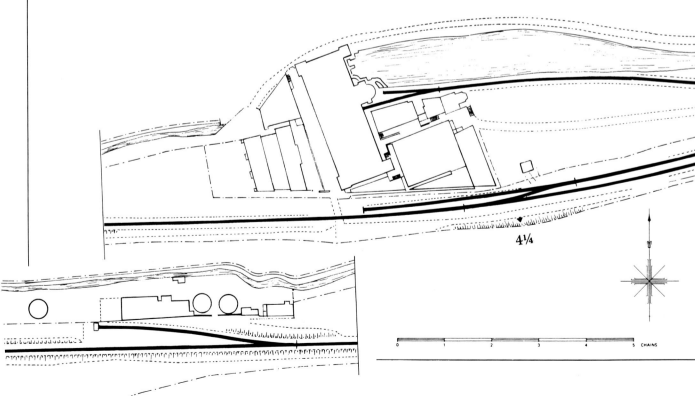

Hurcomb, who lived in a nearby cottage, was the first to raise the alarm, and people hurriedly responded by moving the furniture onto the Common. But there was little anyone could do. The fire had taken such a hold that the hastily organized 'bucket chain' from the millpond to the firemen on the scene was little more than a token gesture. A contemporary account describes a groom from the nearby Heythrop Hunt kennels taking news of the event to the town, the message then being broadcast by the urgently pealing bells of St Mary's Church; it was this alarm that woke William Bliss.

The day was one of immense tragedy for the town, but Bliss was undeterred. He wasted no time rebuilding the mill, appointing the eminent architect of industrial buildings, George Woodhouse, to design the new structure.

Characteristically, William Bliss turned the negative situation into an opportunity, allowing the architecture of the new mill to make a stunning visual statement. When the new Lower Mill was completed within a year, its appearance suggested a hybrid of a traditional textile factory and a grand country house, complete with massive stone balustrades topped with finials. The illusion was completed by its setting beside the Great Common, resembling a naturalistic, landscaped park. This metaphor carried some meaning, for it

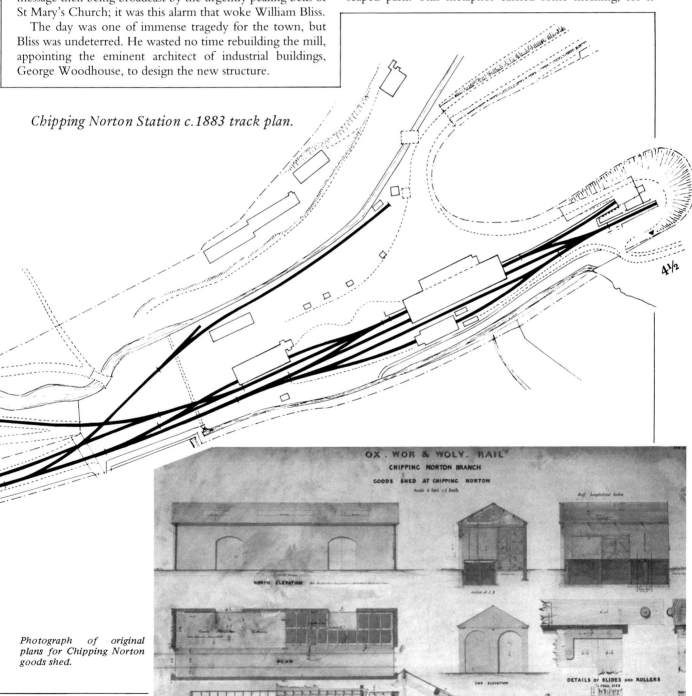

*Chipping Norton Station c.1883 track plan.*

*Photograph of original plans for Chipping Norton goods shed.*

*The 'Bliss Empire' as it appeared on the company's corporate literature, following rebuilding of the 'Lower Mill' in 1872. Compare this view of the terminus with that on page 17.*

revealed Bliss as the paternal lord over his empire, elevating the workplace above the traditional functional environment. However, it could never have been his intention for this 'message' to be taken too seriously, for the centrepiece of this grand design was a huge, preposterous chimney, towering high above the mill and protruding through a lead-clad, ribbed dome. The chimney dominated the surrounding landscape, the whole structure presenting a startling appearance, an impression which is as true today as it was when the mill was constructed in 1872.

The Banbury Guardian blandly announced the completion of the new building in its edition of 16th October 1873:

'CHIPPING NORTON
'New mill at Chipping Norton for Messrs W Bliss & Son, cost £20,000, Architect George Woodhouse Esq, Clerk of Works Mr. Richard Wood, both of Bolton-le-Moors, Lancashire.'

The new mill epitomised the flamboyant character of its owner, and made a powerful advertising image for the company, appearing on its new letterheads. Unfortunately, the boom years were drawing to a close; the years of success that had accompanied Bliss's expanding business were never to be repeated as the textile trade shifted to the north and west of England. However, none of this happened overnight. Even as the new Lower Mill was being paid for out of diminishing returns, William Bliss continued to set the standards for employer/employee relations throughout the district, as illustrated in these two accounts reported in the *Banbury Guardian*:

'June 22 1876
'The employees of Messrs Bliss, the extensive manufacturer of tweed &c, in this town, propose visiting the Crystal Palace on Saturday next, a special train having been chartered for their conveyance.'

'June 29 1876
TRIP TO THE CRYSTAL PALACE
'On Saturday the work people in the employ of Messrs. W. Bliss & Son, to the number of 300, engaged a special train, comprising twelve carriages, to convey them to the Crystal Palace & back, starting at 5.35 in the morning, they arrived at the palace at 9.35 a.m. and returned from the Palace at 7.30, reaching Chipping Norton at 11.45, a good day's outing having been enjoyed by all without any mishap. We are informed.'

Four months later the railway was once more in the local news, and again Bliss's firm occupied the central theme, but sadly, this story did not have a happy ending:

'CHIPPING NORTON
'Thursday October 19 1876
'FATAL ACCIDENT
'On Thursday evening last a melancholy accident happened to a widow, named Sophia Burnham, residing with her nephew in one of Messrs. Bliss's cottages at the Lower Mill. The unfortunate woman, who was very deaf, was returning home up the line, when she was overtaken by the evening train, and received such injuries as resulted in her death a short time after the occurrence. An inquest was held at the Fox Inn on Saturday morning, before Mr Westall, when the following evidence was adduced – Mr Burtonshaw, residing at the Gas Works, stated – on Thursday afternoon, I and my children went down the line for the purpose of getting some blackberries when we overtook Mrs Burnham and a neighbour named Robinson, who accompanied us. We went into some fields adjoining the line and stayed about two hours, all leaving together. Mrs Burnham walked on first, and as we were going along one

of my children had its foot wedged in between the rail and sleeper; at this time we heard the 5.30 train approaching and it was with difficulty that we got its foot free before the train reached us. Mrs Robinson was in front of me and my children, and we heard the whistle blow to warn her, and we also heard it a second time. Owing to a sharp curve in the line I was unable to see the deceased when the train came up, and when I had got a short distance from the signal I saw her lying on the ground, Dr Farwell and another gentleman attending her, Mr Robinson, who also was prevented seeing the train strike the deceased on account of the curve, corroborated the previous witness's evidence. Samuel Bright, the driver of the engine stated – on Thursday evening when we were about 150 yards from the signal post where there is a sharp curve, I saw a woman walking on the side of the line, and clear of the metals. She was going towards Chipping Norton. When we got within 50 or 60 yds of her, I saw her walk on to the ballast and proceed between the line of rails. I at once blew the whistle, reversed the engine and had the breaks applied. Before however, we could stop the train, the engine struck the woman, and when we had come to a standstill I saw her lying behind the train on the line. I got off my engine, and went up to her, and found her very much injured. The poor woman was attended by Mr Farwell, surgeon, who happened to be in the train, but her injuries were of so serious a nature that she died at nine o'clock the same evening. The jury returned a verdict of accidental death.'

In February 1876, seven trains were running daily each way from Chipping Norton to the Junction, with the first departure from the terminus at 7.50 a.m. and the last arrival at 9.13 p.m. At this time, all five main-line trains in each direction – express and local – called at Chipping Norton Junction, and the first branch train, 7.50 a.m. from Chipping Norton, now permitted a 2 hr 35 min journey to

Paddington. In the down direction, the 6.30 p.m. Paddington was due into the Junction at 8.51 p.m., from where a 9.0 p.m. branch departure gave a 2 hr 43 min journey to Chipping Norton.

Five trains ran from Bourton to Chipping Norton Junction in 1876, the first leaving the terminus at 8.40 a.m. and the last service arriving back at 9.15 p.m.; these were expanded to six in 1880. Bourton passengers were not provided with an early connection for London, though the 6.30 p.m. Paddington did allow a 2 hr 39 min journey to Stow, and 2 hr 45 min to Bourton.

Of the five main-line trains calling at Chipping Norton Jct., one each way called only to pick up or set down First class London passengers.

By this time, the main-line goods traffic had increased to nine trains each way, most of which called at the Junction. In addition, there were two conditional trips in each direction, one of which ran from Worcester to Chipping Norton Junction itself, arriving at 4.25 p.m. with goods and coal, and departing for Worcester thirty minutes later with goods and empties.

Although William Bliss's requirement for coal was a major factor in the very existence of the line, it was not until 1884 that a siding was constructed from a point to the west of the goods shed into the mill's grounds, allowing coal wagons to be taken to a convenient location for offloading.

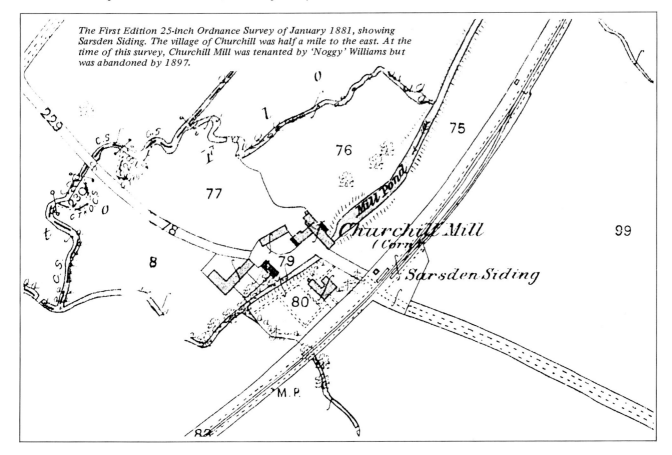

*The First Edition 25-inch Ordnance Survey of January 1881, showing Sarsden Siding. The village of Churchill was half a mile to the east. At the time of this survey, Churchill Mill was tenanted by 'Noggy' Williams but was abandoned by 1897.*

Among the footplate crew at Chipping Norton shed in the late 1870s, in addition to Samuel Bright, were George Wood, also a driver, George Allen King, who remained there until at least 1885, and Thomas Stickley, fireman, who by 1885 was promoted to driver at Chipping Norton. By that year William Munday had joined the complement at Chipping Norton as an engine driver. Also serving at the terminus in 1878 was Thomas Hartley, stationmaster.

The staff at Chipping Norton and the other stations along the two branches would by now have been aware that changes were on the way. During the cold, snow-filled winter of 1880–81, the last stages in the construction of the western section of the Banbury & Cheltenham Direct Railway, seven years in the making, were nearing completion. The cosy existence of the two lines, each performing their basic local function, were drawing to a close, although Chipping Norton would have to wait a further six years before the extension to Banbury was finally opened.

Also at the turn of the decade William Bliss, now aged 70, was making preparations for his own future. He did not reserve a plot in the local graveyard, but in typical generous style, bought three acres and two roods of land from the Regulated Pasture to be designated as the cemetery for the benefit of the people of Chipping Norton. On 29th January 1881 the purchase was made at £150 per acre.

★   ★   ★

Early in the morning of the first day of June, 1881, at Hampen Manor Farm, high up in the Cotswolds, one-year-old Tom Handy was taken across the fields to witness a special event taking place. At 7.20 a.m. the family, who had

farmed there over four generations, gathered to watch as the first passenger train from Cheltenham climbed the 1 in 60 gradient to the summit, which lay beyond the great cutting at the top of Hampen Hill, half a mile to the east, before beginning its long descent through Notgrove to Bourton-on-the-Water, eleven miles away. The long-awaited, much hoped-for link to Cheltenham was open at last.

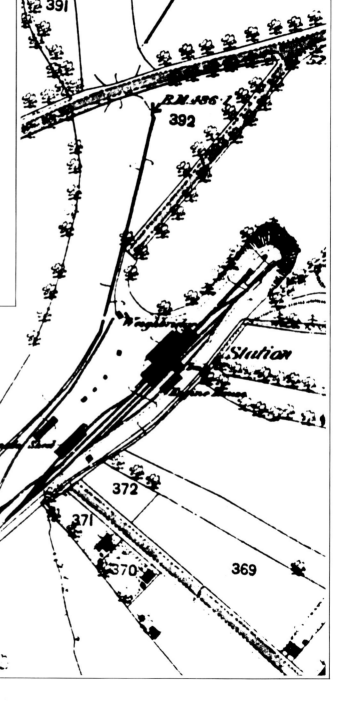

*The First Edition 25-inch Ordnance Survey of Chipping Norton station 1881. The years of Chipping Norton as a terminus were drawing to a close. The alignment for the Banbury and Cheltenham Railway is established, and the bridge carrying the Worcester Road over the proposed line is in place. However, at the time the survey was published, another six years were to pass before the railway finally opened.*

# CHAPTER FIVE

# THE ERA OF THE BANBURY AND CHELTENHAM DIRECT RAILWAY
## 1872–1897

BY the third quarter of the nineteenth century, large portions of the British Isles had been reached by the railway system. Most adverse situations faced by railway engineers had been successfully overcome, often with extreme difficulty. At the beginning of the 1870s, three of the greatest challenges were about to be faced: the bridge crossings of the Tay and Forth in 1870 and 1873 respectively, and the Great Western Railway's Severn Tunnel in 1872. Against this awe-inspiring backdrop of Victorian innovation were put forward large numbers of less-demanding proposals to infill gaps in the railway system. Amongst them was the Banbury & Cheltenham Direct Railway.

The B & CD entered the railway scene in 1872. Use of the term 'Direct' in its title led the company to become a popular subject of railway jokes; railway companies tended to embellish their proposed lines in a variety of ways, ranging from the false portrayal of routes as straight lines on promotional maps to the provision of grand-sounding titles (often incorporating distant places which the project was unlikely ever to reach). Very misleading impressions could be given in this way, glossing over the reality of shared running powers and long, meandering routes.

On first inspection, the Banbury & Cheltenham Direct Railway's proposed route appeared to be anything but direct, its location constrained largely by topography, as had all previous schemes to link the two centres. It also involved running rights over existing lines, namely the Great Western's northern main line between King's Sutton and Banbury, and their line from Gloucester between Hatherley and Cheltenham, although these were fairly short distances. In addition, the proposal made connections with the Great Western's existing branch lines at Bourton-on-the-Water and Chipping Norton. The significance of the term 'Direct' to the Banbury & Cheltenham was the reduction in route miles between those places compared with the existing railways. The Great Western's shortest route between Banbury and Cheltenham in the 1870s was via Oxford, Didcot and Swindon, a distance of about 100 miles. An alternative route for passengers from Banbury to Fenny Compton, the Stratford-on-Avon Junction Railway to Broom, thence by the Midland via Ashchurch to Cheltenham was around 56 miles – considerably shorter, though not a great deal faster. The B & CD's route between the stations in the two towns amounted to 48 miles, hence the claim to its title 'Direct'. The B & CDR was therefore a typical example of a secondary cross-country route, providing a much-needed connection between the north-east and south-west of the country.

The B & CD put forward an impressive proposal. The actual length of new lines was substantial, totalling some thirty-four miles. Provision was to be made for triangular junctions at both the King's Sutton and Cheltenham ends of the line, to enable through running from all directions, and there was to be a direct connection between the eastern and western sections in the form of a flyover at Chipping Norton Junction. The company appointed Edward Wilson as its Engineer; he had an extensive knowledge of the area, particularly the western section. Wilson had originally surveyed for the Bourton-on-the-Water Railway Company's Cheltenham extension, the route of which the new railway was to follow.

However, apart from the link with Edward Wilson, the two companies were quite different. Unlike the Bourton Company, the B & CD did not have the vision and guiding hand of a character such as William Bliss behind it. Without doubt, the B & CD was a speculator's project from the start. The prime motivator behind the proposal was the discovery of large quantities of haematite, a deposit of ironstone, that stretched locally from Northamptonshire into north-west Oxfordshire, along the eastern part of the proposed route. Considerable interest was shown in this mineral due to the anticipated revenue to be made by transporting the ore by rail to the established smelting plants in South Wales.

The company clearly expected some rich pickings from transporting the ironstone, and in anticipation of the massive return they were expecting to make, settled for a keen, perhaps deliberately low, estimate allowed by Edward Wilson of £800,000. The capital of the company was accordingly set at £600,000 in shares and £200,000 in loans.

Compared with some of the major engineering projects that were taking place across the country in the 1870s, the construction of the Banbury & Cheltenham Railway ought to have been straightforward. Its shareholders probably thought it would be, but the opposite was the case. The contract that was to have been completed within five years, as stipulated in the Act of Parliament, took fourteen years to achieve; in that time, four contractors came and went, the costs soared from the original £800,000 to £1,800,000, and the company's affairs were transferred into the hands of a receiver. During that fourteen-year period – which, incidentally, witnessed much loss of life on the workings – eight Acts of Parliament were granted to complete the line, many of which related to design changes. When the Banbury & Cheltenham Direct Railway finally opened in April 1887, there was no customary celebration. To many people, the railway was a bitter disappointment, and even today there are those who harbour a surprisingly deep-seated resentment, remembering their forebears who invested large sums of money in anticipation of a return that never came.

During 1872, the year preceding the Enactment, the infant company was esteemed as the worthy successor to the many abandoned proposals that had gone before, and the company was at the centre of much activity. In that year, the plans and sections were deposited to the clerks of the peace for the counties of Northampton, Oxford and Gloucester, and the necessary land acquisitions began. The Banbury and Cheltenham Direct Railway Bill was prepared for the 1873 Parliamentary session.

A significant event in forming the detailed proposals for the railway was the meeting of the House of Commons' Select Committee, 'appointed to consider and report upon the merits of this Bill' , which assembled on Tuesday, 25th March 1873. Horace Lloyd QC, appearing as Counsel for the promoters of the Bill, opened the case. As the 'Special Reporter' to the *Banbury Guardian* described in the edition of 27th March,

'The object of the Bill was to incorporate a new company for the purpose of giving direct railway communication between Banbury and Cheltenham, two places which though not far distant from each other as the crow flies, could not communicate with each other except by a circuitous route …'

The encouraging news was reported that the proposed line was unopposed for almost its entire length, 'the principal opposition proceeded from a few landowners in the neighbourhood of Cheltenham …'.

Attention then turned to an appraisal of the engineering aspects of the line. In view of the extreme difficulties that would be encountered, the subject was treated with breezy nonchalance …

'Of engineering questions, although the line was more than 34 miles long there was a singular paucity. In fact there was no serious difficulty of any kind. There would be two tunnels, (Dowdeswell and Chipping Norton) but the longest of them would be under a sixth of a mile. The extreme gradient would be 1 in 60 which, having regard to the features of the country, was by no means heavy. It would be a single line, of course, and the estimate of its cost was £600,000.'

Then came the principal selling feature of the scheme: the abundance of ironstone deposits in the vicinity of the proposed railway. As Horace Lloyd explained:

'At present, practically this ironstone could not be sent to South Wales as a commercial speculation, for it could not be forwarded there except by a most roundabout route. If the new line were made, ironstone would be sent in large quantities to South Wales, and the trucks would bring back from thence large quantities of coal. Again, there were a great number of villages and small towns near the proposed line, and the inhabitants would be considerably benefited … a feature which ought not to be overlooked. The promoters of the line were justified in expecting a satisfactory arrangement with the Great Western Company to work it, and they confidently believed they would be able to get the whole of the capital whenever it was wanted.'

In conclusion, the learned counsel appealed to the committee not to reject a scheme which would confer so many benefits on the inhabitants of the district.

There were several witnesses giving evidence in support of the Bill, including William Bliss. John Argall, manager of the Adderbury and Towcester Ironstone Works at Adderbury, was the first witness. He described his investigations into the extent of the ironstone fields between King's Sutton and Chipping Norton, 'which is found in a district 9½ miles in length and varying from 7 to 3 miles in width.' He was convinced that the present cost of carriage of ironstone to South Wales from 5s. to 5s. 7d. a ton could be reduced to 2s. or even 1s. per ton for the carriage were the new railway to be built. Mr Argall judged the railway 'necessary to the development of the iron ore found in the district and that it would open up communication with Northampton and South Wales'.

William Bliss had been a key figure in the promotion of both the Chipping Norton and Bourton Railways. Here, addressing the House of Commons Select Committee for the Banbury and Cheltenham Direct Railway Bill, he appeared almost out of place, his role much diminished. However, it did not stop him doing what he did best: promoting the interests of his town by arguing in favour of the link that he had spent much of his life campaigning for. His evidence made an interesting comparison with that given some 25 years earlier, when addressing the OW & WR in 1845. He deposed:

'I am a member of the firm of Bliss and Son, manufacturers of fancy goods at Chipping Norton. That town is on a branch of the West Midland line of the Great Western. The length of the branch ,is four miles. Our firm employs 800 hands. The wages we pay in the course of the year amounts to something like £30,000. For our manufacturing purposes we use about 5000 tons of coal per annum. We have 20 railway trucks of our own. We pay the Great Western Company a large sum for carriage of goods – over £3000 a year. We pay 4s.3d. a ton for the carriage of coal by the Great Western Railway. It is of great importance to us to get as near access as possible to the coal fields. We are now tied to the Staffordshire coal mines but we want to get to South Wales in order to test the qualities of the different coals. I think we should get coal of better quality and cheaper in price from the South Wales mines. We have not yet had an opportunity. The proposed line would be convenient to us by throwing open to us a large population and a large number of new markets. We should then get our materials from Birmingham. At present they come by the Oxford and Wolverhampton Railway. The new line would open to us the east of England.'

He then added:

'I might as a commercial speculation be induced to invest money in the new railway but not to a large extent, because I have no disposition to take up shares. It is not because I have no confidence in the success of the line'.

The last statement, addressed to Mr Wyatt, contained a certain wary cautiousness concerning speculative investment. This was particularly poignant in light of the effects of the 1866 stock market crash that had befallen Sir Morton Peto and the Bourton Railway Company's proposed extension to Cheltenham seven years earlier.

The next two witnesses, Earl Ducie and Mr Baseley, also declared that they were not subscribers to the undertaking. Mr O'Hara, representing the B & CD, intervened, confirming that there were no local subscribers. He then appealed to those present, implying that the company were equally vulnerable to the vagaries of the financial markets: 'We have paid our deposit of £30,000, which will be absolutely forfeited to the Government if, having got the Act, we fail to make the line. That is the earnest of our sincerity.'

Earl Ducie said:

'I am Lord Lieutenant of the county of Gloucester. I have one estate …between Gloucester and Bristol on the Midland Railway, and another estate between Chipping Norton and Chipping Norton Junction [Sarsden House, which he purchased from James Haughton Langston].'

He then added, with pompous amusement,

'I have the misfortune to live in two districts.

'I have carefully considered the railway accommodation which Gloucester requires. I think this line, as projected, would afford a convenient access to that part of the country in which I am particularly interested. To persons living between Bourton-on-the-Water and Cheltenham it would also prove a very considerable convenience.'

Three witnesses who had been closely associated with the Bourton Railway Company gave their evidence next; these were Thomas Barton, the miller from Bourton, The Rev. Edward Witts and Charles Whitmore QC, all, naturally, in support of the Bill.

Charles Whitmore, Recorder of Gloucester, a County Court Judge, a magistrate for Gloucestershire and a 'director of the little railway which runs to Bourton-on-the-Water', seemed to have very high expectations of what the railway might achieve for Bourton. He said that 'if there were direct communication with Cheltenham that town would doubtless become the metropolis of the district in which he resided, their sessional district being Stow-on-the-Wold. If they had to send a prisoner to gaol, he had to walk to Gloucester, and in consequence of the defective railway communication, he spent the greater part of the week going there and coming back again'. This produced much laughter in the Committee.

Two other witnesses representing the interests of the western section of the line came forward, expressing both the advantages to Gloucester of being placed in direct communication with the east of England, and to Cheltenham being brought within about 34 miles of Oxford.

After the last witness, Mr Grierson, General Manager of the Great Western Railway, had been examined, the Chairman announced that, in the opinion of the committee, the preamble was proved.

The Select Committee resumed its investigation the following day, 'when the clauses were revised and settled'.

Provisions related to the requirements of three separate municipal bodies: the Cheltenham Gas Light Company, the Cheltenham Improvement Commissioners and the Cheltenham Waterworks Company, collectively referred to as the Town Commissioners of Cheltenham. Mr Michael, in representing the Town Commissioners, noted that he had addressed Mr O'Reilly before, when he had acted as Chairman for the Select Committee appointed to report on the merits of the East Gloucestershire Railway Bill in 1864. Now, as then, the Commissioners were concerned that the amenities of their road users should be protected, Mr Michael simply requesting that the original clauses should be inserted into the Bill. Collectively, the Commissioners were

a determined body, and they were very concerned about their affluent and rapidly developing centre. Rightly so; railway companies, if left unchecked, were capable of carving out swathes through the centres of large settlements. The proposed railway was very close to the centre of Cheltenham, and Cheltenham was rapidly expanding in the direction of the proposed railway. The Commissioners were taking a responsible approach to protecting the existing amenities of Cheltenham, while continuing to promote its development.

Mr O'Hara, representing the B & CD, clearly did not wish to make too many concessions to the Commissioners. After some discussion – during which Mr O'Hara was reported as saying that 'Nothing was so mischievous and dangerous as the insertion of special clauses in Private Bills unless the circumstances were of a very peculiar nature' – it was agreed that a number of exceptions to the general rule would be made.

The Select Committee then attended to the particular provisions of the Commissioners, paying scrupulous attention to the detailed arrangements for bridges spanning or crossed by roads leading out of Cheltenham, covering such elements as road widths, approach gradients and the laying and maintenance of mains services. In the lengthy deliberations, nothing was left to chance, the individual responsibilities of the B & CD and the Town Commissioners being agreed down to the last detail.

Two particular provisions presented before the House by the company's counsel were disallowed by the Committee. Firstly, the addition of a clause which would enable the railway companies to be paid by the gas and water companies for watching and superintending any works carried out, over and above the provisions of an existing clause which provided merely for unpaid attendance and payment only as a result of damage to the line.

Secondly, a clause which, had it been agreed to, would effectively repeal an Act of Parliament (namely, the Clauses Consolidation Act of 1869), which did away with a restriction on the issuing of original shares offered at a discount prior to the passing of the Act, yet restricted those that were issued subsequently.

The other clauses were agreed to, and the Chairman was ordered to report the Bill, with the amendments, to the House. The Bill, as amended in Committee, was 'To Incorporate a Company for the Construction of the Banbury and Cheltenham Direct Railway, and for other purposes.'

The railways were described as:

'Railway No.1, fifteen miles and six furlongs in length commencing in the parish of King's Sutton in the county of Northampton by a junction with the Birmingham and Oxford Railway of the Great Western Railway Company near the King's Sutton Station of that railway and terminating in the parish of Chipping Norton in the county of Oxford by a junction with the Chipping Norton Railway of the Great Western Railway Company near the Chipping Norton Station of that railway.

'Railway No. 2, two furlongs eight chains and eighty links in length commencing by a junction with Railway No.1 near its commencement and terminating by a junction with the Birmingham and Oxford

Railway of the Great Western Railway Company about half a mile from the said King's Sutton Station of that railway.

'Railway No. 3, seven furlongs nine chains and fifty links in length commencing in the parish of Churchill in the county of Oxford by a junction with the Chipping Norton Railway of the Great Western Railway Company near the Chipping Norton Junction Station and terminating in the parish of Bledington in the county of Gloucester by a junction with the Bourton-on-the-Water Railway about three-quarters of a mile from the same station.

'Railway No. 4, sixteen miles six furlongs and one chain in length commencing in the parish of Bourton-on-the-Water in the county of Gloucester by a junction with the Bourton-on-the-Water Railway near the termination thereof and terminating in the parish of Cheltenham by a junction with the railway between Cheltenham and Gloucester near Cheltenham.

'Railway No. 5, four furlongs and seven chains in length commencing in the parish of Cheltenham in the county of Gloucester by a junc-tion with Railway No. 4 about three-quarters of a mile from its termination and terminating in the same parish by a junction with the said railway between Cheltenham and Gloucester near Cheltenham aforesaid'.

The B & CD did not have a monopoly on the district. While its Bill was proceeding through Parliament, another for the Banbury & Blockley Railway, which proposed to run westward through the Stour valley, was also being prepared. This was a cut-down version of the hugely ambitious Banbury, Blockley & Ross-on-Wye Railway put forward in 1871. However, the competition withered when the Banbury & Cheltenham Direct received the Royal Assent, which was granted by Parliament on 21st July 1873. This contained a few minor amendments, and the inclusion of a

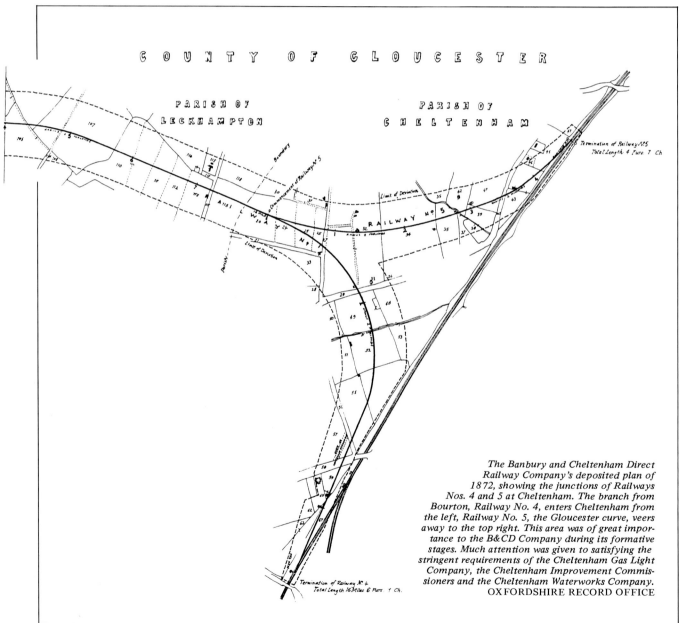

*The Banbury and Cheltenham Direct Railway Company's deposited plan of 1872, showing the junctions of Railways Nos. 4 and 5 at Cheltenham. The branch from Bourton, Railway No. 4, enters Cheltenham from the left, Railway No. 5, the Gloucester curve, veers away to the top right. This area was of great impor-tance to the B&CD Company during its formative stages. Much attention was given to satisfying the stringent requirements of the Cheltenham Gas Light Company, the Cheltenham Improvement Commis-sioners and the Cheltenham Waterworks Company.*
**OXFORDSHIRE RECORD OFFICE**

new Clause 50, which defined the parameters concerning bridges Nos. 1 and 2 over the Oxford Canal at King's Sutton, an element which had been overlooked in the Bill.

The year 1873 saw a boom in railway development, with over a hundred Bills passed by Parliament. Other local railways planned that year included the East Gloucestershire Railway between Witney and Fairford, a rude curtailment of its original ambitious proposal; the East & West Junction Railway, between Towcester and Stratford via Fenny Compton; the Evesham, Redditch & Stratford-on-Avon Junction Railway; and the Swindon, Marlborough & Andover Railway, which would eventually become significant to the B & C in its eventual form, the Midland & South-Western Junction Railway.

The Banbury & Cheltenham Direct Railway Company comprised the following members:

The Rt. Hon. The Earl of Devon, Chairman, of Powderham Castle, Exeter
Seymour Clarke Esq., Vice-Chairman
Lt. Col. Josiah Wilkinson
Lord Alexander Gordon Lennox
Octavius Ommanney Esq.
Hew Dalrymple Esq.

Of these reputable characters, three were described in the company's prospectus as being directors of various railways: Octavius Ommanney of the Salisbury & Dorset, and two others of the London, Brighton & South Coast Railway and the Great Eastern Railway. Lord Lennox was the late General Manager of the Great Northern, and formerly with the GWR, while Hew Dalrymple had an unspecified association with the Clifton Extension Railway. If further evidence were needed to emphasize the speculative nature of the undertaking, suffice it to say that only the distinctively-named Octavius Ommanney lived locally, his address quoted as Bloxham, near Banbury.

In addition to the Board of Directors was a dedicated staff team, including Richard Looker, secretary; Hargrove, Fowler & Blunt of London and John B Looker of Banbury, solicitors; and the bankers, the Consolidated Bank (Limited) of 52 Threadneedle Street, London. The company business alternated between offices at 3 Victoria Street and 31 Lombard Street, London.

The year 1874 was formative for the newly-fledged company. In the middle months, the directors were clearly enjoying the favourable prospects that appeared to lie ahead for their shareholders. On 8th July 1874, in sprightly form, Vice-Chairman Seymour Clarke wrote the following letter to his directors:

'Gentlemen
'The Banbury and Cheltenham Direct Railway forms a very important and much-needed link in the chain of communication between the West and East of England. One of the best arguments in support of this statement is the Map accompanying the Prospectus of the Company, showing, as it does, the rich districts right and left of this connecting Railway which will be brought into such direct communication by the construction of it, instead of the traffic having to pass, as is now the case, on the circuitous routes via Swindon and Didcot.

'The public have long felt the need of this Railway, but railway prospects in general were not sufficiently encouraging to induce local parties, however much they might desire the BANBURY AND CHELTENHAM LINE, to undertake its construction. The success, however, which has recently attended Railway enterprise, and the progress of traffic on most of the Railways of the Kingdom, have entirely altered this state of things.

'The difficulties which new Lines have so often to contend with are absent in the present instance.

'Sometimes a new Line is made to give access to a town locally important only, which being accessible through an unproductive country, can barely yield traffic enough to pay working expenses.

'If worked by an adjoining Company, hard terms are often demanded for the services performed, which have ... to be submitted to, being less damaging than the establishment of a staff of managers and servants, of engines and of carriages, to say nothing of the difficulties involved in [the working of] through traffic ...

'Then again the construction of a new Line often creates rivalry between neighbouring Companies, and after a while, arrangements having been made by the said Companies for a division of the traffic of the district, the new Line is left to care for itself.

'The case of the BANBURY AND CHELTENHAM LINE is, however, wholly different. An agreement is already made between the Company and the Great Western Company, of a very favourable character ... which ... has the full sanction of Parliament.

'This agreement, which is in perpetuity, is evidently intended to be liberal on the part of the Great Western Company. By it the BANBURY AND CHELTENHAM COMPANY are for ever spared the cost of working and management, the supply of engines and other rolling stock, the maintenance and renewal of the Line, stations, and all other works, all liability from accidents, and claims for compensation; all these being covered by the 50 per cent of the gross earnings, retained by the Great Western Company under the agreement for working expenses.

'If therefore the traffic realises your expectations, and of which I have no doubt, the result cannot fail to be highly satisfactory to the Shareholders. Half of whatever is earned is theirs, and there must be a profit, whether their moiety is large or small.

'THE BANBURY AND CHELTENHAM DIRECT RAILWAY starts out of the Great Western at either end, joining the Chipping Norton and the Bourton branches respectively. These two branches were made by parties locally interested in the traffic of the district, but having been subsequently purchased by the Great Western Company, all traffic passing to or from the BANBURY AND CHELTENHAM LINE must benefit that Company, and as the Great Western already find the necessary appliances for working these two branches, very little additional plant would be required for continuing the service between Banbury and Cheltenham.

'With respect to the through traffic to be expected on the Line, it must be obvious that large numbers of Great Western trains will be sent over it, to the mutual benefit of the two concerns. The BANBURY AND CHELTENHAM LINE should be equal ... to that of the Great Western Company; and ... it would benefit the Great Western Company to use the BANBURY AND CHELTENHAM LINE for the conveyance of traffic between the East and West, including, of course – South Wales, with its already immensely developed industry, the thriving and increasing Ports of Bristol and Gloucester and all places west of these points, and the vast districts served by the Great Eastern and Great Northern Companies, as also parts of the Midland and North Western systems.

'In the evidence given before Parliament in support of the Bill, it was stated by the General Manager of the Great Western Company, that they looked favourably on the projected Line; that the Great Western Company had agreed to work it; that the traffic would utilize the two short branches, which form part of the route; and that he had no doubt that through traffic would be carried over it to a considerable extent, as the London and North Western and Great Western Companies had a Parliamentary Agreement, by which they are bound to book through with each other ...

'Rates and fares will be the same, whether the new route or the old circuitous one is used; and the division by mileage, as provided by the agreement, would give so much more per mile, by the shorter route, that the use of the new Line might actually put more money into the coffers of the Great Western Company, than if its own longer Line were used all the way.

'The construction of the BANBURY AND CHELTENHAM LINE will also be important to the Great Western Company as respects the ... much discussed question ... of the separation of ... goods from ... passenger trains, so as to give more security to the travelling public, by avoiding overcrowding on the Line between Gloucester, Swindon and Didcot.

'That being so, if the greatly increasing traffic between South Wales, Bristol, Gloucester &c., and places east of Banbury, can be sent over the new Line at the great saving of distance, how manifestly beneficial it must be to the Great Western Company to avail themselves of it.

'One of the great features of the BANBURY AND CHELTENHAM is that it passes through large and important beds of most valuable ironstone, great quantities of which are sent into Staffordshire, some already finds its way into South Wales by the present circuitous route, and so soon as the facilities afforded by the BANBURY AND CHELTENHAM LINE come into operation, immense quantities will be sent into Wales.

'According to the evidence given before Parliament, the quantity of ironstone sent into the smelting districts will be only limited by the carrying powers of the Company.

'The places benefited by the new Line for traffic in minerals, grain, cattle and agricultural produce, are so important that it cannot be doubted that large quantities must pass over the whole distance between Cheltenham and Banbury, and that the increasing prosperity of the district cannot fail to act beneficially on the future prospects of this concern, and that the success of the undertaking will be greater than could have been supposed possible a few years ago.

'Its position is such that the earnings per mile must be larger than on most other lines, as the facts...show how large a proportion of through traffic shall flow over it, and anyone who knows the country will be aware that the local traffic also will be important.

'After careful consideration I estimate the ironstone
    Traffic to pass over the Line at a minimum of
    18,500 Tons per week, which at 1s. 6d. per ton,
    would yield . . . . . . . . . . . . . . . . . . . . . . . . .72,100 per annum.
The general traffic I place at £25 per mile per week,
    equal to . . . . . . . . . . . . . . . . . . . . . . . . . .45,500 per annum.
Making the total gross earnings . . . . . . . . . . . . . .117,600 per annum.
Less 50 per cent. To Great Western Railway for
    working . . . . . . . . . . . . . . . . . . . . . . . . . .58,800 per annum.
Leaving a minimum nett annual income of . . . . . . .58,800 per annum.
Deducting Interest on Debentures . . . . . . . . . . . . .10,000 per annum.
There will be left available for Dividend to the
    Shareholders of The BANBURY AND
    CHELTENHAM LINE . . . . . . . . . . . . . . . . .48,800 per annum.

'Equal to more than 8 per cent. Per annum on the entire Share Capital of the Company.

Yours obediently,
SEYMOUR CLARKE.

WALTHAMSTOW, E
July 8th 1874'

The working expenses agreement with the Great Western was later adjusted slightly from the 50 per cent figure to 55 per cent of the gross receipts until they reached £25 per mile per week, and 50 per cent when they exceeded that amount.

With the advantages now presented to the investors, the company was ready to start building their line.

## THE FIRST CONTRACT – LAWRENCE
The second half of 1874 was devoted to preparation for the railway, and began with the appointment of Edward Wilson as its Engineer on 24th July 1874. It was recorded that he

'...be paid the sum of £12,000 (£4,000 thereof on the commencement of the formation of the line), such sum [£12,000] to include all the costs, charges and expenses whatsoever and completing the line in accordance with the plans and specifications and with the contract with Mr. Lawrence making plans for buying the land for the purposes of the Company...'

Six weeks later, on 4th September, the contract was made between the company and the contractor, Mr. W. F. Lawrence, 'for the purchase of the land and the construction of the line...Approved...in accordance with Board resolution on July 24th.'

On 12th November 'the Engineer reported that he considered it desirable that land should be acquired for stations at Adderbury, Bloxham, Hook Norton, Chipping Norton, Bourton on the Water, Salperton, Andoversford, and Cheltenham.

At the Board Meeting of 10th December, Seymour Clarke (in the Chair) outlined his meeting with Edward Wilson and the Great Western Railway Company's General Manager, Mr. James Grierson, at Paddington to discuss the position and number of proposed stations. The locations for the stations at Bloxham, Hook Norton, Chipping Norton, Aylworth Down [Notgrove], Andoversford and Leckhampton Road were agreed as marked on the plan.

The minutes record that 'Mr. Grierson thought that though a station at Adderbury would secure a good deal of passenger traffic it would be so near to the end of the Banbury line that it was doubtful if it would be required and it was resolved that the question of a new station at Adderbury be deferred.'

In the 1840s, the southern outskirts of Cheltenham were around a half-mile from the centre of the town, though it had begun to extend southwards about the Bath Road, soon further encouraged by the tramway system. The B & CD company quickly saw an opportunity to suggest that Leckhampton Road could become the Great Western Railway's principal Cheltenham station, particularly as the town was still expanding in that direction. Not having any money allocated for this purpose, they were looking to the Great Western to fund it. The Great Western Board duly discussed the suggestion, and at the B & CD Board meeting of Thursday 31st December, a letter from Mr Grierson was read, referring to the status of Leckhampton Road station; after deliberation, the Board had 'considered that Leckhampton Road would be too far from the centre of town to be satisfactory to the Cheltenham people.'

On 19th November, the subject under discussion had been the future doubling of the line and whether or not it was advisable for the company to bear the extra costs of building the tunnels at Chipping Norton and Sandywell Park (Dowdeswell) to take an additional line of rails. The Engineer was asked to give an appraisal of the comparative costs between the two options. On 8th January he reported that the estimated cost of building the tunnels double would be £10,000 whereas to rebuild them in this form later would cost £28,000. Mr Lawrence was unable to give an estimate for the cost of building the tunnels and bridges to take the double line of rails although he was prepared to carry out the work.

One issue which had been discussed by the Board and with the Great Western was the use of steel rails in lieu of the cheaper iron rails, which had been allowed for in the estimate. The GWR were broadly in favour, provided that suitable arrangements could be made between the companies as to when and where they were to be delivered. Mr Lawrence, meanwhile, had also looked into the possibility of using steel rails, but doubted their being available in time. On 8th January 1875, it was recorded that he required two hundred tons of rails immediately for use within the month. He also stated that he had no land on which to place plant and 'was at a standstill for want of it.' He received his answer more than two weeks later. On 26th January the Board resolved that the line would be laid with iron rails. It is not clear whether the land had become available at that time.

On 4th February 1875 the Board of Directors resolved in favour of the increased width of the tunnels, but the issue was by no means settled.

The ceremonial cutting of the first turf was carried out on Tuesday, 9th February 1875. The *Banbury Guardian* reported:

> 'The first sod of the Banbury and Cheltenham Railway was turned by W. Chamberlin Esq., on his estate at Adderbury, on Tuesday.
> 'The Contractor for the line is Mr. Lawrence, of Bristol, and we understand that this will be pushed on most vigorously. The necessary plant has been deposited at various places along the line which, when opened, cannot fail to be of great convenience to this neighbourhood.'

The initial centres of activity were around the existing railheads of King's Sutton and Chipping Norton in the east, and Bourton and Hatherley to the west. A contemporary account from Chipping Norton describes the scene in the first few months of the construction period:

> 'Chipping Norton awoke one morning to find that it had been invaded by a number of foreign-looking workmen, many of them wearing earrings, and all requiring lodgings. They were navvies who had come to start work on the construction of the tunnel.'

'Navvies' or railway labourers found lodgings wherever they could, often in extremely cramped conditions. Their accommodation ranged from large houses to sheds and barns. Much of the early work on the contract involved building their own barracks-style huts close to the proposed railway workings.

It was very soon apparent that the railway labourers worked and played hard. Another contemporary account describes them as thirsty men, the Railway Inn at New Street, Chipping Norton, being much frequented.

Johnny Charlott, a New Street shopkeeper, saw no reason why he should not share in the prosperity of the publicans and opened what was Chipping Norton's first tea room, apparently strictly for the teetotallers, described as 'an atmosphere of noisy cheerful gossip and backchat where steaming hot pint mugs of tea were served.'

In the public perception, there was activity. However, at this early stage, the B & C directors were aware that progress was not as effective as had been hoped for. On 20th January, Deputy Chairman Seymour Clarke visited the eastern section of the line to assess its progress and consider the locations for stations. He was accompanied by the company's solicitor, Mr Looker, the Secretary, and Edward Wilson's chief assistant engineer. When he reported to the Board on 27th February, he began by describing the progress of the works:

> 'You will be glad to learn that Mr. Lawrence has made a real commencement near Adderbury; we saw men and horses at work tipping earth, plate laying and we met carts along the lanes carting plant to the line. There is a good deal of Contractor's plant, wagons, rails etc at Chipping Norton and at King's Sutton.'

However, his report quickly sounded a worrying note:

> 'The landowners on the eastern section are well disposed – the negotiations are proceeding as satisfactorily as they can be in the almost total absence of the Sections of the land and other information which should be supplied by the Engineer. For want of these particulars the land valuers are very much embarrassed in their negotiations with the proprietors.'

Seymour Clarke's report recommended a station at Adderbury, and agreed the locations for Bloxham and Hook Norton. He then went on to Chipping Norton where he was satisfied that the present 'goods station of the Great Western Company will suffice but a passenger station must be placed at the end of the New Road [New Street] leading to the town, as it would not do for the passenger trains to be backing in and out of the Great Western Station.'

The principal concern highlighted by the survey was the requirement for sidings and ancillary works over and above the passenger accommodation allowed for in the Act, budgeted at £35,000. This aspect of the line's construction appeared to have been overlooked, and now Mr Clarke recommended 'most strongly' that the company take steps to secure the land necessary for this provision while funds were available, to establish and agree the working arrangements with the Great Western. He urged the company to instruct the Engineer to prepare plans at the earliest opportunity, showing how the facilities would be used.

Seymour Clarke again occupied the Chair at the next Board Meeting on 16th March. After dealing with financial transactions, and the reporting of the bank balance at £7945 7s. 9d., the meeting turned to its pressing business.

Several landowners had given the company the right of possession to facilitate construction before the amount of their claim had been agreed. William Chamberlin of Adderbury, and others, had approached the company Solicitor, Mr Looker, expressing concern that their vulnerable position might be used to advantage by the company. The Secretary was instructed to send a letter to the company's land agent, Mr Davids, offering reassurance.

Conversely, and much more serious for the company, situations existed along the line where the contractor was unable to take possession because the landowners were holding out for more money. With typical Victorian restraint, this situation was described as being 'much regretted' by the company. The Secretary was instructed to request the land valuers to advise him of the date of receipt of all necessary plans and sections to enable them to purchase land and the date at which land already in the company's ownership had been purchased.

A letter from Edward Wilson outlined the situation, explaining that possession had been obtained of 30 small portions of land, now handed over to the contractor, though not yet sufficient to be of much use in making any progress.

Seymour Clarke now reported on his visit to the western section of the line, which he made on Wednesday 10th March. He began by describing in greater detail the necessity for passing places, sidings and spurs, with an estimated length of 800 feet being allowed, assuming a train load of thirty wagons, each 20 ft long, plus a 50-foot locomotive.

The abandoned earthworks of the East Gloucestershire Railway in the upper Chelt valley was the main focus of attention. Edward Wilson was in the process of preparing a deviation of the route between Sandywell and Charlton Kings, at the contractor's request, avoiding the authorised route along the course of the East Gloucestershire's abandoned earthworks. The course of the authorised route, and indeed the deviation, was taken through part of the Sandywell Park, at that time occupied as an asylum, but which would revert to residential status on expiration of the current lease. Whether or not the owner of Sandywell Park, Walter Lawrence (no relation to the contractor), was aware of this proposed deviation is not known, but he was now considering a deviation of his own. This was briefly mentioned at the Board Meeting of 27th February.

Seymour Clarke met Mr. W. Lawrence to discuss the matter. The reason for Walter Lawrence's concern over the authorised route is unclear. Face to face with Seymour Clarke, he stressed that the proposed deviation was entirely in the interests of the company, though he believed that the forming of the cuttings through the treacherous land on the north of the turnpike road along the East Gloucestershire route, past Sandywell Park, would be extremely difficult and costly.

The company took Walter Lawrence's views seriously. Clauses 35 and 36 in the Enactment uniquely gave Walter Lawrence the right of pre-emption, or first refusal, to sell the lands acquired by the company for the construction of the railway in the event of the Banbury & Cheltenham not completing within the time allowed. As noted by Seymour Clarke in his report, there were 'many stringent clauses' in the Act relating to the interests of Sandywell Park, 'including the erection of a station at Andoversford, the rebuilding of the Park Lodge and the formation of a new road.'

Mr. Clarke did not rush to a conclusion, and discussed the suggested deviation with the resident engineer, John Wilson (Edward Wilson's nephew) and the contractor, Mr. Lawrence. Mr. Clarke decided that 'the deviation, after careful consideration, [was] not desirable.'

Later, in assessing the merits of Mr. W. Lawrence's proposal, the contractor and Engineer both concurred that the company would not gain anything by the proposed deviation. Upon inspection, it was agreed that were that course to be taken, the tunnel mouth would be brought nearer the mansion, displacing yet more ground for the necessarily wide cutting, and that heavy claims for compensation could be expected.

Seymour Clarke's observations at Sandywell confirmed his view that both of the proposed tunnels should be constructed to take a double line of rails immediately.

His report then turned to the subject of stations. The position at Andoversford was confirmed, but the selection of a site for a station serving the scattered communities of the high Cotswolds was more difficult. The location had loosely been described as Aylworth Down, approximately midway between Bourton and Andoversford, the nearest village being Notgrove. But now the small village of Salperton, two miles to the west and alongside the proposed route, was also being considered. Mr. Clarke had arranged to meet Thomas Beale-Brown of Salperton Park, a Mr. [Conwell?] Rogers of Notgrove and John Waddingham of Guiting Grange (who had been a director of the Bourton Railway Company) to discuss the merits of the two sites at Aylworth Down, otherwise known as Westfield and Salperton.

Unfortunately, Mr Beale-Brown (who owned some 2½ miles of land along the route) was away in Ireland, and the meeting took place without him. One may contemplate the extent to which the lack of representation from Salperton affected the outcome of the meeting. Seymour Clarke reported as follows: 'after hearing the views of the local parties and carefully considering the mode of approach to the two places, I recommend that the station be placed near Westfield, adjoining the old road between Cheltenham and Bourton-on-the-Water.' It is interesting to note that Mr Beale-Brown subsequently made attempts to meet the directors to discuss accommodation arrangements for his land.

In concluding his work of inspection Seymour Clarke wrote in a state of frustration:

'I cannot finish without again expressing my sorrow for the position of inaction in which Mr. Lawrence the Contractor is placed by the inability of the professional men to give him land on which to work.

'Little has been done (as I understand) at the Banbury end, since my former report, and at the Cheltenham end there is as yet no land on which he can commence his operations. Mr. Lawrence said that the pecuniary loss to him was very great, for months past he had men ready to go on, his staff were appointed, the salaries are being paid, all to no purpose, and worse than this is the loss of the most valuable portion of the year for earth work.'

On 1st May 1875 the *Oxford Times* published this report:

'Progress with the Chipping Norton Railway. The Contractors for the new line of the railway are busily engaged in excavating on the lower portion of the Common, and metals have already been laid as far as the turnpike road.'

An eyewitness account describes the same location, stating that 'the bridge which carries the road had been strengthened to allow for excavation under it.'

Evidently, the matter of the two tunnels was not yet closed, and at the Board Meeting of 6th May the subject was again discussed. A week later it was firmly resolved that the tunnels at Sandywell and Chipping Norton would be constructed for a single line. In the event, Sandywell Tunnel was built to take double track.

Mr. Lawrence had now engaged 322 men on the works, but progress was still slow. The directors expressed great dissatisfaction, the frustration emphasized by the contractor's absence from the meeting.

During July, some interest in possible station accommodation was being shown from the communities of Charlton Kings and Great Rollright. The company's response was cool; in the former situation, the Secretary was instructed to reply to Mr Gabb, the Clerk of the Local Board of Charlton Kings, asking how much capital the 'Memorialists' were pre-

pared to contribute towards a station at 'Edward's Lime Kiln'. The Engineer was asked to provide a rough estimate for providing a station at Rollright, and to inform a Mr. Saunders accordingly; he was a determined individual, who had already sent six memorials to the company!

The piecemeal possession of land continued much as before, unfortunately. The contractor's agent and engineer, Alfred Terry, wrote to request possession of Mr Barton's land, Plot 26 at Bourton-on-the-Water, and the Secretary was instructed to write to his agent, Mr. Ritchie, requesting that his immediate attention be given to it.

Mr. Lawrence continued to defend his position regarding the slow progress of the works. Mr. Terry had written again and the statement, which was read at the Board Meeting of 5th August, described the remaining sections of the land 'he urgently required for the construction of the line'. The Secretary was instructed to write to Mr Davids, the B & CD's land agent, expressing their regret 'that so much land between Banbury and Chipping Norton had not yet been arranged for, and request that he will forthwith agree the amount of the purchase money or call in the Board of Trade valuer to fix the amount to be deposited in every case along the line.'

The directors had their own view on where the responsibility for the lack of progress lay. After congratulating the Deputy Chairman on his meticulous report into the state of affairs over the route, the Secretary was instructed to write to Mr. Wilson on behalf of the Board, 'to express their great surprise that the Engineer, whose duty it was to have prevented so ruinous a delay, should have allowed such a state of things to exist without…communicating the circumstances to the Board, and they earnestly trust that the affairs of the Railway will be conducted more vigorously and with greater attention for the future.'

Meanwhile, the Engineer had continued to develop proposals for a major deviation to the south of the East Gloucestershire route between Sandywell Park and Charlton Kings, 'to improve the gradients and avoid a cutting through very treacherous ground.' Walter Lawrence of Sandywell and an adjacent landowner, Mr. Rogers, had written via their solicitors objecting to the proposal. The Secretary was instructed to inform the Engineer.

The contractor, meanwhile, continued to make progress where he could.

In the edition of 19th August, the *Banbury Guardian* made the following announcement:

'CHIPPING NORTON
'BANBURY AND CHELTENHAM DIRECT RAILWAY
'The Contractors for the Banbury and Cheltenham Railway are making great progress with the work, although the recent heavy rains somewhat impeded the work. The bridge at the Common Hollow on the Salford road was so far completed on Thursday afternoon last, as to admit of traffic passing over it.

'We understand that the first vehicle passing over the bridge was the carriage of W.S. Hitchman, Esq., the railway having been completed just as that gentleman's brougham neared the structure on his return from Chipping Norton to Kitebrook House. The first of the two shafts sunk on the Common for the tunnel has now reached a considerable depth,

*The Banbury Guardian, 6th May 1875.*

and extensive machinery is now in course of erection for working the shafts.'

The railway made news again two weeks later when an inquiry took place on Monday, 30th August at The Red Lion Hotel in Banbury to settle a dispute surrounding land taken by the company at Adderbury Mill. The source of the dispute was Mr. Arthur Wilson, a solicitor practising in Banbury, who had bought Adderbury Mill with its accompanying eight acres of land in 1871 for £1,810, a location described by the *Banbury Guardian's* reporter in its edition of September 2nd as 'a place where he could retire to and enjoy a quiet bit of fishing.' This opportunistic case against the B & CD, put forward by Mr. Staveley Hill, was principally the loss of amenity to the property due to the railway bisecting his land, in conjunction with Mr. Wilson's inability to lease the mill because he was unable to receive a clear indication from the company as to the exact course the railway was to take. This latter point did not stand, because it was decided that there had been no notice served upon Mr. Wilson to treat.

The jury was asked to consider 'the loss Mr Wilson would sustain by the severance of the land; the loss to the amenity to the house by putting the ugly and gigantic embankment near it, and burying his apple trees; the loss to the amenity to the property as a whole (which Mr Wilson valued at about £5000) and the loss of the little bit of fishing in the stream'.

Jonas Paxton, on Mr Wilson's behalf, placed the value of his property, at £2,260, and when cross-examined by Mr Littler, the company's Banbury solicitor, he estimated the 'compensation for the nuisance of the twenty feet embankment close to the window of the house, and trains crossing night and day', at £35 per year.

Mr. Wilson was persuasive, but he overstated it somewhat when Paxton informed the court that: 'The embankment would cause the house to be damp, and obstruct the light,' a point which raised a laugh among the jury, who well knew this was a gross exaggeration, the embankment being a good distance away. They had been escorted to Adderbury to see the site for themselves.

Arthur Wilson's case against the company was a typical situation in which an opportunistic individual had fleshed out a flimsy case in order to hold the railway as long as possible, inconveniencing the company to the point where they would settle whatever terms the complainant instructed. Mr. Littler was not impressed and, recognizing the plaintiff's motivation for the case, appealed to the jury's common sense. When he addressed the jury, he did not mince his words:

'…on occasions like these it was always said that railway companies took the cream of a man's land and that the man would give ever so much to get a railway away from his property. Here [is] a man who showed so little interest in the matter that he did not take the trouble to give his assent or dissent when the notices were served. The Parliamentary practice [is] that if a man remain neuter he [has] assented. Here [is] a gentleman who in 1871 bought this mill and property, which he cared so little for that he did not take the trouble to go through it. Mr Wilson paid for the whole estate, £1,810 in 1871, and although there was not the smallest evidence that property had gone up in value in the neighbourhood, he came there – [I] was going to say with the effrontery, and now that [I have said it I will] not withdraw it – because four acres of his land [has] been taken away, and they [have] left him his house, the mill, four acres of land, and stables, and asked £440 more than the whole estate cost him. On this alone [you] should be content to rest [your] verdict as men of common sense. People take wild views of things, but [I have] never heard a wilder view than this. There was a claim of £10 a year for 300 yards of fishing, and if the same amount of compensation [were] to be paid all down the stream the amount would be something considerable. Then they were going to take the ironstone out, [which] would be no nuisance although the railway would be. Things simply [need] to be pointed out to common sense men. Mr. Paxton said he supposed the ironstone was there. If it [is] there, how [are] they to get it away without the railway? Mr Paxton valued the whole estate at £3,600, and asked them for £2,250 for four acres of land, so according to this showing the value of the mill, house etc, remaining to protect Mr Wilson would be £1,350. [I ask] the jury to protect the railway company against such a claim as that. They took half of Mr Wilson's land away and offered him £1000 for it [which I think]…was very fair. Mr Paxton said the embankment would make the house dark, damp, and dreary, but they must remember that the bank is upwards of a hundred yards from the house. [I ask] the jury to take care, the company [are] not compelled to pay extravagantly, and Mr Wilson [did] not take £1,700 when it was offered to him. Remember that the whole expense of the Inquiry [falls] upon the railway company.'

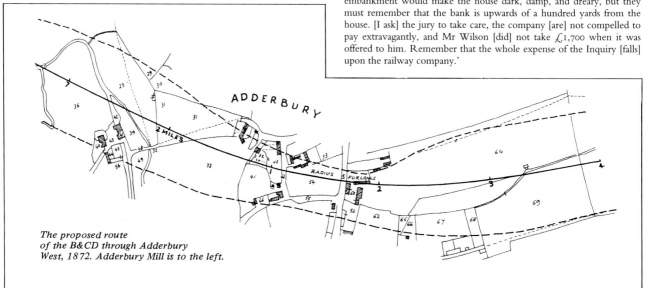

*The proposed route*
*of the B&CD through Adderbury*
*West, 1872. Adderbury Mill is to the left.*

After the room was cleared, the jury deliberated in private for about three-quarters of an hour. Then, the foreman said that the jury had assessed the value of the land at £750; the compensation for damage to be 20 per cent.; for compulsory sale, £150; and for general depreciation of the property, £400 – making a total of £1,300.

In the same edition of the *Banbury Guardian*, a progress report on the Banbury & Cheltenham stated:

'The works in connection with this railway are making rapid progress. The earthwork is now completed to the Great Western Railway at King's Sutton, and it is anticipated by the contractor that the line to Chipping Norton will be opened by next June. The works at the Bourton-on-the-Water and Cheltenham portions are also favourably progressing. The distance between Banbury and Cheltenham is diminished by this route to about one-third the present one via Didcot and Swindon.'

Five weeks later, on Saturday 9th October, the second serious floods in two months occurred across the region as a result of torrential rain, and three lives were lost. The *Banbury Guardian* reported that on Sunday morning the

'water was rushing through the Great Western station like a river, where it rose to a height of two feet above the metals...a canal boat had been sunk, and others forced on to the towing path, and ... a number of sheep had perished...
'From morning to night Banbury Bridge and the Great Western station were the centres of attraction, being visited by crowds of people. From Banbury Bridge, as far as the eye could reach on each side, there was nothing to be seen but water.'

The floods continued as the main news story around the district, and in a caption devoted to the village of Adderbury, it was stated that: 'Here, as at Banbury, a life was lost on Sunday'. A ten year old boy, Arthur Southam, while playing with a number of lads 'on a temporary bridge over the mill stream near Mr Coles' mill, and in the vicinity of the works of the Banbury and Cheltenham Railway', fell into the water and was swept away to his death.

The report stated that 'the Banbury and Cheltenham works were inundated, and some of the plant submerged, wheelbarrows etc. were floating about, while a recently-erected bridge is said to be injured. The works will be considerably retarded through the floods'.

Also in October, William Bliss made a claim against the company for damage to his property in proximity to the line.

At the Board Meeting of 22nd October, the bank balance was stated as £3,010 2s 0d.

The contractor requested that the company would offer for subscription £200,000 five per cent debenture stock to the shareholders in pursuance of the contract.

Plans and Sections of the proposed deviation at Dowdeswell were submitted by the Engineer. The Board approved the proposals, which the contractor 'on account of the nature of the land' stated that he was very anxious to build.

The Board resolved that an application to Parliament would be made to build the deviation, on the proviso that the contractor would undertake the payment of all costs, expenses and incident to such application and to guarantee the company against all payments for compensation for land

etc. and that the completion of the line would not be delayed.

Notification had now been received by the company from the solicitors with reference to the contractor's claim for the issue of debenture stock, and it was agreed that in the event of the company not having sufficient cash in hand or available by the realisation of shares, they may pay the contractor in fully paid up shares at par or face value, and if the whole share capital is exhausted, then in five per cent debentures or debenture stock at his option. The company must offer the shares and debentures or debenture stock when required by the contractor, at his expense, for public or private subscription.

By 4th November, the details of the eight outstanding land acquisitions had been submitted to the Board by Messrs. Hargrove, Fowler and Blunt, the company's London solicitors. The Secretary was instructed to send a copy of Messrs. Hargrove's and Winterbotham's letters to the contractor or his bankers and request on the part of the Board immediate attention thereto.

The Report of the Directors, prepared for the Meeting of the Shareholders at 31 Lombard Street, London on 28th February 1876, was predictably optimistic in its outlook.

'The Directors beg to submit to its Shareholders a Statement of Accounts for the Half Year ending 31st December, 1875.
'The construction of the line is proceeding satisfactorily over its whole length, upwards of 1,800 men being now engaged on the works.
'The Directors considering that a deviation of the Railway near Cheltenham will improve the line and tend to facilitate its completion, have taken the necessary steps to obtain Parliamentary Powers to effect the deviation. The sanction of the Shareholders to this course will be asked at the Special Meeting, of which notice has been given. This change will not involve any increase of cost to the Company.
'It has been found necessary, from the nature of the soil, with the view of avoiding possible heavy claims hereafter, and from other causes, that more land than was originally contemplated should be purchased. The cost of this will be payable by the Company, in addition to the amount of the original contract. Such portions of the whole lands as may not ultimately be required, will be re-sold as surplus lands for the benefit of the Company.
'The Engineer's Report is appended'.

The report announced the regrettable news that Lord Lennox had resigned his seat at the Board, due to the illness of a member of his family, and concluded that the retiring directors, Hew Dalrymple and Octavius Ommanney, would offer themselves for re-election.

The Engineer's Report of 18th February 1876, referred to above, stated:

'The progress made in carrying on the construction of the BANBURY & CHELTENHAM DIRECT RAILWAY has been satisfactory during the last half-year, considering the extreme weather, which rendered it so unfavourable for works of this kind.
'The greater part of the land is now in the hands of the Contractor, who has made fair progress with many of the bridges, culverts, tunnelling, and other work.
'About three-fourths of the permanent rails, sleepers &c., have been brought into the district, also large quantities of plant and other material, which should enable the Contractor to push on the works with great vigour.'

At the Meeting of 28th February, the company, who had now made an application to Parliament for a Bill to deviate from the authorised route between Sandywell and Charlton Kings, now received a letter from Messrs. Hargrove, Fowler and Blunt, notifying them that a Petition had been lodged against the Bill by Walter Lawrence, Richard Rogers, [Conwell?] Rogers and others, including the East Gloucestershire Railway Company.

During the two weeks since the Engineer's report had been written, a further 200 men had been taken on by the contractor, bringing the total to 2,000.

While the plans for the deviation were proceeding (the shareholders having given their consent to it), the company were proposing an alternative route for 'Railway No.3' at Chipping Norton Junction, in the form of a short loop from the Chipping Norton branch to create a junction with the Oxford & Worcester line on the south side of the Bledington road bridge. This was without doubt a cost-saving exercise, and involved dispensing with the costly and labour-intensive construction of the flyover and its associated heavy earthworks on the approach embankments. This idea had been loosely discussed since the previous October, and in November the proposal had been drawn to the attention of the General Manager of the Great Western Railway. William Bliss felt sufficiently strongly about the proposal to write three letters to the company. The nature of his interest is not known, and the directors continually deferred the subject.

In March 1876, the company's Deputy Chairman, Seymour Clarke, died. Francis D. Grey offered to replace him, though the matter was deferred.

Further claims against the company regarding land were made during 1876, both centred on Adderbury. In January, the case which went before an inquiry was that of Edward Railton, owner of seventeen acres of land between Adderbury and Aynho, which had successfully yielded a large quantity of ironstone since its purchase in 1862. Edward Railton transferred the licence of his enfranchisement to Mr. Lloyd in 1869, for it to be worked for fifteen years, the lease held on a payment of 3d. per ton of stone with a surface rent of 5d. a ton. The workings of the B & CD had bisected the property, cutting off the sole access between the workings and the dock at the nearby Oxford Canal (these had been connected by a dedicated tramway, which had been severed by the construction work). The railway reduced the portions of land on either side to one of 11 acres and the other of 6, with 4½ acres of unexcavated stone in the 'landlocked' 6 acre portion.

The loss was difficult to calculate; consideration was given to the removal by the company of the original tramway, and also the worked-out 11-acre portion, an acre of which still required building up for its value as cultivated land to be realised. The B & CD had provided an accommodation crossing linking the two fields, but this was inadequate, as Mr Stockton, who appeared on behalf of Mr Railton, explained:

'This level crossing put Mr Lloyd's working the mine at an end...and when they had great facilities for getting it [the ironstone] away by

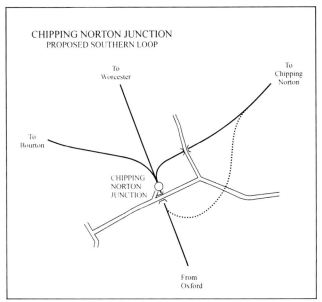

tramway it was worth getting away; but the moment they took away those facilities and brought into operation horses and carts, they immediately destroyed its value as a marketable commodity, and it was no longer worth getting'.

There was no realistic chance that the Board of Trade would sanction the reinstatement of a tramway across the level crossing, and a siding alongside the Banbury and Cheltenham would cost an estimated £900. As Mr Littler, the B & CD's Banbury solicitor, noted, 'It is idle to talk of a siding costing £900'.

This case was adjourned, and later resumed at the Institute of Surveyors, in London. There, the discussions centred on the provision of a bridge across the railway to link the two areas, and the level of compensation due to the inestimable quantity of ironstone worth extracting. Another difficulty was the fact that the claimant had parted with his lease to Mr. Lloyd, and along with it, his rights; the lessee was in a position to claim, but not the landlord, whose only rights involved compensation for lost royalties.

The second claim was related to land that belonged to Mr Chamberlin, on whose ground the first turf was cut fifteen months earlier. It was resolved by the Board of Directors on 15th May that, subject to Mr Chamberlin's valuer, Jonas Paxton, assenting, the question of value of the property would be transferred to John Clutton to settle the claim on the company's behalf as a referee, with Mr Davids to assent to his nomination.

The Engineer had valued the contractor's plant, now on the works, at £79,500, with an estimated £76,000 having already been advanced. The company decided to give a further advance of £3,500. Engineer's Certificate No. 15 was presented to the value of £15,500, with an agreed addition of 20 per cent being added, totalling £18,600. Of this, £13,200 had previously been paid in anticipation, and the outstanding balance of £5,400 was forwarded to the contractor. A further £6,000, including 20 per cent, was added in respect of 500 tons of rails and 200 tons of chairs, all in the course of delivery.

One difficulty for the contractor was the marshalling of plant onto the works at Cheltenham; the contractor had obtained access, but without an agreement of terms with the GWR. The manipulation of materials was an acute problem, particularly in restricted areas when large quantities were being moved. As Mr. Terry, the contractor's manager, observed, 'It would take nearly two months to get the plant and materials on to this company's land from the Cheltenham Station'. The Secretary had negotiated with the Great Western for temporarily leasing of that company's yards to facilitate access. The rates were agreed as current wharfage rates, and the fee of £500 would be paid back to the GWR for use of their facilities to date.

Work on plans for another alteration in the proposed alignment had commenced during May, this time at Hook Norton. The idea put forward was to substitute the vast open cutting through South Hill and the accompanying massive embankments across the tributaries of the Swere for a short tunnel and viaducts. This proposal was not initiated on grounds of cost or engineering (the principal engineering advantage that the gradient would ease from 1 in 60 to 1 in 100) but on speed of construction. Tracings of the new layout were presented to the directors on 1st June for consideration. A week later, the proposals were agreed, subject to the following provisions being met:

1. The tunnel would be made for a double line.
2. The tunnel would be brick lined throughout.
3. No additional cost to the Company would be incurred.
4. That Board of Trade approval will be obtained, together with the consent of the Great Western Railway.

On 20th June, Mr. Lawrence returned an estimate for the cost of constructing the Hook Norton alterations at £25,000 more than that of the authorised arrangement of open cutting and embankments. The works required yet another Act of Parliament to approve their construction, which would not be granted for a further twelve months.

Also in June, provisional arrangements were put in place for the purchase of land at Dowdeswell in preparation for constructing the deviation. The landowners were in agreement with the company, it being reported that 'there only remains to obtain the sanction of Parliament or of the Board of Trade …'

While the company was busy preparing their plans, the works on the ground appeared to have ground to a halt, at least in some quarters. On 22nd June the *Banbury Guardian* published this account:

'CHIPPING NORTON
'The works of the Banbury and Cheltenham Railway here, which for the past fortnight have been in a great measure suspended, are again in active operation.'

These works at Chipping Norton were extremely heavy. A contemporary account describes the meticulous processes involved in building the tunnel:

'The first job was to alter the existing lines to join up with a new section under the Common Bridge and these were added to as the work pro-gressed. Some of the soil, taken out of the tunnel, was burned and used for making mortar. Some distance up the slope, on the outside, a shaft was sunk, through which the soil was drawn up. At the bottom of the slope was an engine house and winding gear as in a coal pit. The additional soil was drawn up the shaft and tipped to form … clay mounds. In the meantime similar work was proceeding from the Rollright end of the tunnel.'

Negotiations were moving ahead over the proposed alterations at Chipping Norton Junction. After discussions with the Great Western, Edward Wilson was asked to prepare estimates for the construction of 'Railway No.3' and the alternative loop, together with the necessary alterations to the station and sidings.

On 19th July 1876, the Solicitor was instructed to serve notices for taking the land in preparation for constructing the deviation at Chipping Norton Junction, while the Engineer had prepared three alternative arrangements for the connection onto the main line, to confer with the Great Western's Engineer.

Since construction began on the railway late in 1874, the works had proceeded without serious mishap. Sadly, that was about to change. The second half of 1876 witnessed four fatal accidents in as many months. Serious accidents were, of course, an accepted consequence of building a heavily-engineered railway such as the Banbury & Cheltenham. However, it may not be inappropriate to consider that as the contractor and his workforce conducted their laborious operations under ever increasing pressure, normally established duties of care were perhaps not always being observed.

The first fatal accident on the railway took place at 7 o'clock in the evening of 19th July. Twenty-year-old Robert Jarvis, from Towcester in Northamptonshire, lodging at Finsbury Place, Chipping Norton, was employed at the tunnel workings. On that evening he was taking a horse-drawn train of empties to the tunnel tip, with Richard Prior as 'breaksman'. Instead of walking with the horse at the head of the train, he decided to ride on the buffer of one of the wagons, resting his legs over the side. As the train of wagons approached its stop at the tunnel entrance, Robert jumped off, ran the twelve yards distance to the head of the train and took the reigns of the horse. This was an unofficial manoeuvre, and it was costly: Robert Jarvis stumbled, and fell onto the tracks in front of the train. He had no time to move clear, and the wagons passed over him, inflicting fatal injuries. He was taken up to the contractor's huts above the tunnel workings at Elmsfield, where he died shortly afterwards.

Two weeks later another fatal accident occurred, this time at Bloxham. On Friday, 4th August, Robert Lamb was killed by a fall of earth in No.8 cutting. Robert Lamb began employment on the Banbury & Cheltenham Railway the previous week, on 28th July, lodging with other navvies at the lodging house at Neithrop, Banbury. Nobody knew where he came from, except that it was some distance away, or what his age was. At the inquest the following day, it was put at about 38 years.

The story of Robert Lamb is a reminder that the Boardroom deliberations that took place in plush offices such as those of 31 Lombard Street in London were far removed from the grim realities of railway construction in the last quarter of the nineteenth century. The life of a navvy was set in a unique, transient world, with its own culture and terminology, which only the contractor and his workforce fully understood. Robert Lamb's accident highlighted the evils of a dangerous, commonly-practised technique called undermining, whereby in constructing a cutting, the labourer dug horizontally into the face of the earth, forming a platform on which to pitch the spoil into the available wagon, removing sufficient material to allow the weight of the soil above to dislodge the unexcavated portion, causing it to fall. This technique was popular because it reduced the amount of excavation required, but it needed a supreme level of vigilance.

At two o'clock in the afternoon, the gangs on No.8 cutting were working in sets of four men to a wagon. Robert Lamb was 'holding for four' and filling the wagon belonging to his 'set', while the other three men were on the top 'stocking'. William Hunt, a labourer, also lodging at Neithrop, was in the next set. He could see that Robert had removed the earth by digging a hole into the side of the cutting, but the 'lift' would not come. Instead, he began to fill the wagon with the dislodged earth. William Hunt looked round as he heard the sound of falling earth, and saw that the 'lift' had then fallen onto his comrade. William Hunt rushed to his aid, and held his head while fellow labourer Thomas Turton, along with others, dug him out. But it was to no avail. Robert Lamb died some ten minutes later.

Two weeks later, on 19th August, another death of a labourer employed on the railway occurred, but this time there was no doubt that the cause was natural. The *Banbury Guardian*, in its edition of 24th August, reported the incident under the heading 'SUDDEN DEATH'. The labourer was Joseph Baker, aged 38, who was employed on the construction of South Hill cutting at Hook Norton. The circumstances surrounding Joseph Baker's death were straightforward. He finished his shift at four o'clock on Friday afternoon and returned to his hut, leaving only to fetch water located 'a ground and a half distant from the hut'.

He went to bed just after eight o'clock (normal for railway labourers) and, as his brother John, also a labourer at work on South Hill cutting, stated at the inquest, 'He was in his usual health and perfectly sober'. However, it was not generally known that Joseph Baker had experienced frequent chest pains during the previous seven or eight years. During the night, at around 1.0 a.m., he suffered a ruptured blood vessel and died almost immediately, and, as the surgeon conducting the examination reported, 'in a natural way'.

The newspaper account gives an interesting glimpse into the accommodation provided by the contractor for the workforce. Joseph Baker was described as living 'in a hut there by the side of the railway'. The building was divided into compartments, which were primarily used for eating and sleeping. Mr Baker's brother, John, inhabited another compartment. How many people were occupying this hut is not known, but an unlikely assortment of no less than five individuals who shared the same room with Joseph Baker is mentioned. These included his nephew, a fellow labourer by the name of James Beard, 'a little boy and two other men'. It is likely that Joseph Baker's accommodation block formed part of a group, forming a community like other similar, temporary 'villages' located close to the centres of construction activity.

Difficulties were beginning to take their toll on the contractor. On 9th August, Mr Lawrence wrote to the company:

'For many months past, as you are aware, I have been suffering from severe financial pressure owing to the very great increase in the quantity of work ... in the construction of the railway.

'The ... unexpected nature of the soil which has necessitated taking very nearly double the quantity of land to allow for extra slopes, cuttings and banks, has occasioned a large amount of the work.'

Mr Lawrence claimed a figure of £133,609 19s 0d for the amount of extra work over and above the Parliamentary quantities, and stated that 'It is absolutely necessary that the Company add to my contract this extra sum ... I cannot go on one day longer under the frightful pressure which the state of things has caused me.'

The directors' response of 16th August was guarded, and the Secretary admitted that were the claim genuine, then it would be reasonable to pay it, but that there were no grounds to do so. The Secretary referred to the previous Agreement of 13th January 1876, in which the company made 'great concessions', agreeing to add £9,333 to the contract as a 'final and complete arrangement' between Mr. Lawrence and the company.

Mr. Looker had written on 30th August, informing Mr. Lawrence that 'subject to ... modifications and the approval of the shareholders ... the Directors are prepared under the pressing exigencies of the case to assent to an addition ... of £215,000.' There were strict conditions, including the proposed substitution of viaduct and tunnel at Hook Norton, to be paid for by the contractor.

Lawrence himself wrote again on 30th August, and requested the sum of £240,000 to be added to the contract for him to complete the line. This figure included the sums to be deducted for payment of interest, the balance of the loan, and balance due on shares. He stressed that 'no provision has been made for profit, it about covers the actual outlay which I shall have to make to complete the contract and no more.'

Amongst this rapid exchange of correspondence, Mr. Lawrence had now received Mr. Looker's letter of the 30th August. He agreed to the terms, stipulating only that as the company had proposed an immediate deduction of the moneys required to pay Mr. Lawrence's shares in full, they were to be given up to him, in exchange for his deposit of £50,000 deferred stock.

The Agreement with Mr. Lawrence, together with the proposed Parliamentary application for borrowing powers to raise the money to support it, was outlined in the Ordinary Half-Yearly Meeting of the Company, with the B & CD Chairman, the Earl of Devon, presiding. The following account was published in the *Banbury Guardian* of Thursday, 7th September 1876:

> 'The report stated that there were now nearly 2000 men engaged on the works and that the section of the railway between Hook Norton and the junction with the Great Western Railway near Banbury would be completed and ready for opening in October, and that a further section at the Cheltenham end would be completed in November next. It also stated that the Directors had found it necessary, in the interests of the Shareholders, to assist the Contractors with advances beyond the Engineer's certificates. The accounts stated that on the stock and share capital the Company had received 508,492. The Chairman (The Earl of Devon), in moving the adoption of the report, owing to the death of Mr. Seymour Clarke, the Deputy Chairman, the Directors had appointed Col. Wilkinson in his place, and Mr. C. K. Dyer in the place of Lord Henry Lennox. He thought that in the next session of Parliament the Company would have to apply for powers to increase their capital. He thought it would be desirable for the Directors to grant an addition to the sum to be paid to the construction under his contract. The Directors proposed to add 215,000 to the contract on account of works, and 85,000 on account of lands, and this would form the subject of their application to Parliament. However, they proposed to deduct from this amount a balance of loans paid to the contractor, and the amount paid in advance of the certificate. The report was adopted, and the Directors were empowered to make a supplementary contract with Mr Lawrence.
>
> 'The proceedings terminated with a vote of thanks to the noble chairman.'

On 6th September a third fatal accident occurred on the railway. The labourer was seventeen-year-old George Fry, son of a tailor from Malmesbury in Wiltshire, who had been working on the railway for the previous eight months. George Fry was working on the South Hill Cutting (No.14), Hook Norton, at around 7.0 p.m. He and Isaac Mills were 'loosing some wagons', the first wagon not being coupled, and Isaac Mills steadied the train with the brake stick. While the loaded train was in motion, George Fry ran between the first and second wagons to couple them. The line was slippery, the blue clay being greasy underfoot. Isaac told him to be careful, but as he attempted to couple the wagons George Fry stumbled. Isaac Mills dropped the brake stick and made a vain attempt to catch his assistant, but it was too late; the wheels of the second and third wagon passed over his thigh. The train of four wagons derailed and fell down the incline.

The incident made big news in the locality because it highlighted the problem of treating injuries of such severity. The press account states that the patient 'was put in Mr Lawrence's cart as soon as possible, with a handkerchief tied around the wound and taken to the Horton Infirmary in Banbury, where he subsequently died. This was clearly embarrassing to the medical authorities. At the Inquiry the examining surgeon, Mr Douglas, expressed uncertainty about what the best course of action would have been, on the one hand saying that 'he thought cases should not be sent to the Infirmary unless there was some chance of recovery', implying that there was none, and on the other, noting that 'if a surgeon had been called in he would have put on a tourniquet and the haemorrhage would have been prevented.' However, when pressed by a juror, who asked whether Mr Fry's life might have been saved had he not been moved, Mr Douglas had to admit: 'I can't say that.' Even so, he added a statement that might sound shocking today, but would have been reasonable enough given the abilities of the medical profession at the time: 'It is no use sending men to die here.'

The surgeon who normally attended the railwaymen was a Dr. Richard Laycock Routh, who lived in Sibford Ferris, a village some three miles north of Hook Norton. As it transpired, the local surgeon was well-known among the railwaymen, but unfortunately the whereabouts of Sibford Ferris was not; nobody was able to reach the surgeon, and he was not called out to the patient.

Meanwhile the progress of the works continued to give great cause for concern. On 5th October, the Engineer's Report stated: '...that works were not proceeding satisfactorily and the plant required considerable sums expended on it for repairs. There appears to be a deficiency in the number of horses on the works to what had been certified...'

In some locations along the railway, the works had stopped altogether. Indeed, the suspension of operations in Chipping Norton tunnel would continue for seven years. There could be no denying that the condition of the works presented a gloomy situation to all concerned, especially taking into account the general sadness felt due to the recent accidents. The press, however, with a timeless ability to determine a mood (though not always an appropriate one), elevated the story of the Banbury & Cheltenham Direct Railway above its present shortcomings. In its edition of 5th October, the *Banbury Guardian* described the breathtaking scale of thirty-four miles of civil engineering as it appeared in the autumn of 1876:

> 'The construction of this line is being vigorously proceeded with. And the following information with regard to it will doubtlessly be read with interest. The line, as our readers are aware, commences near King's Sutton, a junction being formed with the Great Western Railway there. The permanent way has been laid to Adderbury, and at Bloxham a considerable stretch of the line is also completed. At Hook Norton there is the heaviest piece of work along the line, and indeed one of the largest open cuttings yet attempted in England. It is about half a mile long and for a considerable distance is 76 feet deep. About 800,000 cubic yards of stone and clay have in all to be excavated and the necessary width of the cutting at its top will be such that the contractors have been compelled to acquire a width of over 170 yards of land along part of its length. The soil from the cutting is being worked out by locomotive to the "tip" of an enormous embankment by which the line will cross the pretty valley of Hook Norton. This embankment, including two short viaducts, will be about ¾ of a mile in length and in its highest point no less than 85 ft. in height. Its formation will require nearly a million cubic yards of soil. Work is being pushed on here as rapidly as possible but it is necessarily a slow process and this portion of the line will probably delay the completion of the Chipping Norton to Banbury section long after the date at which the Cheltenham to Bourton section will have been completed. At Chipping Norton, there is a tunnel which will be about 484 yards long, through a wet clay with boulders. Upwards of 240 yards of this have been driven through, part of the soil being worked up by means of a shaft, and the other being taken out a heading on the further side of the hill, to form the embankments beyond.
>
> 'The railway from Chipping Norton to Bourton-on-the-Water is utilised. From Bourton-on-the-Water to Andoversford the line follows generally the route proposed by the abandoned Bourton-on-the-Water scheme of 1862, and runs not quite parallel with the Stow turnpike road.

Good progress is being made with the works between these places which are of necessity heavy, the line passing for much of the distance through heavy cutting or over as heavy embankment. Many of the cuttings are through stone, every yard of which has to be blasted, but the embankments which the excavated soil go to form, are slowly creeping out over the intervening valleys. In places the permanent way has been completed for a considerable distance and at Bourton upwards of a mile is thus finished ready for use. The summit level of this section of the line is near Hampen Brake [west of Salperton] where the line is 638 feet above the level of the junction at Hatherley. Thence it gradually descends to Bourton where it is 288 feet above the same level. The heaviest cutting between Bourton and Cheltenham is near the Bone mill at Hampen Hill where it is 54 ft. deep and the bank just below the turnpike road, into which the excavated soil is now being tipped is 62 ft. high. In the 16½ miles of which the Bourton – Cheltenham section consists, there are no less than 70 bridges and 30 culverts for streams, containing 39,000 cubic yards of brickwork or masonry. A large proportion of this work has been done, and appears to be remarkably well done throughout.

'Between Andoversford and Whitehorn nothing has been done, the work having been delayed by litigation with the East Gloucestershire Company. The litigation has resulted in the decision that the company will have to pay compensation for the abandoned works, though the amount has not yet been declared. The Banbury and Cheltenham Company have, however, decided on adhering to the deviation for which they sought the counsel of Parliament, and have now arranged with all the landowners. By this deviation, instead of crossing the London Road at the foot of Dowdeswell on a gigantic embankment, the line will be carried along the right hand side of the road, until, after passing, by cutting and tunnel, through the crest of Dowdeswell Hill, it will emerge beyond Sandywell and pass over the road, not far from the Andoversford Inn. This deviation will undoubtedly be a public convenience, as the throwing of the turnpike road at the foot of the hill into a dark tunnel 150 yards long – as proposed by the East Gloucestershire route – will be avoided and the line will be kept further from the road. The opening up of new ground will, it is also believed, be less costly than the adaptation and repair of the East Gloucestershire property.

'The railway terminates at Hatherley in a junction with the existing line between Cheltenham and Gloucester. The total length of the new line exclusive of the part already worked between Bourton and Chipping Norton, is a little over 32 miles, 16½ between Cheltenham and Bourton and a little under 16 miles between Chipping Norton and King's Sutton. Along the whole of the two sections there are no less than 130 bridges, and fifty culverts for streams, requiring 85,000 cubic yards of brickwork or masonry in their construction. There are two tunnels, the one under part of Sandywell Park, 250 yards long; the other at Chipping Norton, 484 yards long. The latter is more than half finished. There are thirty-three cuttings between Cheltenham and Bourton, and twenty-three between Chipping Norton and Banbury. There will be three stations on each section of the line, beyond the terminal stations already existing. On the Cheltenham section the stations are, at Leckhampton Road, at Andoversford and at Westfield; and on the Chipping Norton portion, stations are at Hook Norton, Bloxham, and Adderbury. The steepest gradients upon the line are on the Cheltenham section, as the line rises over the Cotswolds. The gradient of 1 in 60 prevails for 2½ miles, and there are others of 1 in 70. About £500,000 has been as yet expended on the line, including the purchase, of, with one or two trifling exceptions, the whole of the land. About 70 miles of fencing have been formed; about a million cubic yards of earth and rock have been excavated; about 40,000 cubic yards of brickwork and masonry have been erected, and about 200 tons of ironwork and girders have been placed in position. The permanent way has been laid for about ten miles and temporary rails for about the same length. Nearly 5000 tons of permanent rails are required to lay the whole of the railway, and these are all on the line; while the whole of the permanent sleepers needed, some 60,000, are also upon the ground. There are likewise seven locomotives at work and one hundred and twenty horses. The plant of the contractor in use upon the works would probably be moderately estimated at £90,000, while the 2000 or so of navvies and workmen at work along the line absorb between £2,000 and £3,000 a week in wages. Probably about 3/5ths of the railway has been completed. The date at which the

whole line will be opened, must, from the heavy nature of the works at Hook Norton, be somewhat remote, but the Bourton and Cheltenham section will be completed, at the present rate of progress, before Christmas, 1877.'

The scale of the works as described indicate how great a challenge the project was turning out to be. The contractor's difficulties, hinted at before, were now revealed. On 6th October, 'with reference to the unsatisfactory progress of the works, the state of the plant, and the Contractor's admission as to his financial difficulties', the Board formally gave notice to Mr. Lawrence, to terminate the contract.

The Board, with Col. Josiah Wilkinson in the Chair, resolved to relinquish Mr. Lawrence of his contractual obligations by the following Monday, 9th October. The Secretary was instructed to suspend the notice for an additional week, allowing the contractor to continue the works to the Engineer's satisfaction.

Unfortunately for all concerned, the company were obliged to serve notice to Mr. Lawrence, although the precise details are not available.

Meanwhile, on 20th October, another fatal accident occurred in the South Hill cutting at Hook Norton. John James Gilkes, a labourer, was killed by a fall of earth whilst shovelling spoil into a wagon. On this occasion, the surgeon from Sibford Ferris, Dr. Richard Routh, was called, but he was unable to apply any medical aid to save the man's life, such was the severity of his injuries.

By early November, the terms of Mr. Lawrence's retirement were settled, although the parting was not amicable, and he would go on to take legal action against the B & CD. Mr. Lawrence's manager, Alfred Terry, was appointed to act as contractor's agent pro tem. (*pro tempore* – for the time being).

The urgent priority for the Board when they met on 3rd November was the objective to complete the sections between King's Sutton and Hook Norton, Bourton and Salperton, and Leckhampton to the junction with the Great Western, by the end of the year.

Mr. Terry took up the cause with enthusiasm, stating optimistically that in carrying out these instructions, about sixty horses, locomotives, 200 tons of rails and two-thirds of the men were now surplus to requirements, and could be discharged.

The company did not respond immediately, and the Board were taken by surprise when they discovered that sometime between Saturday 18th and Monday 20th November, a quantity of rails, chairs and other materials (pledged to the Credit Foncier of England), had been removed by the Great Western from the B & CD's compound at Bridgewater Siding, in Cheltenham. The usual lengthy exchanges of correspondence took place as the company anxiously sought to find the reasons for the disappearance.

At the Board Meeting of 21st December, a letter was read from the Cheltenham Waterworks Company requesting the B & CD to pay an outstanding claim against them. It seems the company were reluctant to do so. Mr Looker advised the

Board that were the claim to remain unpaid the company might be required to relinquish the lease of the Bridgewater Siding, necessitating removal of the materials stored there. Clearly this was no idle threat, and doubtless the company directors remembered that a quantity of their materials had already disappeared from that siding. To make sure the B & CD understood their position, Mr Looker said that the legal interests of the Cheltenham Water Works and the owners of Bridgewater Siding were under the supervision of the same solicitor.

On that bleak note, the year 1876 closed over the business of the B & CD. Morale was low at every level, from the Boardroom to the rock face. The company were without a contractor, short of funds, still without an Enactment to exercise borrowing powers to raise more capital, and continually harried by the demands of landowners along the length of the line. Such was the process of constructing a railway in Victorian England.

## TROUBLED TIMES – ALFRED TERRY

The year 1877 began with a spell of bad weather across the region. On Thursday 4th January the *Banbury Guardian* reported that 'the floods were very high here, as high as at any previous time this season'. Many of the local railways were affected by flooding and it was reported that 'the landslip at Harbury continued to increase on both sides of the tunnel and large numbers of men were sent for, fifty leaving this neighbourhood.' The works of the Banbury & Cheltenham Railway were also affected, the account stating that one of the bridges had given way.

Contractual problems continued to dog the company. On 8th January the Board rejected Mr. Terry's tender for the completion of the works as initiated in November. Two weeks later, the Board resolved that Mr. Terry and Messrs Lovatt & Dixon should be invited to tender for the construction of the remaining sections. The company attached severe restrictions – namely that the contractor would have to comply with an understanding that were the company to suspend the works at any time, the contractor should have no recourse to claim compensation – the Engineer would notify the contractor of the amount due for the works executed, and the contractor would have no claim beyond the amount certified.

Despite the uncomfortable arrangements set out by the company, the two contractors obligingly returned the tenders. The figures were set out at the Board Meeting of 5th February.

| Tenders Received | Terry £ | Lovatt £ |
|---|---|---|
| King's Sutton to Hook Norton | 46,550 | 49,000 |
| Hook Norton and Cheltenham | 300,000 | 298,000 |
| | 346,550 | 347,000 |

The Board were not satisfied with Terry's estimate, and asked him to reconsider, pricing for the whole works. He duly complied, and on 19th February the revised sum had been returned, reduced to £322,900. The directors must have felt some relief that matters were moving forwards again, and that they were at last able to report some positive action to the Half-Yearly Ordinary General Meeting of the Shareholders two days later. The report was published as follows:

### 'Banbury and Cheltenham Direct Railway

'The half-yearly Ordinary General Meeting of the Shareholders in the above company was held yesterday (Wednesday) under the presidency of the Earl of Devon, the Chairman of the Company. The report stated that with regard to the paragraph in the last half-year's report and the Contractor's statement that the section of the line between Hook Norton and the junction with the Great Western Railway at King's Sutton would be complete and ready for opening by October last, and a further section at the Cheltenham end by November last the Board regretted that neither of the statements had been realised. Notwithstanding the large concession made to him by the Supplemental Contract, approved at the last meeting, the Contractor was unable to carry on the works, and the Directors were compelled in the interests of the Shareholders to cancel the contract without prejudice to the liability of the Contractor's surety. Since the cancelling of the contract the Directors have carried on the works with the staff of the company. The Chairman then moved the adoption of the report, and in doing so regretted that the Contractor's statement had not been verified. The supplemental contract was entered into, in the hope that the assistance thus rendered would have enabled him to complete his contract. Since that contract had been cancelled the Directors had taken other means to find another contractor, and they have now – though not actually completed – carried through to a considerable extent, and with every prospect of success, an arrangement with another contractor, on terms which they believe would be satisfactory. They had every reason to believe that their bill would pass. The engineer's report fully explained the position and the progress of the undertaking, and he hoped that it would not be considered an unsatisfactory statement, remembering their difficulties. He concluded by moving the adoption of the report, which was seconded by Colonel J. Wilkinson. After a discussion in which great dissatisfaction was expressed at the report, it was adopted; an amendment by Mr. Allen – referring it to a Committee of the Directors and Shareholders, with power to communicate with the Great Western or some other railway company, with the view of purchasing the line – falling through not being seconded. The retiring Directors and the retiring auditor were then reappointed. A special meeting was then held, when the Company's bill before Parliament was approved. The meeting separated with a vote of thanks to the chairman.'

Edward Wilson, the Engineer, had assessed Mr Terry's tender and submitted a report to the directors dated 23rd March, 1877, which was read at the Board Meeting the same day. He made the following evaluation:

'I have already informed the Directors that if a Contract for these works, based upon cash payments was submitted to Public Competition, probably upwards of 15 per cent would be saved and I still retain this opinion.

'It is most important however that the works should be carried on from the present time up to the passing of the Act now before Parliament and until the new capital can be issued; but as the Company are not in a position to pay for this work, some extra cost must doubtless be incurred to prevent the still more serious loss to the Company through the works coming to a standstill.

'Mr. Terry undertakes to execute the works during the period named for the extent of £30,000 for which he is to receive Lloyds Bonds.

'Taking this into consideration … I think the Directors would be justified in accepting Mr. Terry's tender if they feel quite satisfied with the security he offers for his duly carrying out the works.'

The Engineer supplemented the report by adding the following comments:

'If the works were stopped they might be damaged to the extent of at least £10,000 and it being considered that the difference between issuing the new stock with the works in progress as against issuing the same with the works stopped would far exceed the sum the Engineer considered the tender was in excess of what a Contractor would do the work for cash.'

The directors were of the opinion that no contractor would complete the King's Sutton – Hook Norton section on the basis of being paid in Lloyds Bonds unless the contract also included the remainder of the line. They therefore accepted Terry's tender subject to a satisfactory outcome of the enquiry into the contractor's sureties, the works to be completed by the end of August.

Also at the meeting: the fees of the directors were reduced to £1,000 per annum, to take effect from the previous Christmas to the opening of the line.

The works must have been virtually at a standstill through most of the spring season while the Engineer and Mr. Terry negotiated the terms of the draft contract. At the Board Meeting of 10th May, it was recorded that the directors were not convinced 'as to the desirability of entering into the contract with Mr Terry' and wanted to know which terms and conditions were in dispute. Another development, requiring the contractor's consent, was accepting payment in Lloyds Bonds for constructing an undisclosed portion of the line, without stipulating for the execution of the remainder. The Secretary was instructed to inform Mr Terry and ask if he would accept the contract on the basis of the schedule of prices, which he had agreed with the Engineer.

Two weeks later, the Board resolved that the company would not enter into a contract with Mr. Terry until his proposed sureties had been approved and the Heads of Agreement in connection with the tender had been settled.

Another week went by. On 1st June it was reported that the Heads of Agreement were now approved by the Board of Directors and the contract documents were signed. Mr Terry's proposed insurers, Mr Ashwell of Bedford and Mr Murgatroyd of Skipton, were approved and accepted.

The widely accepted view was that an early opening date of the King's Sutton to Hook Norton section to goods traffic was expected, and various parties were starting to show an interest in it. The Great Western wrote, suggesting opening the section for the conveyance of coal, corn, etc. A Mr.

Sayer had also written in connection with traffic, asking the company to consider allowing him to rent a siding at Bloxham station for dealing in coal traffic. The company were not in the position to consider these arrangements, and in reply to the Great Western the company stated that they did not intend using Great Western rolling stock.

Meanwhile, the Bill was being attended to in Parliament; on 27th June, a House of Lords Committee met to discuss it. On 5th July, the *Banbury Guardian* dutifully reported:

'Banbury and Cheltenham Direct Railway Bill
'This bill came before a Committee of the House of Lords on Wednesday last, consisting of Viscount Lifford (Chairman), the Marquess of Northampton, Lord Carysfoot, Lord Ellenborough and Lord Carew.

'Mr. Littler, QC, and Mr. O'Hara appeared for the Promoter and Mr. Shireswell for Mr. Chamberlin, of Adderbury, through a portion of his land the line runs, and who opposed the extension of time asked in the Bill.

'Mr. Littler, in opening the case for the promoters, said the line was commenced in 1873, and was at present in an unfinished state. Up to the present date the whole of the share capital of the undertaking – £800,000 – had been spent in constructing the railway about one half of which was made, and nearly all the land required had been paid for. Unlooked for difficulties had arisen to interfere with the progress of the work: there had been landslips and floods on them and the difficulties connected with the works of excavation at many parts had been great. The bill asked for power to enable the company to make a certain deviation in the line, which nobody opposed, and which would be for the public interest; for an extension of time of three years for the purchase of the land; and a further extension of time of four years for the completion of the line, which they hope to complete by the 21st of July 1881; and; further the company asked for the power to enable them to raise £400,000, which was necessary to finish the line. No opposition was raised to the latter proposal by any shareholder, one of whom, he might state, was the noble lord, the Chairman of the Committees of the House of Lords. It was proposed to raise the £400,000 by debentures or debenture stock, which would rank next to the existing debentures and before

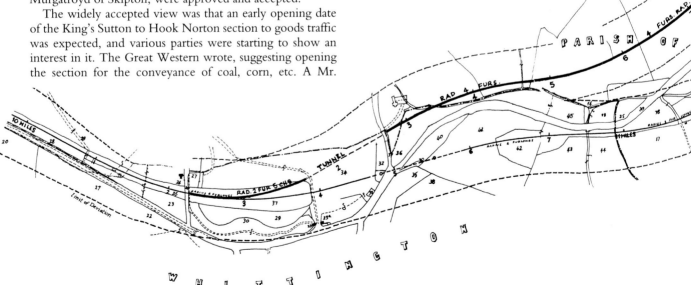

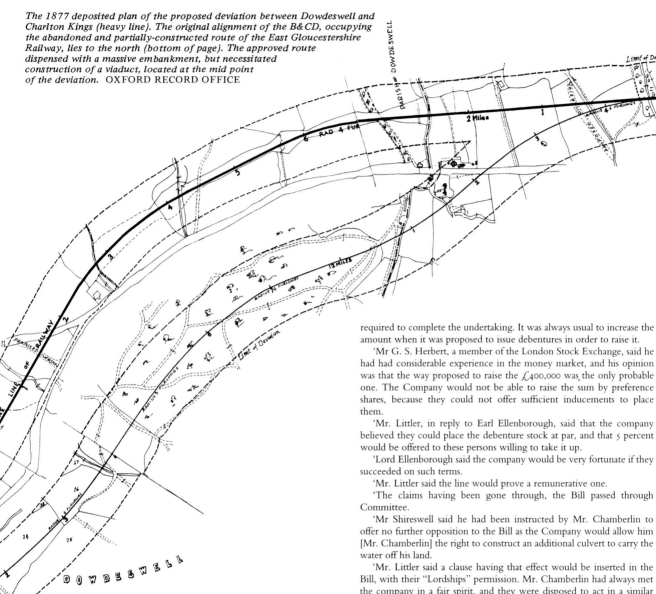

*The 1877 deposited plan of the proposed deviation between Dowdeswell and Charlton Kings (heavy line). The original alignment of the B&CD, occupying the abandoned and partially-constructed route of the East Gloucestershire Railway, lies to the north (bottom of page). The approved route dispensed with a massive embankment, but necessitated construction of a viaduct, located at the mid point of the deviation.* OXFORD RECORD OFFICE

the ordinary share capital. The company had no place of such shares. It was impossible to otherwise get the money except at a price, which, as a gentleman had said before the Committee of the House of Commons, would be nearly all discount – at something like 70 or 80 percent.

'The company had been advised that there would be no difficulty in raising the money as proposed, The East London Railway Company having raised a similar sum in the same way; and he might add that the Witney Railway Company in 1872, and the Newport Tramway Company so far back as 1870 had raised in like manner smaller sums. The only opponent of the bill was Mr. Chamberlin, a landowner, who complained that the line remained so long unfinished, and he therefore opposed the extension of time for the completion of the line. But the fact was the Company could not help themselves.

'Mr. Littler then called Mr. Edward Wilson, C.E., who explained the progress of the works of construction since their commencement. Already £800,000 had been spent, and £360,000 or £380,000 was still required to complete the undertaking. It was always usual to increase the amount when it was proposed to issue debentures in order to raise it.

'Mr G. S. Herbert, a member of the London Stock Exchange, said he had had considerable experience in the money market, and his opinion was that the way proposed to raise the £400,000 was the only probable one. The Company would not be able to raise the sum by preference shares, because they could not offer sufficient inducements to place them.

'Mr. Littler, in reply to Earl Ellenborough, said that the company believed they could place the debenture stock at par, and that 5 percent would be offered to these persons willing to take it up.

'Lord Ellenborough said the company would be very fortunate if they succeeded on such terms.

'Mr. Littler said the line would prove a remunerative one.

'The claims having been gone through, the Bill passed through Committee.

'Mr Shireswell said he had been instructed by Mr. Chamberlin to offer no further opposition to the Bill as the Company would allow him [Mr. Chamberlin] the right to construct an additional culvert to carry the water off his land.

'Mr. Littler said a clause having that effect would be inserted in the Bill, with their "Lordships" permission. Mr. Chamberlin had always met the company in a fair spirit, and they were disposed to act in a similar manner towards him.

'Their "lordships" having been deliberated, the Chairman said it had been made clear that the money was required to complete the line, and as no shareholder opposed the proposal the Committee would allow it and the other powers asked for.'

The Banbury and Cheltenham Direct Railway Act, 1877, (40 & 41 VICT.) passed into law on 23rd July 1877.

'An Act to empower the Banbury and Cheltenham Direct Railway Company to make a deviation of their authorised Railway, and to make a new Railway, and to execute other powers, and to raise further Money, and to extend the Time limited for the Construction of their authorised Railway; and for other purposes.'

The deviation at Dowdeswell was approved, and described as being a little over 2¼ miles in length, whilst the company was empowered to abandon the length of route authorised by the 1873 Act that was bypassed by the new alignment.

SUBSCRIPTION FOR

# £400,000 PERPETUAL FIVE PER CENT. DEBENTURE STOCK

OF THE

## BANBURY AND CHELTENHAM DIRECT RAILWAY COMPANY,

Authorised by the Company's Act of Parliament 1877.

---

### THIS LINE WILL BE WORKED, MAINTAINED, AND MANAGED IN PERPETUITY

BY THE

# GREAT WESTERN RAILWAY COMPANY

Under an Agreement Confirmed by Act of Parliament.

---

By the Act of Parliament authorising the issue of the above-mentioned Debenture Stock, it is enacted that The GREAT WESTERN RAILWAY COMPANY shall, subject to the provisions of clause 32 of the Act of 1877, as fully set out on page 3 of this Prospectus, at the times provided by Article 23 of the said Agreement, pay the proportion of the gross receipts payable to the Company, or so much thereof as may be sufficient to provide for the interest for the preceding half-year, on the Debenture Stock for the time being created and issued under this Act to a separate account of the Company, to be called The Banbury and Cheltenham Direct Railway 1877 Debenture Stock Account.

---

### DIRECTORS.

*Chairman and Managing Director,*

JAMES STAATS FORBES, Esq.,

*Chairman of the London, Chatham & Dover Railway, and Metropolitan District Railway.*

COLONEL JOSIAH WILKINSON,

*Director of the North Staffordshire Railway.*

HEW DALRYMPLE, Esq.

*Director of the Bristol Port and Channel Dock.*

CHARLES KEMP DYER, Esq.

*Lloyd's and St. Albans.*

OCTAVIUS OMMANNEY, Esq.

*Director of the Salisbury & Dorset Railway.*

---

The Directors of the BANBURY AND CHELTENHAM DIRECT RAILWAY COMPANY are prepared to receive applications for £400,000 PERPETUAL FIVE PER CENT. 1877 DEBENTURE STOCK, authorised by the Company's Act of Parliament 1877 to be raised on security of the undertaking.

The Interest will be payable half-yearly, on 15th March and 15th September in each year, the

Another clause allowed for protection of the interests of the East Gloucestershire Railway's lands in respect of the deviation. This concerned the award under the names of Walter Marr Brydone and Richard Hall that had been made on 29th December 1876.

Similarly, the interests of the owners of Sandywell Park with respect to the deviation were protected, in particular the existing agreements entered into between the company and Walter Lawrence, of the Manor House, Sevenhampton, and to an award or supplemental award of Richard Hall of Westminster. However, the time for completing the purchase of the land to be acquired by the company was extended until six months from the passing of the Act, and the time for completing the railway and works until two years from the same date.

The new loop at Chipping Norton Junction was also covered. This was some 1¼-mile in length.

In connection with this railway, the interests of Earl Ducie of Sarsden House were satisfied:

'In constructing the new railway by this Act authorised through the lands belonging to the Right Honourable the Earl of Ducie in the parish of Churchill, in the county of Oxford, the Company shall make, for the use and accommodation of the owner and occupier for the time being of the said lands, a bridge over the railway, with suitable approaches, and a roadway 12 feet wide, in the field numbered on the deposited plans 21, in the said parish (the said bridge to be capable of bearing a steam traction engine), and a bridge under the railway, with an arch 12 feet wide and 7 feet 6 inches high in the centre, in the field numbered on the said plans 7, in the same parish.'

The original proposal for the alterations at Hook Norton, first considered fourteen months earlier, were now authorised, subject to compliance with the original Act, the Railways Clauses Consolidation Act of 1845, or the Railways Clauses Act of 1863.

'...the Company may, in the construction of the Railway No.1 described in and authorised by the Act of 1873, substitute tunnel for open cutting between the points on the deposited plans...'

In addition, the tunnel at Chipping Norton was authorised to be lengthened by about 150 yards at its southern end.

William Chamberlin at Adderbury received very precisely-stipulated accommodation works from the company, authorisation being given to provide a culvert and drain, and to 'Turf or sow with grass seed the embankment' in fields specified in Adderbury West. The company was to complete all accommodation works on the lands to the satisfaction of William Chamberlin's surveyor, 'on or before the 21st day of July 1878.'

At the other end of the line, Thomas Beale Brown was given assurance that the completion of his accommodation works at Salperton would not be subject to the extension of time of five years given in the Act, which stipulated completion by 21st July 1881.

The company was given authorisation to 'create and issue debenture stock...from time to time...to the amount of four hundred thousand pounds, subject to the provisions of Part III of the Companies Clauses Act, 1863; and such debenture stock shall be distinguished as 1877 Debenture

Stock, and the same and the interest thereon shall rank after all mortgages and debenture stock, and the interest thereon respectively, granted or created...by the Company in pursuance of the powers of the Act of 1873.'

This Agreement stated that the works authorised by the 1877 Act were put forward to hasten construction. Evidently the moving of large quantities of soil was considered to be more time-consuming than the building of the tunnels and viaducts.

Notice of the passing of the 1877 Act was received as encouragement that the works would progress again.

On 26th July the *Banbury Guardian* reported:

'CHIPPING NORTON
'THE BANBURY AND CHELTENHAM RAILWAY – We understand that active preparations are now being made for resuming the work on this line, which has now been in abeyance about twelve months.'

Also on 26th July the company instructed Alfred Terry to concentrate his efforts on completing the King's Sutton to Hook Norton section of Railway No.1, to allow goods traffic to run between those places, and then to continue the construction of Chipping Norton tunnel at a moderate speed, at the discretion of the Engineer, to prevent decay of the existing works.

On 17th August the company, clearly in financial difficulties, now proposed varying the terms of Alfred Terry's contract, suggesting an increase in the amount of moneys retained by the company from 5 per cent to 10 per cent.

Mr. Terry was also asked whether he had the financial strength to receive payments in Lloyds Bonds up to £30,000, in accordance with the terms of the contract; he asked for time to consider the conditions. Due to the tenuous nature of the agreement between the two parties, the sealing of the contract still having been deferred, operations along the route were conducted in a somewhat piecemeal fashion.

The anxious position in which Alfred Terry found himself is painfully evident in his letter addressed to Col. Wilkinson, dated 22 August.

'Dear Sir,
'I beg permission to call your attention to the very serious embarrassment I am being subjected to, in connection with my Contract for the completion of your Company's works – owing to the continual postponement of my Contract deed having signed – it is impossible to believe, that when instructed by the Board, at their meeting of the 28th of June last, to take possession of the works (and the heads of the contract were signed). It was their intention into the cruel position I now find myself, by having been led into that step.
'I need scarcely recapitulate. The struggles and anxieties I have gone through during the past 18 months in connection with these works, and more especially so during the last nine months – of negotiating for the Contract. I have submitted altogether seven tenders – have competed with the different Contractors invited by the Board to tender for the works, and as in every case – as you are aware – my figures have been the lowest – the last tender of February 3rd which I received...had been accepted, has been discussed – and discussed nearly weekly since that date, innumerable modifications have been made to meet the Board's – and Engineer's views. I have been allowed, with the full...knowledge of the Board and the Company's officials, to make arrangements for carrying on the work – to arrange terms with sureties – instructed to proceed

with the works in my own name – had my first month's work measured and certified for by the Engineer in due course, and received pay in cash – the respective solicitors have that – and arranged and agreed Contract deed – yet at the last moment, from a statement having made that I have no Contract with the Company – my means of procuring financial assistance for the issue, have to a great extent been diverted from me, and at the present moment after being distinctly put in possession of the work by the Board – I find myself left to make the best of a bitter fight to keep faith with the liabilities of the Contract.

'I would, by your especial attention to the position I have been placed in and trust that the question of the deed being signed will be settled at once. A considerable amount is now due from the Company for liabilities assumed by me – since the 3rd February last – and which is withheld simply by reason of the deed not been completed.

Yours faithfully
Alfred Terry.'

At the meeting of the Board of Directors on 14th September, Alfred Terry reported that 'the source on which he had relied for obtaining cash for the Lloyds bonds to enable him to complete the contract had failed him; that the wages of the men were unpaid…he was entirely unable to obtain any money to pay the men…and that unless some immediate steps were taken to raise the sum of £1,000 a riot would take place and the property of the company be destroyed'.

The company then advanced £1,000 on the security of the unpaid instalments of debenture stock applied for, and a cheque for £1,000 was handed to Mr Terry.

Four days later, the company informed Terry that he had broken his engagement, and handed him a letter asking him to give up the contract, which he declined to sign. Formal notice was given, but in an aimless manner, the contract with Alfred Terry continued to run. On 27th September, he was asked to commence work on the cutting at Milcombe, between Bloxham and Hook Norton, but on 3rd November the engineers informed the Board that the works had not been proceeding to their satisfaction. Terry then admitted he was unable to continue with the contract.

The company took possession of the works, and formal notice was given to the contractor, so ending Alfred Terry's short-lived and unhappy association with the Banbury & Cheltenham Direct Railway Company.

The termination of Terry's contract marked the point at which construction work ceased on the eastern section between King's Sutton and Chipping Norton. The works were suspended and would not be progressed, but simply maintained at their existing level, for the next six years.

Other notable changes took place in the latter half of the year. On 23rd August, Mr. James Staats Forbes was appointed as acting General Manager, and a week later, the company's Engineer, Edward Wilson, died. Messrs. Macintyre, Wilson & Russell were temporarily appointed as engineers on 20th September. On 19th October 1877, the Earl of Devon resigned after a five-month period of ill-health. Colonel Josiah Wilkinson took his place and on 25th of that month Mr. Forbes formally became Managing Director and Chairman of the Company.

Preparations for the transfer of shares to B & CDR debenture stock took place during November. On the 9th the Secretary submitted applications which totalled £110,000. Particular attention was given to protecting the monies against the claims of execution creditors and the requirement that all parties agree to postpone their claims for further consideration so that the principal part of the monies received in respect of the allotment would be allocated solely to the railway works. The directors set out the terms as follows:

'The Directors have advertised the issue of £400,000 Perpetual 5 per cent Debenture Stock authorised by their Act of past session and upon the terms of the prospectus. A large sum has been applied for by the public and the time has arrived when the allotments must be made or the money paid or application returned.'

It was stressed that 'nothing could justify their receiving the money to be applied in paying the company's debts if the undertaking could not be carried on towards completion'.

Once the terms for the allotment of debenture stock were agreed, the company deferred the allocation and began the serious process of selecting a suitable contractor for completing Railway No.4, the Bourton and Cheltenham section, the priority being to earn revenue as quickly as possible and give value to the debenture stock.

Of the suitable candidates interviewed, a Mr. Charles Lucas declined to tender. On 16th November, the company approached Henry Lovatt, who had much experience running large contracts for the Great Western Railway Company. Lovatt agreed to complete Bourton & Cheltenham for the lump sum of £157,000, the loan of £17,000 upon the rails being paid off, and the rails of an equivalent value being transferred to him in part payment.

The company wasted no time, and accepted his tender the following day.

Lovatt agreed to purchase the redundant plant from the B & CD for £20,000, giving credit for that sum at the end of the contract on account of his contract price. There was also an undertaking to accept £20,000 in 1877 debenture stock on further account of his contract, the stock to be redeemed by the company at par out of the proceeds of any future issue after £20,000 shall have been first retained by the company of the issue.

The tender was accepted subject to the allotment of debenture stock being made, but the allotment was not made. The Chairman stressed that the result of holding off for the company would be an almost worthless share capital, endangering the £200,000 first charge debenture stock.

On Friday 23rd November, eighteen 1877 debenture stock certificates to the value of £14,900 were signed in the company's seal book.

The company's redundant plant had been held by a Mr. George Berkeley, on a deposit of £14,000, as a collateral security. On 6th December, the company paid the amount plus £281 1s 5d interest, now saving the 4 per cent interest rate.

At the same time, an agreement was made to pay off a loan of £17,000 to release the company from 'the serious amount of interest' being paid on a collateral security for the rails. A cheque was handed to the Secretary of the company concerned.

The company sold the existing plant to Mr Lovatt for £20,000, as a protection against claims.

Lovatt's price of £157,000 for completing Railway No.4 was made up of £100,000 in cash, £20,000 in debenture stock, £20,000 in plant, and £17,000 allotted to the permanent way. The sum of £13,000 was allowed to guard against earth slips at Dowdeswell, any savings being returned to the company.

The terms of the contract were agreed, final sealing of the document only waiting on Mr. Lawrence's insurers granting their assent. The contract was finally made on 6th December 1877.

No further details have come to light concerning the contract with Mr Lovatt, as the fluctuating financial situation generally discouraged investment.

The company, meanwhile, spent the early part of 1878 settling seemingly interminable land claims and continuing to pay various parties' deposits on permanent way materials, thus freeing Lovatt to take possession of them. The Great Western were instructed to release their hold of materials, which included rails, chairs and bolts, excepting 186 tons 2 cwt 23 lbs of rails lying on the Great Western's premises at Cheltenham, which that company had withheld as security for a claim made against the B & CD. Terms for rental of the Great Western's property at Bourton and Cheltenham were also revised to £15 per year.

Company business throughout the year was concerned with trifling matters. They were approached in April by a Mr Pottinger with a request that he might purchase Whitley Villa, a building belonging to the company (which was probably vacant) for £850. This move quickly alerted the company to secure a tenant to occupy the premises, which took place two months later.

In May 1878 the company must have been surprised to learn that a Mr. Henry Biggerstaff had presented a petition for winding up the company, the notice being published in the *Daily News* edition of the 16th May. No reasons were given. The petition was abandoned, formal notice being given by the petitioner's solicitors on 20th May, the notice having been published and advertised under a misapprehension.

During the latter part of the year 1878, more financial difficulties arose for the company, and in November the works were terminated, conditions for this being agreed on 20th December, and settled with the contractor at the Board Meeting three days later. A resolution was passed before Mr. Lovatt and his solicitor to the effect that the works would be suspended, and at the company's request the contractor agreed to 'continue them to the extent necessary to prevent deterioration'. On terms which were generous to the contractor, the B & CD resolved to compensate him for any loss sustained by the partial suspension.

The company's Minute Books are silent for the next two months, then on 21st February 1879 Mr. Lovatt gave notice to the company to cancel the contract. He arranged the claim for works undertaken to date (the agreed sum of £12,000 and £121,350 compensation would not be settled for another six months). He was also asked to consider and report the cost for completing the works between Cheltenham and Bourton. His minimal role was now restricted to maintaining the existing works, to be reviewed after three months.

Various landowners were enforcing the company to pay for purchasing the lands taken for the railway, and the B & CD's solicitor was instructed to see if arrangements could be made for any of them to take the 1877 debenture stock.

Meanwhile, the company was negotiating working arrangements with the Great Western. A problem had developed since the B & CD had accepted Henry Lovatt's tender to complete the Railway No.4, Bourton to Cheltenham, in advance of Railway No.1. The B & CD fully expected the Great Western to manage the operation of Railway No.4 from its opening, but the GWR contended that the working arrangements proposed by the company would be invalid until the remaining sections were opened, the arrangements applying to the term 'railway' as a singular and not 'railways' defining a series of separate lines. It is likely that the interpretation of the agreement could be argued either way, although the fact that the Great Western (supposedly an ally) had called the B & CD's interpretation of it into question would not have seemed fair to the struggling concern. The problem was potentially extremely serious, and the B & CD sought legal counsel to define the correct interpretation of the agreement.

On 27th March, the company's legal advisor responded and found that the weight of evidence lay in favour of the B & CD, noting that the interpretation of the Agreement made between the companies accepted that one or more sections of the line would be opened separately and independently of the others and that the shareholders would not have invested in the enterprise without expecting the opened section to be worked. He stated his case as follows:

'I think that the Agreement means that the Great Western Railway Co. are to work a section even if it does not pay them.

'I think that on the section being finished it must be phased.

'On being passed I think that the holders of the Debentures are entitled to have it worked.

'The interest is charged on the tolls taken on that section and the Great Western Co. must deduct the amount paid from the sums payable to the Banbury Co.'

Negotiations with the Great Western solicitors are not recorded, neither are the terms of settlement, but the nature of the proceedings can be imagined. The outcome, as history has shown, is that the Bourton to Cheltenham section was opened seven years ahead of the eastern portion and worked by the Great Western from the outset. For a company plagued by trouble, the news of the resolution in its favour must have been received with a great sense of relief.

## HENRY LOVATT AND RAILWAY NO. 4

By the end of May 1879, the company were taking steps to apply for Parliamentary powers to raise further capital to complete Railway No.4, Bourton to Cheltenham, and on 5th June a petition for leave to introduce the company's third Bill was sealed.

Mr Lovatt was paid £893 8s 5d for the maintenance of the works from 20th February to 23rd May, which included pumping to the Chipping Norton tunnel workings. He was instructed to maintain the works for a further three months, subject to the Enactment being granted. Anticipating this, detailed arrangements were made to agree the terms of his contract both to complete Railway No.4, and to pay for the works carried out on it to date.

It was agreed that the due amount for works executed on Railway No.4 including the retention monies would remain secured by the rails and permanent way materials ready to be laid down, and the £10,000 debenture stock, on the proviso

that the stock should not be sold within two years of the opening of that portion of the line; the permanent way items were to remain unsold for three months from the date of the Agreement.

Payment to the contractor for suspension of the works between 20th December and 20th February was agreed as £3,294 6s 9d.

It was not until another three months had passed that an agreed revised figure was determined for the construction of the Bourton to Cheltenham section. The company had received Parliamentary powers to raise capital up to £600,000 on 11th August for the completion of that section. On 18th August, Henry Lovatt agreed to construct Railway No.4 for the sum of £82,000, of which £50,000 was to be paid cash and the remaining £32,000 in debenture stock at 80.

The contract was made, and by October Mr. Lovatt had submitted his first invoice to the Company for £5,000.

This action highlighted a problem the company had overlooked, namely that the Engineer, Edward Wilson & Co., had not formally been re-engaged by the company since suspension of the works the previous November, and therefore was not in a position to certify that the invoice submitted by the contractor was correct. In a letter to the directors dated 30th September, the resident engineer made much of the unpaid work, which the company had done, and added an unrealised truth that the obligation to pay the wages of the engineers who checked the work was equal in importance to the payment of the contractor for carrying it out. This situation did not remain unresolved for long. Terms for reimbursement of past work were agreed, and the engineers were re-engaged for overseeing the construction of the railway.

Henry Lovatt began work on Railway No.4 in a businesslike manner, and concentrated his efforts throughout the winter of 1879–80 on the tunnel at Dowdeswell, alongside the abandoned earthworks of the East Gloucestershire scheme.

There were considerable difficulties between the B & CD and the Great Western concerning the construction of the Gloucester curve at Cheltenham, the disagreement being resolved only through another costly Act of Parliament. The problem was of so severe a nature that it required the appointment of an Arbitrator to resolve it.

There were problems at Bourton, too. The original agreement between the two companies stipulated that the B & CD would pay for the provision of a new station, to replace the original one built seventeen years earlier, but the B & CD now suggested that a new station was not necessary. Instead, they proposed retaining the existing facilities but paying for 'additional accommodation', which the Great Western's General Manager's Office regarded as 'having only been made with the view of saving expense to the Banbury Company.' The GWR's General Manager, Mr Grierson, was broadly in favour of negotiating a way forward, but the suggestion that the Great Western should construct the works at their own expense and charge the B & CD interest, or rent for the works, 'could not possibly be entertained.' The Great Western were not inclined to offer charity towards the B & CD, and on 30th August 1880 they responded to the latter's proposal, reminding the company that:

'After the course adopted with respect to the junction at Cheltenham, the Directors of this Company might not be disposed to approve of similar concessions again.'

The B & CD prepared plans for Bourton station and submitted them to the GWR on 21st August. No allowance had been made for enlargement, or the provision of an engine shed, but the Great Western made little comment, simply suggesting that one of the facing points at the Chipping Norton end might be dispensed with.

This B & CD proposal was estimated to cost about £2,000, although the figure soon rose to £4,800 after Mr Grierson requested that a new goods shed be provided, and other works carried out. The GW offered £1,000, but the B & CD countered by offering to deposit £2,000, the Great Western engineer to apportion the costs between the companies accordingly.

Meanwhile, internal matters also preoccupied the company. On 20th September 1880, Captain Hoare resigned from the Board, the £500 of deferred stock being transferred to Mr. E.G. Davis. Also in September, James Staats Forbes, the company's General Manager, refused to accept the terms of his revised salary, stating that he had 'quite made up his mind not to allow himself to be placed in a worse position …' He wanted to accept stock at the value of £130,000 at 50, and the company were not prepared to issue it except at 80. The Board recognised that the stock was not presently worth that, but expected it to realise that value two or three years hence. Mr Forbes' services were invaluable to the company, and the Board did not want to lose him. On 16th September, the Deputy Chairman, George Allen, wrote to him:

'I hope that we shall hear from you tomorrow that in consideration you think our proposal to be the fairest that can be made, and that you accept it and will do your best to pull the Company through.

'We have all been disappointed and have all made sacrifices.

'We expected to get all the 1877 Debenture Stock placed – we did not.

'We expected to get the last £200,000 we wanted – we did not.

'We expected to sell our iron rails well – we did not.

'We expected to have had a part of the line open long ago – we did not.

'My time is as valuable to me as yours is to you. I have not received one penny for three years work and anxiety, and what is more I shall not until the line is safe.

'You on the contrary have received a sum which sunk would produce a handsome annuity on your life and can if you like make the payment we offer a valuable one.

'We want on the other hand every pound we have for our absolute existence, to complete the Bourton section, to keep ourselves going, to promote the new Bill &c.

'But whatever your decision is do pray let us have it at once that we may do what we can – without your help if we are not to have it; with it if we are. I trust sincerely it may be the latter.

'I write reluctantly and without the knowledge of anyone knowing that every hour is precious, and being weak enough to feel for the large body of Shareholders and others who are now suffering from the former mismanagement and misfortune.'

Mr Forbes did not reply to this or other letters and telegrams urgently requiring his attention. By now there was a risk of the works having to be stopped because the cheques could not be paid out. George Allen wrote to a Robert Baxter stressing the importance of an immediate resolution and suggesting that 'if, through his omission to make proper arrangements during his absence … Mr Lovatt's Contract is again broken and the opening of the line again indefinitely postponed, he will become personally liable.'

The directors took steps to anticipate Mr Forbes withdrawing from the company, and recognised that the funds held in his name as a trustee jointly with co-director Mr. Mackay would need to be transferred to one of the other directors. He was given until 1st November to decide. The decision is not recorded, but inspection of the Board minutes reveals that James Staats Forbes continued in office, and is shown in *Bradshaw's* as being the Chairman until 1882.

Work continued on the section as the date scheduled for opening of the line – also 1st November – approached, although it would prove to be premature. On 23rd October 1880 the First Notice was announced, the Engineer reporting to the Board of Trade that the railway would be ready for public traffic in about a month. An agreement with the Great Western over the provision of facilities at Bourton, including 'an alteration beneficial to this Company' had now been reached, subject to Mr. Grierson's approval.

But the month of November arrived, then passed, and the line remained unopened. The Great Western continued to request additional facilities for their use, including a water tank at Andoversford, which delayed the long-awaited opening.

On 16th February 1881, the Second Notice, stating the readiness of the line, was withdrawn. The Engineer reported to the Board of trade that '… a substitute notice will be sent when the works are a little more complete.'

A contract for providing signals had been made with the Gloucester Wagon Company. On 23rd February the Great Western confirmed that the single line would be worked on the train staff and ticket system in conjunction with the block telegraph.

At long last, on 28th March 1881, Col. J.H. Rich of the Board of Trade reported on his inspection of the line, and stated that the line

'was single throughout, with sidings and loop lines at the Junctions and at Andoversford station, which is the only place fitted as a passing place.'

The permanent way was constructed of double-headed rail at 80 lbs per yard, fished, and wooden keys were fixed in cast-iron chairs weighing 36 lbs each. Chairs were fastened with screw bolts to wooden sleepers, which were spaced at a gauge of 8 sleepers to every 23 feet of rail, each sleeper being 9 ft x 10 in x 5 in.

The inspector reported that all sixty-three bridges were built of brick and stone except for six underbridges and seven overbridges of wrought-iron girders on brick abutments. Dowdeswell viaduct consisted of 13 arches, each of

40 ft span. Sandywell Tunnel, at 385 yards, was noted as being substantially constructed and sufficiently strong, although the appearance was marred by defective brickwork.

He also noted specific items requiring attention. At Lansdown Junction cabin, a separate distant signal was to be installed, instead of slotting the existing home signals controlling the new line and the Midland line from Cheltenham to Gloucester, and Cheltenham to Bourton. Safety points were required at the Cheltenham loop, gauge rods were required to stock rails, and connecting rods were to be installed between points.

At other stations, curves were to be taken out of lines, whilst the timber footbridge required strengthening at Charlton Kings. The platform fencing was to be completed at Andoversford, and the distant signal for Stow was to be placed a minimum of 650 yards from the home signal at Bourton.

General items needing attention included the provision of clocks in all stations and signal cabins; gauge rods to the stock rails near facing points; gridirons over the culvert openings; and repositioning of rails near the platform faces so that the carriage steps would pass within 2 inches of the edge.

A means of watering and turning the engines was requested. The Great Western's proposed operating mode was accepted, but the inspector questioned the practicalities of working over such a great length of single line with only the one passing place, at Andoversford.

Colonel Rich noted his concern over the lack of protection given to the railway from falls of stone in the rock cuttings, and mentioned the occurrence of slips at the tunnel approaches. Correcting measures for the latter included forming drainage channels into the cutting slopes, and inserting land drains to prevent water percolation from the adjacent properties; the drainage channels were to be filled with stone and the cutting slopes to be supported at their base on stone walls.

Because of the incomplete state of the works, the BoT submitted that the Bourton to Cheltenham section could not be opened for passenger traffic without danger to the public.

The Board of Trade report proved to be a defining moment as far as Henry Lovatt's contract was concerned, and he refused to do any more work. The BoT's requirement for expensive earthworks at Dowdeswell Tunnel was the factor; he reasoned that he was entitled to a large claim for the extra works, which had been ordered by the Engineer, to rectify problems there.

Evidently, Lovatt was perceived to occupy a commanding position because, surprisingly, the B & CD did not negotiate terms. They simply asked the Engineer to report the sum Mr. Lovatt would charge the company to comply with the requirements of the Board of Trade and the Great Western. The agreed sum, which covered additional works to Bourton station and maintenance of the line for 12 months, including repairs to landslips, was £6,000.

By 26th April, the Board of Trade was advised that all the outstanding requirements had been met except for engine turntables at Bourton and Chipping Norton Junction. The BoT stated that temporary facilities were not acceptable. After Colonel Rich continued to express dissatisfaction, a resolution was agreed: the company made arrangements to dispense with the turntable at Bourton.

The opening was now scheduled for Wednesday, 1st June.

On 25th May, the GWR issued a directive to the company concerning the working of trains without adequate turning facilities, to be effective until the turntable became operational at Chipping Norton Junction:

> '…The line shall be worked by means of tank engines or by engines running in their proper direction, that the trains shall stop at all stations upon the line and that they shall be timed to run at a reasonable speed [on] the line when the engine is running tender first.'

Railway No.4 of the Banbury & Cheltenham Direct Railway, between Bourton-on-the-Water and Cheltenham, was at last opened on Wednesday, 1st June 1881.

On 2nd August, traffic receipts were reported as £567, which included the conveyance of over nine thousand passengers and five hundred tons of goods.

On 22nd and 24th September, George Allen and Mr Looker, the company Secretary, had inspected the new line as a response to having received 'many complaints', and were able to gather the information first hand from those sources. Mr Looker met with Great Western officials at Paddington on the 27th to discuss the issues that had been raised. These were diverse, ranging from the improvement of the train service, to providing a level crossing free of charge at Notgrove for the use of Thomas Beale Brown. They also included items such as through coach working via Chipping Norton Junction, Sunday services, printed return tickets between London and Cheltenham, issuing of cheap tickets during the Cheltenham cricket week, reduction of coal traffic rates to compete with the Midland Railway traffic at Cheltenham, reduction in the rate of brick conveyance from Andoversford and establishing the rate charged for conveying skins from Stow-on-the-Wold. What the skins belonged to has not been ascertained.

By the middle months of 1882, the new railway had shaken down nicely into its operation. On 1st June, exactly one year after the opening, the Board of Trade Inspector again visited the line. When he reported to the Great Western Engineer the outstanding works to be completed, they were estimated to cost no more than £120. However, slips at Dowdeswell continued to cause concern for all those involved. Mr Lovatt's claim finally settled at £7,381 3s. 8d. According to the Engineer, the slips were attributed 'in a great measure to the severe treatment by the working company in running at high speed a 45 ton engine over the newly made line.'

# BANBURY & CHELTENHAM DIRECT RAILWAY.

## OPENING OF THE CHELTENHAM TO BOURTON SECTION.

[*From the " Cheltenham Examiner," Wednesday, June 8, 1881.*]

The completed section of the Banbury and Cheltenham Railway, between Cheltenham and Bourton-on-the Water, was opened for traffic on Wednesday last, the First of June. There was no formality at the opening. Indeed, the absence of ceremonial of any kind was one of the most remarkable features of a day which might fairly claim to be a "red letter" one in the railway calendar of the locality. It is thirty-four years since the opening of a railway of direct importance to Cheltenham took place, and then the completion of the Great Western branch from Swindon to Cheltenham was celebrated by fete trains and banquets and such-like evidences of public rejoicing. In the interval there has been an almost perennial effort on the part of the district to obtain further accommodation in the direction which the Banbury and Cheltenham Railway will serve, but after so many years' waiting and disappointment the line on Wednesday was opened without any attempt at official celebration, and as though the occasion were anything rather than a day of rejoicing to those having control of the undertaking. The people of the locality did show their interest in the occasion by the simple process of patronising the trains run during the day, but never was a line opened, we should think, with a greater appearance of desire on the part of the controlling power to check inconvenient enthusiasm and to make the opening as matter-of-fact and prosaic as possible. The new line, by its alliance with the Great Western Company, is under that Company's absolute direction, the Banbury and Cheltenham Company merely receiving a moiety of the traffic receipts from their under-taking, and the credit or otherwise of the opening arrangements rests therefore entirely with the Great Western Company. Notwithstanding all the delay that has taken place in the use of the line by the public, less than a week's official notice of the date of opening was given, and so little effort was made to make the traffic arrangements known, that on the day before the opening there were not half a dozen time-bills in the town, and the public were chiefly dependent on the publication of the time-tables in the columns of the Press, on the evening prior to and on the day of opening, for any information on the subject. But for the energy of the Deputy-Chairman of the Banbury and Cheltenham Company (Mr. Allen), who with the Secretary (Mr. Looker), was in town on the day before the opening, the publicity given to the arrangements would have been less even than it was. If any overture had been made to the Corporation with that view, we believe that the Mayor of Cheltenham would have been pleased to take part in a formal opening of the undertaking, and it is to be regretted that some such inauguration of it was not provided for.

The first train left the St. James's-square station at 6.30 in the morning. It consisted of eleven carriages well filled with passengers, chiefly booked for Leckhampton and Charlton Kings, people determined to have a first ride on the new line. Among the passengers booked through were Mr. Allen, the deputy chairman of the Banbury and Cheltenham Company, Mr. J. S. McIntyre (a member of the firm of Messrs. E. Wilson & Co., the engineers of the line), Mr. Looker, the Secretary, and two or three representatives of the local press, among whom one gentleman had chosen this route to reach Epsom for the Derby. As the train passed out of the station it fired its own salute of honour in the shape of a number of fog signals which had been placed along the rails. There was little in the way of incident to record *en route*. People had gathered on the bridges and at the stations to watch the train go by, and by these it was occasionally cheered, but it was not until nearing Bourton that any other demonstration was made. Some of the houses near to the line there had flags displayed, and at a prettily situated little seat on the left hand side of the way, before reaching Bourton, there were some effective decorations, including a pretty floral arch,

standing in the park-like field in front of the house, with the word "Success" emblazoned upon it. At Bourton station there was a crowd of the people of the little town, by whom the train was lustily cheered as it approached. The station offices had been tastefully decorated with flowers by the daughters of the host of the neighbouring hotel (Mr. Stokes) who had placed along the waiting shed on the up platform the legend "Long life to Lovatt,"—Mr. Lovatt being, we need hardly add, the contractor of the line,—and over the booking office on the down side the words, "Success to our New Line." The majority of the passengers left the train at Bourton and enjoyed a stroll through the quiet town and along the banks of the lovely stream which is the attraction of the place, but others, after a late breakfast at Mr. Stokey's comfortable hostelry, travelled on over the old line, by Chipping Norton junction, to Oxford, and spent the remainder of the day in the University city. Two or three went on to London, two of these, on their way to the Derby, gaining half an hour as compared with those, on a similiar errand bent, who chose the first train by the Swindon route for their journey.

The later trains in the day carried large freights, and the excitement at the stations along the route became greater as the day wore on. There was, however, no incident calling for record. The weather was warm and fine, and the change of temperature from the valley to the high ground at Andoversford and Notgrove was pleasant, but the heat made the atmosphere very hazy, and the lovely view to be obtained on a clear day from the Dowdeswell valley was scarcely seen at its best. The travelling arrangements were well carried out, and we should not be doing justice if we did not acknowledge the courtesy and good temper with which Mr Cooke, the station master, and the officials at St. James's-square station, discharged the extra and somewhat trying duties which the opening of the new line, and the general ignorance of its fares and arrangements on the part of the passengers, threw upon them.

---

We have very recently given particulars of the route of the new line, in connection with the Government inspection, and the report we then published has been generally adopted by our contemporaries. For the information of those, however, who may wish to read it in connection with the opening of the line we may here repeat that the new line, after travelling over the Great Western branch to the main Midland-and-Great-Western line at Lansdown, passes for a short distance over the joint track before branching off through Hatherley towards Leckhampton. Originally the junction was intended to be made by two branches, like the arms of the letter Y, one (that already made) diverging towards Cheltenham, and the other sweeping towards Gloucester, along which through fast trains were intended to pass, without the delay of running into and backing out of the St. James's square station. The second branch is only partly formed, and work has long been discontinued upon it, but the piers of the girder bridge, by which it will be carried over the Hatherley-road, are standing, and its completion would be comparatively a light work at any time. Whether or not it will be completed will depend probably on the future alliances of the line. As originally planned too, the arm towards Cheltenham joined the Great Western line on the Cheltenham side of the Lansdown junction so as to touch the Great Western branch alone, but during its estrangement from the Great Western the new company got the arm shortened so as to join the joint track of the Midland and Great Western companies. Thus nothing but the sanction of Parliament is required to make a connection with the Midland system. The two arms of the Y will converge near the Alma-road, on the late Mr. Winterbotham's property.

The completed branch crosses the Hatherley-road to this point by a girder bridge, and similar bridges span the Alma-road and one or two other roads on the Hatherley estate before the line passes by cutting under the road from Cheltenham to Shurdington, the Moorend Park, and the Leckhampton-roads. Upon this latter road is the Leckhampton station. The platform is about 300 feet in length. On the side nearer the town there is the usual station accommodation, and there is on the same side some provision for wharfage, though it is scarcely equal to what we believe will be the need as the traffic with the hills is developed. Still chiefly in cutting, but with glimpses of pretty scenery around, the line proceeds towards Charlton Kings station, the first passing station on the line, placed at the point where the Cirencester-road crosses the track, and not far from the foot of the hill. Thence the line passes in cutting above the village of Charlton Kings. It then rises by gradients of about 1 in 70, cutting through outlying ridges of the hill and passing over the intervening ravines, necessitating a succession of heavy work in cuttings and embankment, which the nature of the soil, a treacherous, heavy clay, has made the more difficult to the contractors. At the back of Whithorne, the pretty residence of Col. Holmes, the work has been very heavy, through the subsidence from time to time of the high embankment, but the soil has now settled, it is believed, at its natural angle, and no further difficulty is apprehended. The effect has been to spread the base of the embankment a long way out towards the London road, which here runs parallel with the line. The long slope is planted with shrubs, the roots of which will be useful in binding the soil, while their appearance will be pretty. The view from the line at this point is very fine. Facing up the line, the wooded top of Dowdeswell, with its pretty Church and Court among the trees, can be seen, and the first glimpse is here obtained of the intervening viaduct. On the left one looks down on Col. Holmes's gable-ended house, with its well kept lawns; beyond this is the London road, its white surface dotted with passing traffic; and still beyond, rise the hills on the other side of the Chelt valley. On the right is a wooded gorge, with its watercourse. Turning towards the town, a good view of the open valley of the Severn is gained, and of the suburbs of Cheltenham. There is constant variation as the line still rises up the valley of the Chelt stream. At other places similar engineering difficulties have been met with to those at Col. Holmes's, a more serious one being at Woodbank, just before the viaduct is reached. The subsidence of the embankment here has carried out the base some 200 feet or so towards the road, but this also has now been conquered, and no further settlement is feared. The embankment at Woodbank terminates in the viaduct, which carries the line over the Dowdeswell Hill road and the ravine down which the main stream of the Chelt runs. Originally it was intended to cross the London road on a high embankment, some way nearer Cheltenham than Woodbank, as proposed by the old East Gloucestershire scheme, and to ascend the Dowdeswell valley on the left hand side of the road. But by the course adopted, the London road is not interfered with, and the line crosses from Woodbank to the high ground on the opposite side of the ravine on a viaduct running parallel with the road. This viaduct is the most interesting work on this section of the line. From below it is of light appearance, but closer acquaintance satisfies one that this appearance is due to the proportions of the design and not to any lack of solidity. As a fact, it is particularly strong. The bricks were all made upon the line, and are laid in mortar largely compounded of blue clay and ballast. This has set like iron. The viaduct, with its abutments, is about 548 feet long. It has twelve openings, each of 40 feet span, and the highest arch, from the bed of the brook running below, to the crown, is 70 feet in height. About a million-and-a-half of bricks have been used in the construction of the via-

duct. Beyond the viaduct the line again emerges on an embankment, soon, however, again to pass into a cutting, which ends with a tunnel under Sandywell-park, at the top of Dowdeswell Hill. This tunnel is 385 yards long, bricked throughout, and has taken about 3½ millions of bricks in its construction. A little distance from the outlet of the tunnel the line again reaches the open country, and Andoversford station, a few hundred yards from the Andoversford inn, is on an embankment. This is also a passing station, the rails here being double. Between the stations the line is a single one, though the overhead bridges and tunnel have been made for a double line, and sufficient land acquired for that purpose. The works on the section of the line beyond Andoversford are heavy, though very different to those on the earlier section of the line. Up the Dowdeswell Valley the difficulty was found in the peculiar soapy clay of the district. When excavated it is almost as hard as stone, but when exposed to the air and damp it slakes like lime, and becomes of the consistency of soap. But beyond Andoversford the excavations are almost all through rock, in some places so hard that every yard of it had to be blasted. Here was no danger of shifting of cuttings or embankments. Two and a half miles or so beyond Andoversford Notgrove (Westfield as it was at first named) station is reached. The work about here is very heavy. At the top of Hampen Hill the line reaches its highest point, 634 feet above the junction at Lansdown. It crosses the summit in a cutting of an extreme depth of 62 feet through the solid oolite; the sides are a mass of rugged stone which seems almost to overhang the way, and is suggestive of rich store for geologists. This Hampen Hill cutting is the deepest cutting along the line; it is three quarters of a mile long, and for a good portion of its length 54 feet deep. The embankment which grows out of it towards Notgrove is also the highest on the section. From the summit of Hampen Hill there is a steady decline to Bourton, which is still 288 feet above the level of the Lansdown junction. At Bourton the new line finds its continuation in the line from Bourton to Chipping Norton junction, and the only work here done by the new company has been in the enlargement of the station, and adapting it for through service.

To complete the project of the Banbury and Cheltenham Company, the section between Chipping Norton and Banbury has yet to be completed. Considerable progress has been made with it, and the Company have a Bill in Parliament authorising the raising of the capital to complete this portion. Though not perhaps as heavy throughout, some portions of the line are even heavier than any this side of Bourton, and the cutting and embankment at Hook Norton are among the heaviest works of their kind in England. When this section is completed a new country will be opened up and a direct access be given to the eastern counties.

The following are the fares for the single journey:

| From Cheltenham to | 1st Class. s. d. | | 2nd Class. s. d. | | 3rd Class. s. d. |
|---|---|---|---|---|---|
| Leckhampton ... | 0 8 | ... | 0 5 | ... | 0 3½ |
| Charlton ... ... | 1 0 | ... | 0 8 | ... | 0 5 |
| Andoversford ... | 1 8 | ... | 1 1 | ... | 0 9½ |
| Notgrove ... ... | 2 8 | ... | 1 10 | ... | 1 3½ |
| Bourton-on-Water ... | 3 9 | ... | 2 7 | ... | 1 9½ |
| Stow ... ... ... | 4 4 | ... | 3 0 | ... | 2 1½ |
| Chipping Norton Junc. | 6 2 | ... | 4 3 | ... | 2 6½ |

To Oxford the fares by way of Didcot are—1st, 12s. 6d.; 2nd, 9s. 9d.; 3rd, 5s. 11½d. By the new route they will be—1st, 9s. 11d.; 2nd, 7s. 3d.; 3rd, 4s. 9½d. These fares, we believe, are all above the ordinary fares for the mileage covered, and probably one of the first efforts to make the new line really what it should be, will be a struggle with the Great Western over the charges it makes over the line it has adopted.

## CHARLES ECKERSLEY DANIEL – RAILWAY NO. 1

Now that the Bourton to Cheltenham section was successfully operating, attention once again turned to the uncompleted sixteen miles of railway between King's Sutton and Chipping Norton. The works had languished during five years' suspension, and now positive steps were being taken to resume construction of the remaining link that would provide the vital connection between Banbury and Cheltenham.

The company Secretary had informed *Bradshaw's Directories* in September 1880 that the section was about half-finished, nine miles having been completed, excepting stations and signals. An overview of the line early in 1882 revealed that the trackbed was well advanced between King's Sutton and Bloxham, with bridges at Milton, Bloxham, Milcombe and Wigginton all in place. No work had been carried out at Bloxham station. The trackbed continued westward towards Hook Norton where it terminated abruptly at the Milcombe Road. The railway did not exist

### BOURTON-ON-THE-WATER AND CHELTENHAM BRANCH.

**DOWN TRAINS — WEEK DAYS ONLY.**

| STATIONS | 1 Passr. A.M. | 2 Goods A.M. | 3 Passr. A.M. | 4 Passr. P.M. | 5 Passr. P.M. | 6 Goods P.M. | 7 Passr. P.M. |
|---|---|---|---|---|---|---|---|
| Chipping Norton Jn. dep. | 8X50 | 9 0 | 9 42 | 1X 0 | 5X24 | 6 40 | 8 58 |
| Stow-on-the-Wold .. arr. | — | 9 15 | — | — | — | 6 55 | — |
| ... dep. | 9 0 | 9 30 | 9 52 | 1 10 | 5 34 | 7 5 | 9 6 |
| Bourton-on-the-Wtr. arr. | — | 9 40 | — | — | — | 7X15 | — |
| ... dep. | 9 8 | 10X48 | 10 0 | 1 20 | 5 42 | — | 9 14 |
| Notgrove ........... arr. | — | 11 5 | — | — | — | — | — |
| ... dep. | 9 20 | 11 15 | 10 12 | 1 33 | 5 57 | — | 9 26 |
| Andoversford ........ arr. | — | 11 30 | — | — | — | — | — |
| ... dep. | 9 33 | 12 15 | 10X25 | 1 46 | 6 11 | — | 9 37 |
| Charlton Kings .... arr. | — | — | — | — | — | — | — |
| ... dep. | 9 44 | 12 35 | 10 37 | 1 58 | 6 23 | — | 9 47 |
| Leckhampton ........ arr. | — | — | — | — | — | — | — |
| ... dep. | 9 51 | 12 55 | 10 43 | 2 5 | 6 29 | — | 9 53 |
| Lansdowne Junction ,, | 9X57 | 1 0 | 10X50 | 2X12 | 6X36 | — | 9 57 |
| Cheltenham ......... arr. | 10 0 | 1 5 | 10 53 | 2 15 | 6 39 | — | 10 0 |

**UP TRAINS — WEEK DAYS ONLY.**

| STATIONS | 1 Passr. A.M. | 2 Goods A.M. | 3 Passr. A.M. | 4 Passr. A.M. | 5 Goods P.M. | 6 Passr. P.M. | 7 Passr. P.M. |
|---|---|---|---|---|---|---|---|
| Cheltenham ........ dep. | 6 50 | — | 10 0 | 11 20 | 2 5 | 3 15 | 6 50 |
| Lansdowne Junction ,, | 6 53 | — | 10X 3 | 11X23 | 2X17 | 3 18 | 6X53 |
| Leckhampton ........ arr. | — | — | — | — | — | — | — |
| ... dep. | 6 59 | — | 10 9 | 11 29 | 2 40 | 3 24 | 6 59 |
| Charlton Kings ...... arr. | — | — | — | — | — | — | — |
| ... dep. | 7 4 | — | 10 14 | 11 34 | 2 45 | 3 29 | 7 4 |
| Andoversford ....... arr. | — | — | — | — | 3 10 | — | — |
| ... dep. | 7 14 | — | 10X25 | 11X44 | 3•50 | 3•39 | 7 14 |
| Notgrove ........... arr. | — | — | — | — | 4 5 | — | — |
| ... dep. | 7 25 | — | 10 36 | 11 55 | 4 15 | 3 50 | 7 25 |
| Bourton-on-the-Wtr ... arr. | — | — | — | — | 4 30 | — | — |
| ... dep. | 7 37 | 7 45 | 10X48 | 12 7 | 4 50 | 4 2 | 7X37 |
| Stow-on-the-Wold ... arr. | — | 7 53 | — | — | 4 58 | — | — |
| ... dep. | 7 45 | 8 0 | 10 55 | 12 15 | 5 8 | 4 10 | 7 45 |
| Chipping Norton Jn. arr. | 7 55 | 8X15 | 11 5 | 12X25 | 5X23 | 4 20 | 7 55 |

**TICKET COLOUR.**
Round. Pink.
Square. White.
Triangular. Blue.
Half Circle. Yellow.
Round. Green.

**SINGLE LINE WORKED BY TRAIN STAFF AND BLOCK TELEGRAPH AS UNDER:— Staff. Between**
Chipping Norton Junction and Bourton-on-the-Water.
Bourton-on-the-Water and Notgrove.
Notgrove and Andoversford.
Andoversford and Charlton Kings.
Charlton Kings and Lansdowne Junction.

#### CROSSING OF TRAINS.

Trains stop at Bourton-on-the-Water, Notgrove, Charlton Kings, Andoversford, and Lansdowne Junction to cross Staff or Ticket.

7.45 a.m. Goods from Bourton-on-the-Water and the 8.50 a.m. Passenger Train from Chipping Norton Junc. at Chipping Norton Junc.

| | | | | | | | |
|---|---|---|---|---|---|---|---|
| 10. 0 a.m. Train from Cheltenham, and the 8.50 a.m. from Chipping Norton Junc. cross at | | | | | | | Andoversford. |
| 10. 0 ,, ,, ,, ,, 9.42 ,, ,, ,, | | | | | | | Andoversford. |
| 11.30 ,, ,, ,, ,, 9. 0 ,, ,, ,, | | | | | | | Bourton-on-the-Water. |
| 11.30 ,, ,, ,, ,, 9. 0 ,, ,, ,, | | | | | | | Andoversford. |
| 11.55 ,, ,, ,, ,, 9.42 ,, ,, ,, | | | | | | | Lansdowne Junc. |
| 2. 5 p.m. ,, ,, ,, ,, 1. 0 p.m. ,, ,, ,, | | | | | | | Chipping Norton Jn. |
| 2. 5 ,, ,, ,, ,, 1. 0 ,, ,, ,, | | | | | | | Lansdowne Junc. |

and crosses the 5.24 p.m. Passenger from Chipping Norton Junction at Chipping Norton Junction.
6.50 p.m. Train from Cheltenham, and the 5.24 p.m. from Chipping Norton Junction, cross at Lansdowne shunts at Andoversford for the 3.15 p.m. Passenger from Cheltenham to Junc.

6.50 p.m. Train from Cheltenham, and the 6.40 p.m. from Chipping Norton Junction cross at Bourton-on-the-Water.

The Gradients on this Line are heavy, viz. :—
From Cheltenham to Andoversford ...... 1 in 80 Up.
,, Andoversford to Notgrove ...... 1 in 80.
,, Notgrove to Bourton-on-the-Water ...... 1 in 60 Down.

Instructions as to working the Bourton-on-Water and Cheltenham Branch, see p. 55.

*GWR Service Timetable, October 1881.*

# BANBURY AND CHELTENHAM DIRECT RAILWAY.

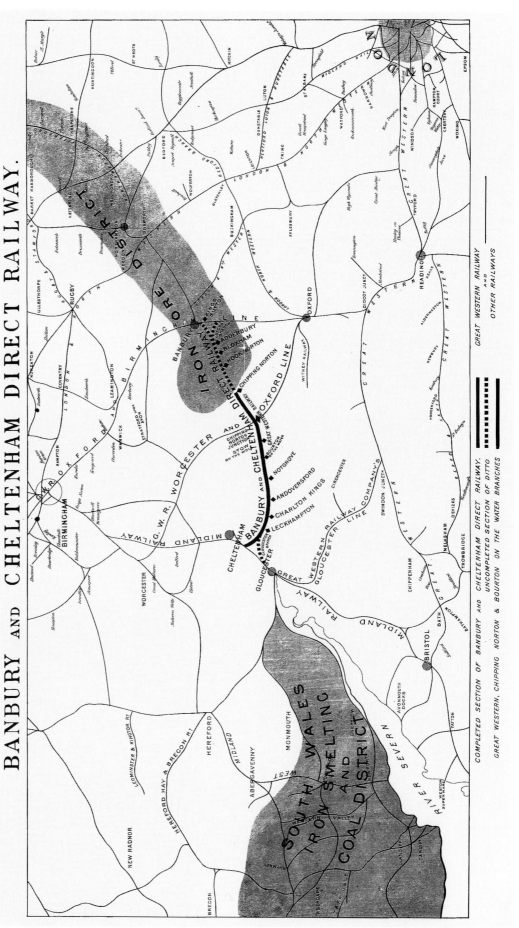

COMPLETED SECTION OF BANBURY AND CHELTENHAM DIRECT RAILWAY.
UNCOMPLETED SECTION OF DITTO

GREAT WESTERN RAILWAY
AND
OTHER RAILWAYS

GREAT WESTERN, CHIPPING NORTON & BOURTON ON THE WATER BRANCHES

A promotional map published in 1881 to draw the investors' attention to the link between the iron ore (supply) and the iron smelting (production) regions. In this presentation they appear tantalisingly close; the message – that the uncompleted eastern section of the B&CD prevented the successful engaging of these processes – is obvious.

AUTHOR'S COLLECTION

for the next two miles until South Hill was reached, where the partially completed cutting was prominent in the landscape. West of Hook Norton the works were patchy, and although the bridge abutments were in place, some of the accompanying earthworks were not, the former presenting a curious appearance as they rose out of the virgin landscape. The tunnel works at Chipping Norton had not yet been driven through, and the spoil forming the embankments to the north of the bore had reached halfway to Choicehill.

Plans for the work of completing Railway No.1 were developed during the early part of the year. The company put great effort into a promotional campaign, including maps of the proposed route and a prospectus. Critical to the success of the scheme was the support of the investors, as revealed in this letter written on 18th March by the Chairman, George Allen:

'I beg to remind you that you have not yet favoured me with a reply to my letter to you of March 8th.

'It is so obviously to the interest of all the Stockholders that the work should be commenced at once that I must again urge upon you the necessity that exists for every Stockholder at once coming forward.

'Unless everyone who is in a position to do so will help to a moderate extent, there is no chance that the Line will be proceeded with.

'I trust, therefore, you will fill up the form of application appended hereto and let me have it by Wednesday next'.

Detailed contractual arrangements were made throughout the summer months. On 20th June, the Board met to discuss the terms of a possible contract with Charles Eckersley Daniel, who was keen to take advantage of the favourable weather to hasten construction and offered to start work within seven days. The Board needed time, naturally, to assess the tender, and invited Henry Lovatt to comment on its merits. Mr Lovatt recommended the adoption of Daniel's tender subject to modifications, which were then agreed. The contract between the company and Charles Eckersley Daniel was sealed and exchanged on 15th August 1882.

Also during the summer, developments occurred within the company. On 26th June, Mr Guinness resigned his position as director, and five weeks later, on 3rd August, George Allen also resigned. George Allen continued to offer his services, acting as Receiver and Manager of the company. On 6th October, Frederick Bond was elected a director, along with General Sir Michael Kennedy, who occupied the position of Chairman. Lt. Col. Josiah Wilkinson was appointed Deputy Chairman and Walter Webb & Co. became the company solicitors. On 18th October, William Wilson of Wilson & MacIntyre was appointed as Engineer, the firm's payment for expenses of the remaining works being £3,600, to include the salary of a resident engineer and preparation of carrying out the works to the approval of the Board of Trade.

On the terms of William Wilson's appointment, agreed with the company, the Engineer gave an instruction to

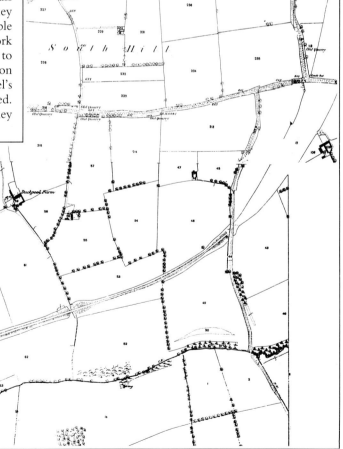

*The 1891 First Edition Ordnance Survey, showing the partially completed earthworks south of Hook Norton. Construction of the tunnel through South Hill, as authorised by the enactment of 1877, had almost certainly not been commenced.*

*The 1881 Ordnance Survey of the Hook Norton district. The area later designated for the station is still under the orchards of East End, and the site of the two viaducts and the embankment that would link them, not yet begun, lie to the left of Park Farm.*

Charles Eckersley Daniel for him to proceed with the construction of the railway.

By January 1883, the preparation of the contract works was well under way but there were many items undecided. The final position of Hook Norton station was still to be resolved; its originally proposed location, possibly on the north side of the Milcombe road, was now considered to be too far from the village.

At the same time, an assessment was made as to the condition of Chipping Norton tunnel. The Engineer reported to the Board on 16th January that the water had been pumped out of the workings, and on the extent of his observations, the brickwork had not been seriously damaged by its effects. He noted that a mismatch existed between the amount of work actually completed and that detailed in the last progress section received. A quantity of that work now required rebuilding.

While final preparations were carried out, expectation was high throughout the region that the works would at last be recommenced.

On 22nd February the *Banbury Guardian* reported:

'BANBURY AND CHELTENHAM RAILWAY
'Probability of early resumption of the work in connection with the construction of this long-delayed line of railway. For several weeks past material has been duly deposited on the ground in the shape of sleepers, &c, and on Sunday evening last a special train was run from Bourton-on-the-Water, by which about thirty tip wagons were conveyed.'

Four days after the *Banbury Guardian* issued this report, the death occurred of William Bliss, who had championed the causes of the Chipping Norton branch and the Bourton-on-the-Water Railway. He was 72. It may not be known whether or not his passing registered as significant to the Board of the B & CD; their present concerns were on a vastly different scale to the struggles which Bliss and the handful of determined individuals from Chipping Norton had overcome thirty years earlier. However, the two branches had made the Banbury and Cheltenham connection possible. Indeed, it was his vision for the extension of those railways that became the prime objective, which was now being followed through. Sadly, Bliss did not live to see it fulfilled; four gruelling years were still to pass before that end would be achieved.

A modest inscription on the simply-adorned stone chest stated:

'Here rest in hope, the remains of William Bliss of this town...the memory of the just is blessed. "I know that my redeemer liveth".'

His wife of 44 years, Esther, had predeceased him by three months. She was 74.

The chest was placed in an appropriately symbolic position within the cemetery that Bliss had given to the town of Chipping Norton. Located on a tract of land known as the Prime Downs, or Primsdown, the entire panorama of the town's hillside elevation could be seen. In view were the built artefacts of a life spent serving the people of Chipping Norton – the unmistakable edifice of the Lower Mill to the south, with its dominating chimney; the functional chimney of the Upper Mill to the east; the Baptist church opposite; the avenue of horse chestnuts along the Worcester Road; and the cemetery itself. Encircling the base of the hill and out of sight was the new railway connecting the Chipping Norton branch to the tunnel workings, these being clearly visible 200 yards distant and shored up with timber, as they had been left seven years' earlier.

Ironically, as Bliss was laid to rest, the wheels were once again set in motion to complete the railway. Within three days, the tunnel workings were brought to life as construction began again on Railway No.1.

The *Banbury Guardian* reported in its edition of 1st March:

'The resumption of work, which has been *in statu quo* for several years past, is now an accomplished fact, a number of men are employed in excavating a road for the running of ballast trucks thereon, in order to take away the excavated material from the tunnel works. The early part of next week will see work in full swing. The contract for the tunnel work, and also for the excavation of the cuttings, having been taken within the past few days.'

Chipping Norton continued to be the main focus of attention for the construction works. A local press account for 3rd May describes:

'THE RAILWAY WORKS
'Miners are now busily engaged in excavating for the tunnel of the Banbury and Cheltenham Railway. A new shaft has been sunk opposite the cemetery, and from this point a heading being made to the centre shaft, and from thence to the portion which was arched in prior to the work being stopped some seven years since. The earth taken from the Salford end is being conveyed in tip-trucks by a locomotive to fill up the bottom between Choicehill and the part of the permanent way completed at the time above referred to. In order to further facilitate the work, a second locomotive arrived on Tuesday, which was with considerable difficulty drawn over the tunnel hill by two ponderous traction engines.'

A contemporary eyewitness account adds further to the description of the tunnel workings at this time:

'There was a second shaft near the further (Rollright) end … The bulk of the soil was taken to the brow of the hill on a line specially laid there and it was drawn up there by a steel cable laid from the station to the power house. The material was used at the Rollright end of the tunnel to make the embankments.'

A large quantity of bricks intended to be used for lining the tunnel was diverted into building houses to accommodate Charles Eckersley Daniel's workforce at Nos.38, 40 and 42 West End, Chipping Norton. It was said that the first load was purchased by the builder; the rest he 'won'; this was a profitable spin-off. Stories have circulated of similar incidents taking place in the villages of Over Norton and Hook Norton.

The heavy plant kept arriving at the workings; this was further reported by the *Banbury Guardian* on 31st May:

'BANBURY AND CHELTENHAM RAILWAY.
'Great progress is now being made with the Banbury and Cheltenham Railway, and on Saturday a monster portable engine of 35 h.p. was brought from Bloxham for the purpose of drawing up the material by means of wire ropes from the station.'

Moving of heavy plant onto the Banbury & Cheltenham workings presented a logistical problem for the contractor, namely that the six miles between Hook Norton and Chipping Norton could not be accessed by rail. The area to the east side of Hook Norton, designated for the two viaducts, was still a yawning gap, and neither of the tunnels at Chipping Norton and South Hill had yet been driven through.

While this situation existed, the contractor had no alternative but to transport plant and materials over the hills by road, a potentially dangerous procedure over the steep, unmetalled surfaces. The local highways were extensively used for this purpose, an example being the transportation of wrought-iron girders to the Choicehill road bridge at Little Rollright, which were brought in from Chipping Norton. As a result of these movements, many complaints were made by Highway Boards and individuals about the contractor's plant, mainly traction engines, cutting up the local roads.

A measure of the extreme difficulty encountered by Daniel's workforce at this time is revealed in this eyewitness account, vividly recalled many years later:

'A small railway engine weighing 18–20 tons was brought to Chipping Norton [station] and had to be taken to Hook Norton by road. There were no heavy lorries to carry it, so twenty horses were hitched to it and it started up New Street – not a hard surfaced road as now, but one of white crumbling stone which became deeply rutted by the heavy engine wheels.

'Having safely negotiated New Street it was found that it could not turn left to go along the Middle Road. The horses had to be driven across the square and turned gradually until the horses and engine were parallel with and close to Top Side. Then it continued on its way to Hook Norton. The engine had no brakes to prevent it from overrunning the horses when going down hill, so men known as spraggers went alongside it carrying spraggs – that is – stout pieces of wood used to check the revolution of the wheels by inserting them between the spokes.'

On 1st August, the heads of terms were set out between the company and the contractor for a supplementary contract, including the additional works as authorised seven years previously in the Act of 18th July 1877, as follows:

Substitution of two viaducts for embankment 14 at Hook Norton.
Substitution of tunnel for works executed in cutting.
Increasing the tunnel length at Chipping Norton from 484 yards to 715 yards

It also included:

Abandonment of Railway No.2, the south curve at King's Sutton.
Abandonment of works in Cutting 13 at South Hill, Hook Norton and lands acquired to build the deviation of the same cutting as authorised by the Enactment of 1877.

The alignment of the proposed railway at Hook Norton was causing problems. A further revised section was approved by Parliament in 1881, but was not built.

Interestingly, the agreement gave notice for the abandonment of works executed at the proposed station site, indicating that a start had been made on the original location set

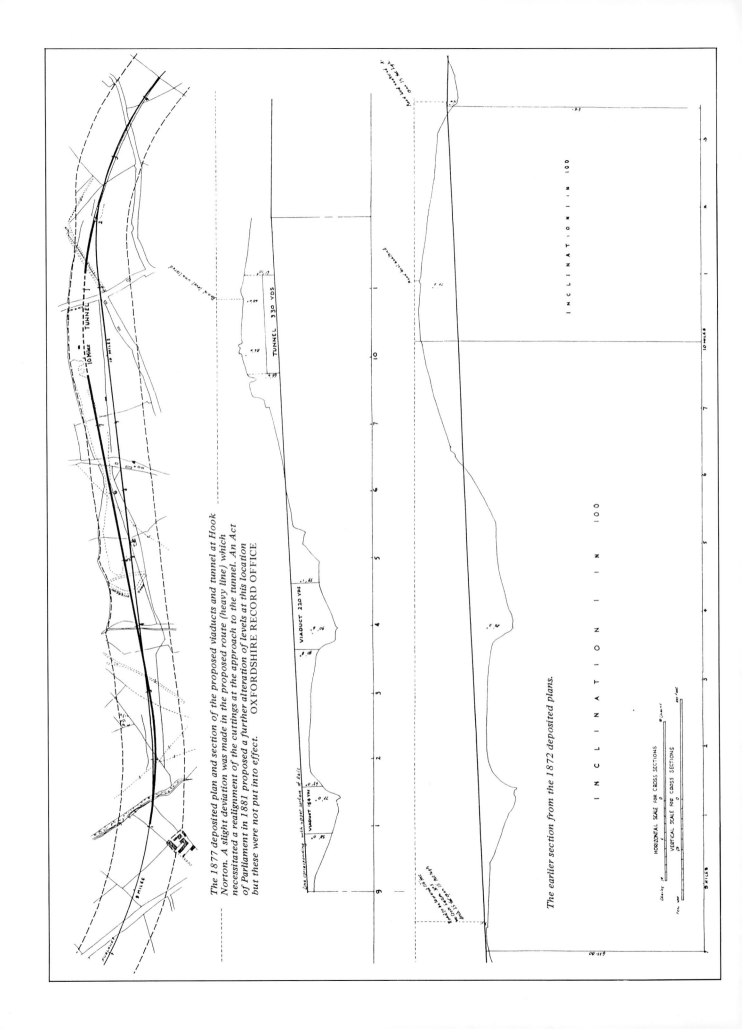

The 1877 deposited plan and section of the proposed viaducts and tunnel at Hook Norton. A slight deviation was made in the proposed route (heavy line) which necessitated a realignment of the cuttings at the approach to the tunnel. An Act of Parliament in 1881 proposed a further alteration of levels at this location but these were not put into effect.   OXFORDSHIRE RECORD OFFICE

The earlier section from the 1872 deposited plans.

*This photograph, taken during the construction of South Hill cutting No. 14 at Hook Norton, shows the north portal of the tunnel. The stone retaining walls are visible on the extreme left and drainage channels are also evident. It seems likely that the picture was taken in April or May 1886.*

COLLECTION
M. QUARTERMAIN

aside on the north of the Milcombe road before the decision was made to relocate to the south. The sum for these works was agreed as £5,703, giving a total contract value of £241,250.

By now it was clear that quantities of lands were now surplus, and available for resale. The deeds relating to these were passed from George Allen, who had relinquished his post as director, to the solicitor, J B Looker.

At the Board meeting of 25th September 1883, a resolution was made to pay an advance of £2,000, covering plant, to Mr Daniel. The current value of the plant actually on the works was valued at £20,000. Of the £10,000 already advanced, £4,780 had been repaid.

Preparations were being made for the accommodation works required at Banbury and King's Sutton; in these, the possibility of King's Sutton being the principal exchange station was discussed with the Great Western. In any event, it was recognized that the amount of payment by the B & CD should take into account the greater increase in staff levels required at King's Sutton than would be needed at Banbury. The Engineer had met the Great Western officials, and the cost of upgrading the facilities at King's Sutton station for exchange of traffic was quoted as £4,075.

The company agreed to approve, subject to negotiating a rebate calculated on the basis of the relative cost of the traffic alternatively being worked out of Banbury.

An important subject under discussion during the second half of the year was the completion of Railway No.5, the Gloucester curve at Hatherley. This had not been finished in 1881, and proposals were put forward at a Board meeting on 28th August (at which Henry Lovatt, now a director of the company, was present) for the contractor to complete it, 'in accordance with the deposited plans...and in compliance with the requirements of the Board of Trade.' In November, the B & CD had approached the Great Western over the possibility of constructing it for a double line. As it happened, the loop would not be completed in that form for another twenty-three years. In the meantime, the Great Western undertook to construct the south curve as a 'siding' for the passage of locomotives.

Meanwhile, works were progressing in the original goods yard at Chipping Norton. An arrangement existed for the employees of Bliss's tweed manufactory in the form of a right of way across the line at the western end of the station. On 21st December the Board discussed a subtle suggestion put forward by the Great Western that arrangements should be made for the route to be diverted, although doubtless the B & CD would try to find a way to avoid paying for it. Indeed, the right of way remained throughout the lifetime of the railway, and though its users took their lives in their hands as they crossed the station yard, risking injury from shunting manoeuvres and approaching trains, there has never

*Although not obvious, this photograph of Bloxham shows the Banbury & Cheltenham Railway under construction. Taken from St. Mary's Church spire, on a summer mid-day c.1881, the railway runs from left to right, east to west, in the background. The Barford road bridge was already in place and the cutting was advanced, but there were no houses yet constructed alongside the Barford Road. The buildings of Manor Farm feature in the foreground.*

COLLECTION DAVID GIBBARD

been any reported instance of an accident occurring there. The right of way is still in use today, some 25 yards to the east of its original position, between the buildings of the Chipping Norton Industrial estate, though no longer with any risk of accident caused by trains!

Works on the tunnel at Chipping Norton were now proceeding rapidly. The date of the event is uncertain, but the simply-described account by an observer tells of the moment the tunnel was driven through: 'Diggers from each end met exactly in the middle when a man crawled through the hole.' The workings were not without incident. On 8th December 1883, an engine driver, Alfred Simpson, aged 19, was killed after attempting to sprag (brake) the progress of a train near the tunnel workings.

The year 1884 brought yet more financial difficulties for the company, and during the early part of the year the works were again suspended. They resumed in May, but not before an application had been made by the company to appoint a Receiver for the plant, after it was discovered that Charles Eckersley Daniel had started to remove it from the works.

These financial difficulties alerted the B & CD to take prompt action, and on 28th May the Board instructed the Engineer to report the extent of the works. On 2nd June 1884, after a thorough investigation, William Wilson reported the following details:

'The line between King's Sutton and Hook Norton is almost finished. The road is completely ballasted and the permanent way laid. At Bloxham Station the sidings are being put down, but the goods shed and cattle pens remain to be done. The station at Adderbury is in nearly the same state of progress … Between King's Sutton and Bloxham there are some … slopes which will require soiling. Hook Norton Station is built nearly up to the level of the doors. A well, close by, has been sunk to a depth of 45 feet and lined with brick. The approach to the station is nearly finished.

'As regards Viaduct No.1, one of the abutments is finished and the other one is about 7 feet above the ground; the concrete foundations for two piers are laid and are ready to be built on; the two remaining piers are respectively 11 feet and 18 feet above the ground. All the ironwork for two spans is on the ground but not yet riveted.

'The steam power at work on this viaduct I found to consist of 3 cranes, one traction engine for hauling stone, one mortar mill, and a pump for feeding the engines. There is also a considerable quantity of stone properly dressed and ready for imminent use on the site of the works.

'The side cuttings between Viaducts Nos.1 and 2 are being excavated by about 40 men.

'As regards Viaduct No.2, the two abutments are finished with the exception of the padstones for the girders which require to be fixed on one of them; three piers are completed, two piers are built up to their full heights with the exception of about 3 ft, and two piers require about 43 feet and 34 feet to be added to them respectively.

'All the ironwork for this viaduct is on the ground in various stages of completion, some being riveted, some simply bolted together for riveting, and some not yet put together.

'The steam power at work on this viaduct consists of 4 steam cranes, one traction engine for hauling stone, besides cranes not worked by steam. There are also some scaling ladders on the ground for the purpose of fixing the lifting apparatus on the piers.

'Bank No.15 is being pushed forward, and there are about 80 men employed in building No.14. In this cutting there is a steam crane which is being used to load the stone which is being built into the piers and abutments of the viaducts. There are also 3 locomotives for hauling the tipping wagons in this portion of the works.

'Hook Norton tunnel is being ballasted at one end, the other end requires about 50 yds to be lined to complete it.

'Cutting No.14a, is progressing rapidly, the steam navvy making good work.

'Chipping Norton tunnel is complete with the exception of the face at the station end. There are about 30,000 bricks on the ground, and the contractor has 11 locomotives, 12 horses and about 650 men at work.

'I have made a careful back measurement so as to ascertain the amount of work remaining to be done to complete Rly. No.1 and Rly. No.1 mineral traffic, and the cost of the same according to the schedule prices. This I estimate to be          £35,037
          And for Rly No. 5     £ 3,733
          Making a total sum of     £38,770

The report closed by indicating that a 15-yard portion of unpaid work had been carried out in Chipping Norton tunnel.

On 9th June, the Board formalised the obvious – that the completion scheduled for July would not be achieved. The directors reported that '… it has become necessary to extend the time for the completion of the railway to the 30th August next.'

A fresh allotment of 1881 debenture stock was made to the shareholders.

William Wilson returned to Hook Norton in the hope of discovering that good progress had been made. However, in his report of 13th June there was little to add to the previous, there being slight increases in the number of men employed on the works, the rate of masonry executed, and the progression of the embankment.

At the Board meeting of 17th June, an agreement was made with Mr. Daniel. The question as to the setting-off of plant and retention accounts was settled by the Chairman.

When the B & CD Board met on 1st July, they expressed great dissatisfaction with the progress of the works. The Engineer was 'called upon to require the Contractor to proceed with greatest vigour, with a view to ensuring completion in accordance with the terms of the Contract.'

Also discussed was an Agreement with the ever-progressive municipal authorities of Cheltenham, who were rapidly extending their amenities into the surrounding region. The company gave approval to the Corporation of Cheltenham to lay water mains under the line at Dowdeswell.

On the same date, the Secretary was instructed to send letters of regret with cheques for return of the deposit to all applicants of 1881 debenture stock who had not received an allotment.

Slow progress of the works continued to give cause for concern to the Board. On 29th July it was recorded that: 'The Contractor is not pushing on the works with the vigour which is absolutely necessary to enable him to complete within the terms of his Contract, and that the Engineer be requested to use the powers he possesses under the contract to secure such a rate of progress as will complete the works within the Contract period and to report on the progress of the works weekly…'

Doubtless, the Engineer felt as powerless as the Board. However, he dutifully reported to that body, and on 13th August presented the sum of £3,000 in accordance with Certificate No.21 for works executed by Mr Daniel, stating that:

'The amount I am sorry to find shows no increase on my last certificate, for the works in hand are confined to the same limited area, and owing to the awkward position and cramped space, it is impossible to push them on so fast as it would have been if the amount to be done were spread over a larger mileage. I am urging the Contractor in every way to push on with some of the other works and I have made arrangements to go over the line with him…with the intention of pointing out to him where the work can be accelerated…'

The Engineer noted that the eastern face of Chipping Norton tunnel had been commenced, and would soon be completed. The station had not been started, although the earthwork forming the junction was nearly complete. As regards Hook Norton tunnel, he reported that it was 'now quite complete, and lined to its total length, requiring only the faces at either end, which must remain unbuilt until the cuttings are out.'

Regarding the condition of the northern viaduct No.1, the Engineer reported:

'There has been an increase to the force of men and machinery, and the masonry is making fairly good progress. Both abutments are finished with the exception of the bedstones, and the intermediate piers are in course of construction, and up to the heights shown on section. There has been within the last few days a further delivery of the ironwork and, as it is all now completed at the works, I hope to see it all on the ground by the time the piers are up, ready to receive it.'

…and for Viaduct No.2:

'Some further progress has been made, the bed stones and weathered courses have been fixed in the abutments and on all the piers except two which are not yet up to the heights shown in section. All the scaffolding and machinery for hoisting the girders is in place, and ready for lifting the ironwork which is all delivered, and I quite expect to see the lifting and fixing commenced next week.'

In August, the company decided to complete the King's Sutton to Bloxham section to the required standard for passenger operation. On the 26th the directors resolved that the Chairman would arrange with Mr. Daniel to complete that portion with the least practicable delay; the Bloxham to Hook Norton section would follow on. The Board of Trade inspection was carried out on Thursday 25th August 1884.

The Engineer reported to the company that the inspector only required some slight alterations in the signalling and locking gear, and small additions including station clocks and lamps, which were promised to be completed by mid-October.

Motive power for testing the bridges on the completed section was provided by the Great Western, who notified the company that payment for this was outstanding. Although the Board of Trade had passed the line as safe for passenger use, no trains were run until the opening on 6th April 1887.

Also in September, Mr Saunders, who had launched a determined campaign to promote a station for Great

Rollright as long ago as 1875, now made a fresh approach to the company on the 23rd, simply asking 'that a station should be placed between Chipping Norton and Hook Norton.' The Engineer was asked to ascertain the most suitable position.

The Engineer duly reported his assessment of the works on 13th October, noting that

'the amount of masonry executed this month is less than has been done in previous months, but a very considerable amount of stone has been brought on the site of the viaducts, and dressed ready to be used in the piers as soon as some necessary alterations have been made to the hoisting gear.

'On Viaduct No.2, a third pair of girders has been lifted and placed in position, and preparations are well advanced for lifting the fourth pair...'

On 14th October, the Secretary reported that he had visited the line the previous Saturday and observed that the progress of the works appeared very slow. His concern was also shared by the B & CD Board. On the 21st the directors expressed their dissatisfaction in regard to the progress made, especially the masonry, 'on the completion of which the prospect of an early closing of the work entirely depends.'

This observation was not an exaggeration. Building the viaducts must have seemed interminable to the observer. A contemporary eyewitness account reinforces the impression of slowness:

'The girders were put into position after they were brought from Banbury. They were so heavy and the viaducts so high that the pace of lifting was almost imperceptible.'

From the contractor's perspective, the work was being conducted as fast as possible, given the confined location, the limitations of the available technology and the enormity of the task.

By the end of October, the company took steps to protect their contractual interests. On 24th, advised by their legal counsel, the Secretary drafted a notice to be served upon the contractor under Clause 17 of the contract. The company also commenced action against the trustees.

The notice had been served by 18th November; Charles Eckersley Daniel reciprocated by serving notice to the company in accordance with a corresponding Clause 18.

Little difference had been made in the rate of progress of the works according to the Engineer's report of 14th November. No fresh building operations had been carried out on No.1 Viaduct; some masons engaged on work at No.2 Viaduct were transferred to No.1 and were now dressing some of the piers. On Viaduct No.2, six feet had been added to Pier No.3, while Pier No.4 had now reached full height. The scaffolding required for lifting the girders of Span No.1 was in position. William Wilson made attempts to meet Mr Daniel, but his efforts were continually thwarted by the contractor's 'pressing engagements'.

Meanwhile, the courts had granted an injunction restraining Mr. Daniel from removing materials from the company's land. At the same time, the Secretary offered to be indemnified against any claims or loss in connection with liability for damages that might accrue to the contractor, were the order for injunction to be set aside.

Arrangements to proceed with the contract occupied the company into 1885, though the draft Agreement and the proposed sum estimated by the Engineer for the completion of the line was not accepted by Mr. Daniel. The Chief Clerk deferred the case until 23rd February, the postponement giving time for the contractor to prepare to answer the affidavits. The arrangements put forward for the contractor were as follows:

1. The existing Contract and Agreements to be cancelled.
2. All matters of dispute to be referred to arbitration, the arbitrator to be John Fowler, or, failing him, the person designated by the Chairman of the Institute of Civil Engineers.
3. A reference to the work being commenced as soon as practicable would be limited by what is due from either party to the other.
4. No claim for penalties by the Company or for damages by Mr Daniel would be permitted.
5. Any award to be payable 30 days after opening of the railway throughout.
6. The Company agree to have the line completed at cost price by a superintendent of the works, who would be a servant of the Company, to be completed as rapidly as funds will permit.
7. A clause would be inserted stating that the Trustees have duly accounted for all funds received to date.
8. Trustees and Company to raise the necessary sums to provide funds for the works.

The negotiations with Mr Daniel were left to the Chairman and Henry Lovatt to conclude.

On 10th March, the company requested a number of revisions to Mr Daniel's agreement. These included a requirement that the contractor, and not the trustees, was to be the borrower, and work was to be completed within four months of commencement.

The company incorporated a clause stating that a timekeeper would be appointed and a cashier to pay wages; the sums to be deducted from Engineer's certificates.

Apart from the business of completing the massive works at Hook Norton, the company had a number of other matters to resolve during the first half of 1885, from the vital Bill which went before Parliament in February, to the mundane repairs to lineside fencing after cattle had strayed on to the line. Other items included, in January, the provision of water supply at Leckhampton station 'from the side of the railway between Leckhampton and Charlton Kings', and, in May, the report that the B & CD had cut off a means of access across the Common at Chipping Norton, isolating the water supply – a temporary means of carting the water was put into place. Also at Chipping Norton, damage had been caused to the bridge carrying the Worcester Road over the railway; the repairs were to be charged to the mayor of the town. Ironically, this bridge was the first to be completed by the company, and had been in existence for ten years; no passenger train had yet passed beneath it, and now it was in need of repair.

Financial difficulties prevailed, and the necessary agreement with Charles Eckersley Daniel could not be reached. In March 1885, the contractor terminated his three-year involvement in building the railway and commenced legal proceedings against the B & CD company.

The materials were advanced for sale by F Homan on 9th April, at Hook Norton and Chipping Norton. Included among the locomotives were 9 six- and four-coupled tank locos, 8-, 10-, 11-, 12-, 13- and 15½-inch cylinders by Hunslet Engine Co. Ltd, Fox, Walker & Co. and the Worcester Engine Co.

## LOVATT ONCE MORE

Following the failure to reach agreement with Daniel, the company immediately set to work discussing the best means to complete the railway. The opinion of an independent Engineer was sought to assess the priorities of work and determine the costs, and on 24th April the terms of settlement were agreed between the company and Mr Daniel. Mr MacIntyre, the Engineer acting in an independent capacity, estimated the sum for completion of the works as £46,000. He allowed ¼ per cent of the estimated cost, £115, to cover the Engineer's stand-alone fee.

By 27th May, the Board had made the necessary arrangements. All that remained outstanding was the means by which the capital was to be raised. On that day the directors wrote to the investors, outlining their position:

THE BANBURY AND CHELTENHAM DIRECT RAILWAY COMPANY
'Mr C E Daniel, the Contractor, having failed to finish the Railway in accordance with the terms of his Contract, and having suspended the works when they were on the point of completion, the Directors were compelled to take legal proceedings to cancel his Contract and release the Stocks and Securities of the Company, which under the terms thereof were held by Trustees to provide for the payments to him.

'The Directors, knowing the enormous advantage to the Stock and Shareholders of getting this important System of Railway completed and opened for traffic, have been trying for some time past to avoid the great and inevitable delay of protracted litigation, and to put an end to all differences by referring them to Arbitration, on condition that the Contract should be absolutely cancelled and the Securities hypothecated for it released.

'I am glad to inform you that these negotiations have at length resulted in an arrangement by which the Trustees now hold the securities above referred to absolutely free and available for the completion of the Railway.

'The Board have therefore anxiously considered what is now the best course to adopt to secure the completion and opening of the entire Line at the earliest possible moment, and to this end they appealed to their colleague Mr Lovatt, the well-known Contractor for Public Works, who completed the Cheltenham Section of this Railway, and who is the largest Stockholder in the Company, holding nearly £60,000 Debenture Stock. Yielding to the desires of the Board Mr. Lovatt has, in the most handsome manner, offered, while retaining his position as Director, to personally superintend the Works to their completion, and this without receiving any profit or compensation whatsoever. He stipulates only that in raising the necessary funds the Stocks of the Company already issued shall not be depreciated by the Stocks available for completing the Railway being offered for subscription at an unduly low price.

'The Directors…have undertaken to agree to the Stipulation he makes by depositing with Trustees, for realization when the Bonds become due, the Stocks available for the completion of the Railway, and in the meantime to issue Bonds against the said Stock, payable with interest one year after date.

'The Stockholders are invited to subscribe for the Bonds…by lending to the Company…at a remunerative rate of interest…the sum necessary…to secure the entire completion of the Line, which, as they are aware, will then be worked in perpetuity by the Great Western Railway.

'To complete the Line, and in terms of the Agreement with the Great Western Railway Company to maintain it afterwards for one year, will require at cost price £40,000.'

On 22nd July, an indenture was made between the B & CD, Charles Eckersley Daniel, Richard Billingsley Looker (the company Solicitor) and two of the company directors, Henry Lovatt and John Wilson. This took the form of a deed settling the certain disputes and litigation between the company and Daniel, and set out the terms of Henry Lovatt's employment.

Henry Lovatt had agreed to lend all plant necessary for completing the works without profit.

On 6th August 1885, an agreement supplemental to the indenture was made between Mr Looker, John Wilson and Henry Lovatt stipulating the terms relating to the use of plant and equipment:

'That the plant would be provided by Mr Lovatt for the completion of Railway No.1, and No.5, the Gloucester curve.
'The plant will be returned to Henry Lovatt upon completion.
'The Contractor will be paid out of any funds subject to the terms of the Indenture.
'The surety against loss or depreciation of plant due to ordinary wear and tear including loss on resale to a value not exceeding £2,500 was given as Mr Arthur Trevor Crowe of Sunderland.
'Repairs to the plant will be paid out of the trust fund and if not able to be paid out of that source then the moneys shall be deducted by Mr. Lovatt from any moneys due to him for subscription for bonds.'

With the agreement signed and sealed, the work once more got under way. The company advertised that they had made arrangements to complete the railway, and had taken on a number of hands.

For the next eight months, work focused almost exclusively on the completion of the two viaducts. When Charles Eckersley Daniel had left them five months before, they were visibly unfinished, surrounded with quantities of plant, including a massive steam crane, heaps of undressed and dressed stone, ironwork for the girders, and scaffolding.

Viaduct No. 2 was the more complete, with the girders of spans Nos. 5 to 8 in place, scaffolding surrounding span No. 1 in readiness for hoisting the girders, and piers 2 and 3 within the final few feet of their bedstones.

Viaduct No. 1 with its five spans was less complete, all the piers were at various stages of completion, with the ironwork lying on the ground.

The essential completion of the Banbury & Cheltenham Direct Railway had narrowed down to an area no more than two miles in length. The viaducts and their accompanying embankments were the last crucial elements remaining to complete the Banbury and Cheltenham connection, and as such the gargantuan structures had become the centre of attention. Everybody involved was acutely aware that the line would not be complete until the day that a train was able to cross the valley.

Henry Lovatt approached the task with vigour. Employing a manager to oversee the works, the last girders of No.2 Viaduct were quickly raised and by mid-October 1885 the permanent way was being laid on it. Another six weeks work was required to complete the structure.

*This photograph, showing an abutment of one of the Hook Norton viaducts, may have been taken in October 1885 when Lovatt took over the completion of the works. One of the roller bearings, which were positioned on top of the abutment for the girders to be mounted onto, can be seen lying on the ground by the figure on the left. The girder work can also be seen beside the abutment pier. The stonework was constructed first, the embankment, which almost surrounded the structure, being built later.*    COLLECTION M. QUARTERMAIN

Attention then turned to completing Viaduct No.1. The piers were raised at the rate of 2 ft 6 in per day, with a maximum of 16 masons employed in dressing and setting the stone. With 700 cubic yards of stone remaining to be placed, Lovatt expected to complete Viaduct No.1 by the end of the year.

In the vicinity, a massive earth-moving operation was taking place as 450 labourers, aided by ample plant and equipment, were tipping 76,000 cubic yards of earth into the embankment between the station and No.1 Viaduct. The bank between the viaducts was still under construction, with completion anticipated for the end of January.

As the year drew to a close, a potential problem in the form of frosts threatened the construction. The resident engineer, Mr Holt, had been appointed to oversee the completion of Railway No.1 and the Chairman, General Sir Michael Kennedy, pressed him to complete the masonry of No.1 Viaduct before a risk of frost damage set in. The contractor worked hard, taking advantage of mild spells in the

weather, and the piers of Viaduct No.1 crept ever upwards. Still the weather held.

The end of November brought rain.

Then disaster struck.

On the morning of Thursday, 3rd December 1885, six men were erecting a gantry at the top of Pier No.1, on a site known as Hyatt's Orchard. The gantry was a working platform arranged round the pier, comprising a framework of uprights, cross braces and rakers, or raking shores, the latter used to support the structure. These utilised mortice and tenon joints, held together with iron bolts. Gantries were erected in an organized sequence, stability being maintained by securing temporary stays. The last components to be assembled were the rakers, which could only be inserted once the stays were removed. So placed, the gantry could safely take the weight of the platform or baulk above.

During the morning, the men assembled the gantry until it was supported with two rakers on the east side, and six temporary stays. One of the workmen, John Burden, had descended the ladder to attach a supply of iron pins to the 'sledge' or cradle, which was then hauled to the top by means of a rope and pulley. When the foreman engineer, Henry Rogers, unhitched the sledge, he realised that the pins were the wrong type to secure the timbers that were about to be fixed – but it did not matter; they weren't needed yet.

At this point, the so-called 'human element' came into play. Henry Rogers had ordered removal of the remaining temporary stays; this was normally carried out in conjunction with the fixing of the rakers, the latter being installed in turn as each stay was removed. However, it was not unusual for the stays to be removed first, and Henry Rogers had already constructed five gantries in that manner.

John Burden scaled the ladder to the top of the pier as Rogers was knocking out the last stay. Also on the pier that morning were the foreman's cousin, Isaiah Rogers, Thomas Lee, Charles Hicks of the nearby village of Great Rollright, and 28-year-old Edward Emery Gaskins. The men set to work installing the remaining rakers, a process that varied according to the habits of the foreman responsible. Some insisted that the side rakers had to be installed first, others opted for those at the ends. In this situation, the east end rakers were already in position, and so the workmen reached for a corresponding raker for the west end of the platform from a load of timbers stacked on the top of the pier. Unfortunately, the required raker was at the bottom of the stack, and there followed an argument as to which one should be put in first. After some disagreement, the men settled on one of the side rakers. Rogers directed Charles Hicks and Edward Gaskins to remove the pulley blocks from the derrick or crane, which was alongside the pier, and transfer them to the pulley attached to the top beam of the gantry, ready to lift the raker into position. Again, this was not unusual, as the pulley on the gantry was capable of lifting up to 6 cwt this way. After Hicks and Gaskins had 'slung the pulley blocks', they attached the raker and lifted it clear of the top of the pier. The timber weighed between 2 and 3 cwt. For a moment it was poised, clear of the masonry, one end ten feet above the gantry level, the other resting on the cross beam upon which Hicks and Gaskins were sitting. The two men guided the beam down. As it came to rest on the platform, the gantry collapsed and fell more than sixty feet to the ground, together with Charles Hicks and Edward Gaskins. Onlookers rushed to their assistance, but it was to no avail – the two workmen lay buried under the broken timbers. Gaskins died almost immediately and Hicks died in the early hours of the following morning.

The inquest on 5th December, as the *Banbury Guardian* reported, was 'protracted', and lasted several hours. When it resumed three days later, in the Wesleyan Schoolroom, Banbury, much discussion surrounded the inconsistent practices involving construction of gantries. Eventually, a verdict of Accidental Death was returned on the two workmen. However, it may be surmised that this was not an accident, as the circumstances indicated a failure in the duty to take adequate care. The pressure to complete must have been a contributory factor. It may be noted that of the alternative methods available for installing the rakers, the workmen appear to have chosen those that required the minimum effort expended in the shortest possible time.

Probably no one of those actions was by itself capable of causing the gantry to fall – the cumulative effects of each in turn may have been sufficient to do so. The circumstances are a reminder that railway construction in the nineteenth century was conducted in a dangerous, highly pressured environment. Misjudgements could be costly. An additional factor in the sad sequence of events, mentioned at the inquest, may have been the effect of wet weather loosening the timber joints, making them unstable.

The weather continued to hamper progress throughout the winter of 1885–6, particularly on No1 viaduct. When the resident engineer reported on 13th April 1886 that the viaduct was complete (the last girders of spans 4 and 5 had been lifted during the week), he noted that 'the long and exceptionally severe winter that we have experienced and which has only lately left us, has been the cause of serious delay... during three months the frost was so keen and persistent that it was almost impossible to make any show with the masonry.' He added that the works 'have been as diligently and unceasingly persevered with as the weather would allow, so... it may safely be said that the bulk of them are completed and another three months of fine weather will go far towards completing them altogether.'

Of the outstanding earthworks, the largest was the massive embankment at the south end of Hook Norton station. This was the only earthwork to have been built in its entirety

ALAN BRAIN

since construction resumed the previous August. By April it comprised some 100,000 cubic yards of earth, with a further 20,000 cubic yards outstanding. The bank was made up of spoil from cutting No.14 East, at South Hill, and was conveyed by train across No. 2 viaduct. In his report, Mr Holt dared to venture an optimistic outlook, stating that 'In fact, with the exception of a gap of about 300 yards at No.1 viaduct, an engine can now run all the way from King's Sutton to Chipping Norton.'

With the earthworks and the permanent way almost complete, and apart from the signalling connections still to be made (the contract for the signalling had been let, and the materials for the cabins were in course of preparation), attention now turned to the last important element to complete the line: the station accommodation at Chipping Norton.

The same engineer's report described the progress at that location made during April:

'Stream diversion under lines is completed; both platform walls are finished; station buildings are in progress; the cutting at this point has been excavated; station yard is formed and permanent way and points and crossings are being laid down and ballasted; Mr Bliss's road diversion has been formed; installed and fenced; two troublesome slips have been dealt with and stopped.'

The works progressed throughout the summer months, and on 2nd August the Engineer, William Wilson, reported:

'The station buildings, platforms and footbridge over the line are all very nearly completed, a week's work will finish everything excepting the signal work which cannot be finally completed until the Great Western Company have laid in their new sidings and junctions which they are now doing, and which they should finish in about a fortnight.

'I have given the subject my most careful consideration, and I think the works are all being properly carried out, and with good weather I confidently believe that everything will be completed ready for Government Inspection in one month from this date.'

On 1st September, the company sent their Second Notice to the Railway Department of the Board of Trade, anticipating the works being ready for inspection during the 13th or 14th of that month. Once more, weather delayed completion of the remaining items and the Engineer wrote to the company, asking the Board to inform the BoT that 'the line would not be ready for inspection before the 23rd or 24th...and ask them to postpone inspection until after the 23rd.'

A few days later, Maj. Gen. Hutchinson of the Board of Trade made the inspection, and on the 29th the report was drafted. It stated:

'The new line is single, but the land has been purchased and the overbridges constructed for a double line of rails.

'There are two new stations, provided with the necessary accommodation and each arranged as passing places with double platforms, at Hook Norton and Chipping Norton, the latter will take the place of the existing Chipping Norton Station, the lines connected with which will become a goods yard.

'The steepest gradient...has an inclination of 1 in 83, and the strongest curve has a radius of 16 chains.

'The permanent way is similar to that of the portion between King's Sutton and Bloxham and the line is well ballasted. On the viaducts bridge rails on longitudinals have been used to facilitate the construction...the width at formation level is 18 ft.

'There are several deep cuttings and high banks, the greatest depth and height being 75 and 58 ft respectively.

'The works on the line are heavy and comprise:
1. Nine overbridges, all constructed in brickwork, widest span 31 ft.
2. Fifteen underbridges all built with brick abutments – eight (widest span 15 ft) with brick arched tops; seven (widest span 42 ft) with wrought iron girder tops.
3. Two viaducts, one of 5 spans and the other of eight spans of 100 ft each, the parapet length being 78 ft and 91 ft respectively. These have been constructed with stone piers and abutments carrying wrought iron Whipple Murphy girders, cross girders and rail bearers.
4. Two tunnels lined throughout in brickwork, 418 and 715 yds long respectively.
5. Ten large culverts, widest 6 ft, all constructed of brickwork, except the east [side] at Chipping Norton Station, where the top is formed with rolled girders supported on brick walls.

'These works appear to have been substantially constructed and to be standing well except in the case of the abutments of some of the bridges which have been built for some years and where the face bricks have more or less perished. The repairs to these abutments have been in some cases completed and others are in progress, it being intended to make them all good. The wrought iron and the piers of the viaducts are fine, substantial pieces of work.

'Most of the road bridges are of very great theoretical strength, and give very slight deflections under test. The viaduct girders have also sufficient theoretical strength, the deflection of these girders, when loaded with three heavy engines, tested between .6 and .9 of an inch, rather more than it is customary to find with ordinary lattice girders of similar depth and span.

'The fencing is of post and rail with some portions of clay bank.

'The signal arrangements have been properly carried out in the cabin at Hook Norton and in two at Chipping Norton.

At Hook Norton there are 13 working levers and 2 spare levers
At Chipping Norton A there are 10 working levers and 2 spare levers
At Chipping Norton B there are 10 working levers and 2 spare levers

'The line is to be worked by the Great Western Railway Company with their ticket and staff, combined with the Absolute Block system and a satisfactory undertaking to this effect (which shall include that for the line between King's Sutton and Bloxham, not yet supplied) given under sign and seal by the Banbury and Cheltenham Company and concurred on (under sign and seal) by the Great Western Company, should be given without loss of time.

'The requirements are as follows:
1. A hand rail is required on each girder of the underbridge at Hook Norton Station; a check rail on the...curves of the up line...is also needed; the platform requires completion and a fence at the back of the down platform.
2. At Chipping Norton Cabin B a compensator should be provided for No. 12 distant signal.
3. Clocks at the stations and in the signal cabins are required.
4. Some fencing at 8m. 50 chains has to be completed.
5. The pointing and facing of the abutments of the bridges should be completed without loss of time.
6. The position of the gas works siding close to the advanced signal at Chipping Norton Cabin A should be interlocked with the train staff, or brought closer to the cabin to be worked from it.

'Subject to the prompt completion of these requirements, and a satisfactory undertaking as to the mode of working the line, the opening of the line between Bloxham and Chipping Norton need not, I submit, be objected to.'

The works were proceeded with and on 18th October 1886 it was reported that they had been carried out as required by the inspection.

At last, the Banbury & Cheltenham Direct Railway was complete.

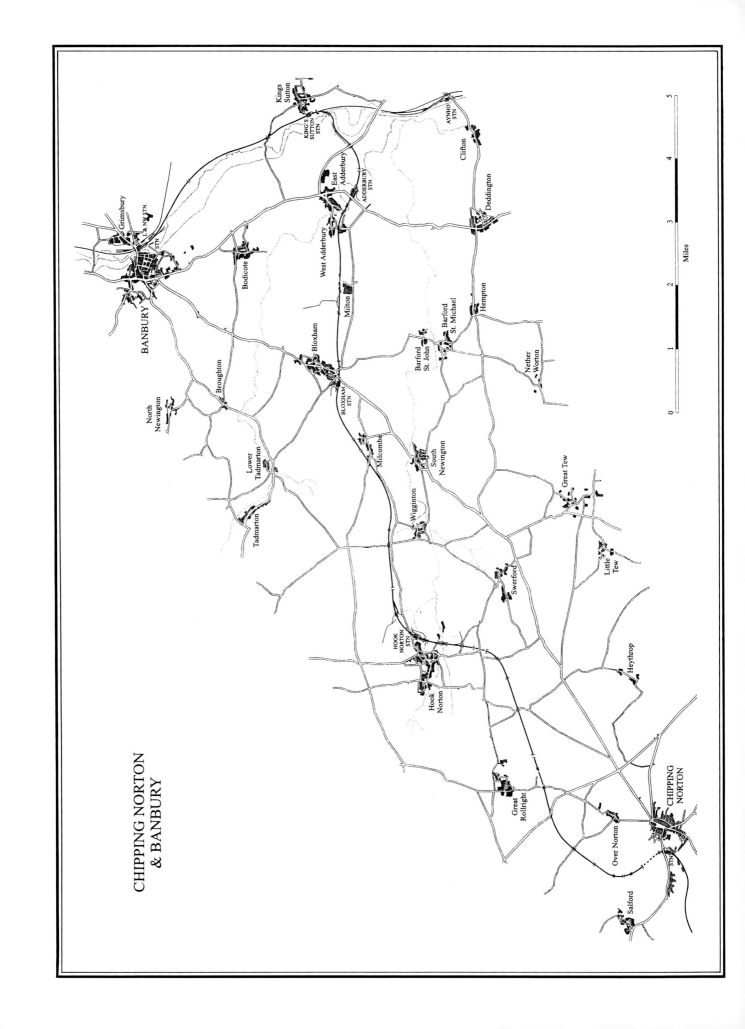

CHIPPING NORTON
& BANBURY

Without doubt, it was a triumph of civil engineering. To the bystander, observing the railway, the new works presented a magnificent sight. Viewed from the slopes of South Hill, the golden stone of the slender viaduct piers at Hook Norton were so bright, they almost looked unreal. From beside the quiet, dusty road at Choicehill, the bare earth slopes of the great embankment stretched impressively away towards Chipping Norton. Seen from the elevated positions above Limekiln Farm, The Walk and Cow Lane in the upper Swere valley – and everywhere – the new railway, with its fences, telegraph poles, freshly-laid ballast, gleaming rails, was in pristine condition. Ready for operations to begin.

The Great Western finalised arrangements.

The weeks passed.

The year 1887 arrived.

Small details, such as an undertaking to widen the yard at Hook Norton Station, were agreed, but still the line remained unopened.

On 8th February, Mr Lovatt reported to the Board that officials of the Great Western Railway were going over the line the next day with a view to it being opened on 1st March; the date came and went.

However, the company had continued to make further small adjustments to the line, which may have had an effect on the validity of the inspection carried out the previous September. On 30th March, the Secretary wrote to the Board of Trade concerning an alteration at Bloxham.

'Since the line was inspected by Major General Hutchinson on 29th September last, an alteration has been made in the connection of a siding at Bloxham.

'If you consider it necessary to have this inspected, I shall be very gratefully obliged if you can arrange for the inspection at a very early date, as we are most anxious to have the line opened in time for the Easter Holiday traffic next week.'

On the following day, the Secretary again wrote to the BoT, seeking permission to open the line before Easter. Preparations had been made for the opening on that same day!

Another small problem had been revealed by Col. Rich at Chipping Norton, to which the GWR responded on 1st April:

'In Colonel Rich's Report, he referred to some points leading into the Gas Company sidings at Chipping Norton, near to the junction between the Banbury & Cheltenham Railway and this Company's railway at this place, and saying that they should either be brought nearer to the box, or be interlocked with the train staff.

'I beg to state that the latter course has been adopted, and that the work concerned will be completed by the date of opening.'

The quicker, less expensive option had been adopted.

Despite these minor problems, the opening was sanctioned, and this was recorded in Great Western correspondence dated 4th April. The entry also confirmed the working arrangements as 'train staff and ticket in conjunction with the block telegraph'.

At 4 o'clock in the afternoon of Tuesday, 5th April, the official announcement was made – the railway would open the following morning. A sudden flurry of activity took place during the evening as a few timebills were circulated in Chipping Norton.

The next morning, the first scheduled passenger train from Banbury left King's Sutton station at around 7.7 a.m. and turned westwards onto the new branch, calling at Adderbury, Bloxham and Hook Norton. On the road bridge at Chipping Norton, a crowd gathered expectantly, leaning over the parapet to catch the first glimpse of the train as it emerged from Chipping Norton Tunnel. The rumbling of wheels on rails in the confined space of the bore heralded its approach as it coasted down the gradient, and then, at 7.48 a.m., the train appeared out of the darkness, slowed, and came to a stand at Chipping Norton station.

On 6th April 1887, the Banbury & Cheltenham Direct Railway had finally opened.

The *Banbury Guardian* faithfully reported the event:

'The Railway was opened for passenger traffic yesterday but there was no public demonstration of any kind to celebrate the occasion ... we may mention that the distance between Banbury and Cheltenham is 51 miles shorter than by the existing route, and there is a saving of 41 miles between Banbury and Gloucester. Mr William Wilson, of Deans Yard, Westminster, was the engineer of the line. The new line was fairly well patronised yesterday, and doubtless would have been more so if longer notice of the opening of the line had been given.'

The vicar of Adderbury mentioned the opening in his parish magazine:

'The opening of the Banbury and Cheltenham Railway the week before Easter, although long expected, took the public at last rather by surprise. A village may well be proud of possessing a Railway Station; and a record of the opening of it, being a decided step forward in civilisation, deserves a place in the Parish Magazine ... We shall all welcome the railway as affording the inhabitants of Adderbury additional convenience for travelling on business or pleasure.'

For the people of Hook Norton, the opening of the line gave them a special opportunity, as recorded by Margaret Dickens in her book: *A History of Hook Norton*:

'The railway was opened in time for the Hook Norton people to give up their own bonfire at the Queen's Jubilee, and make use of a special late train, which enabled them to enjoy the fireworks at Banbury.'

The railway proved quite an attraction during the Easter holiday, as reported by the *Banbury Guardian*:

'The beautiful weather that prevailed on Easter Monday was all that could be desired for holiday seekers ... those who had time for pleasure availed themselves of a ride for the first time on the new line of railway. The arrival of the trains was eagerly watched by crowds of people and, judging from the numbers going to and fro, the new company must have been very well patronised. In the afternoon, too, a little rival bell-ringing was being performed, first by the Bloxham hands, and afterwards by the Cropredy ringers ...'

As regards the changes at Bloxham, Col. Rich reported on 27th April that alterations were required in the interlocking of points and signals. Subject to those changes, he recommended that the BoT should approve the alterations at Bloxham.

Shortly after the opening of the railway, the newly-formed Hook Norton Ironstone Partnership made an excavation in a field between Hook Norton station and that part

# BANBURY AND CHELTENHAM BRANCH

## (Including Chipping Norton and Bourton-on-the-Water).

**SINGLE LINE.**

| Distance. | DOWN TRAINS. WEEK DAYS ONLY. | | 1 | 2 | 3 | 4 | 5 | 6 | 7 | 8 | 9 | 10 | 11 | 12 | 13 | 14 | 15 |
|---|---|---|---|---|---|---|---|---|---|---|---|---|---|---|---|---|---|
| | | | Passenger. | Passenger. | Goods. | Goods. | Passenger. | Passenger. | Passenger. | Passenger. | Passenger. | Passenger. | Passenger. | Passenger. | Passenger. | | |
| | | | AM. | AM. | AM. | AM. | AM. | PM. | AM. | PM. | PM. | PM. | PM. | PM. | PM. | | |
| — | Leamington | dep. | 6 15 | | | | | | | | | 3 27 | | | 7 0 | | |
| 6 | Southam Road | „ | 6 29 | | | | | | | | | — | | | — | | |
| 11 | Fenny Compton | „ | — | | | | | | | | | 3 47 | | | — | | |
| 16¼ | Cropredy | „ | 6 47 | | | | | | | | | — | | | — | | |
| 19¾ | Banbury | arr. | 6 56 | | | | | | | | | 4 4 | | | 7 34 | | |
| | | dep. | 6 58 | | 9 30 | | | | 11 35 | | | 4 6 | | | 7 36 | | |
| 23½ | King's Sutton | arr. | 7 6 | | 9 38 | | | | 11 43 | | | 4 14 | | | 7 44 | | |
| | | dep. | 7 7 | | 9X 45 | | | | 11 44 | | | 4 15 | | | 7 45 | | |
| 25½ | Adderbury | arr. | 7 12 | | 9 50 | | | | 11 49 | | | 4 20 | | | 7 50 | | |
| | | dep. | 7 13 | | 9 55 | | | | 11 50 | | | 4 21 | | | 7 51 | | |
| 28½ | Bloxham | arr. | 7 21 | | 10 4 | | | | 11 58 | | | 4 29 | | | 7 59 | | |
| | | dep. | 7 22 | | 10 11 | | | | 12X 2 | | | 4 30 | | | 8 0 | | |
| 32½ | Hook Norton | arr. | 7 32 | | 10 20 | | | | 12 12 | | | 4 40 | | | 8 10 | | |
| | | dep. | 7 33 | | | | | | 12 13 | | | 4 41 | | | 8 11 | | |
| 39 | Chipping Norton | arr. | 7 48 | | | | | | 12 28 | | | 4 56 | | | 8 26 | | |
| | | dep. | 7 50 | 8 X25 | | | 10X55 | 12 10 | 12 30 | 2 55 | 4 15 | 4X59 | 6 25 | 7 40 | 8X28 | | |
| 41¾ | Sarsden Siding | | — | — | | | — | — | — | — | — | — | — | — | — | | |
| 43½ | Chipping Norton Junction | arr. | 8X 2 | 8 35 | | | 11 5 | 12 25 | 12 40 | 3 10 | 4X30 | 5X10 | 6 40 | 7X52 | 8X40 | | |
| | | dep. | 8 X47 | | | 9 0 | | | 12 55 | | | 5X25 | | | 9 0 | | |
| 48 | Stow-on-the-Wold | arr. | 8 57 | | | 9 15 | | | 1 5 | | | 5 35 | | | 9 10 | | |
| | | dep. | 8 58 | | | 9 30 | | | 1 7 | | | 5 37 | | | 9 11 | | |
| 50¼ | Bourton-on-Water | arr. | 9 3 | | | 9X 40 | | | 1 12 | | | 5 42 | | | 9 16 | | |
| | | dep. | 9 5 | | | 10 48 | | | 1 15 | | | 5 45 | | | 9 18 | | |
| 55¼ | Notgrove and Westfield | arr. | 9 18 | | | 11 5 | | | 1 29 | | | 5 59 | | | 9 31 | | |
| | | dep. | 9 19 | | | 11 15 | | | 1 31 | | | 6 0 | | | 9 32 | | |
| 60 | Andoversford | arr. | 9 29 | | | 11 30 | | | 1 41 | | | 6 10 | | | 9 42 | | |
| | | dep. | 9 31 | | | 12 15 | | | 1 44 | | | 6 12 | | | 9 44 | | |
| 63¼ | Charlton Kings | arr. | 9 40 | | | 12 27 | | | 1 54 | | | 6 22 | | | 9 53 | | |
| | | dep. | 9 41 | | | 12 35 | | | 1 56 | | | 6 23 | | | 9 54 | | |
| 64¾ | Leckhampton | arr. | 9 45 | | | 12 42 | | | 2 0 | | | 6 27 | | | 9 58 | | |
| | | dep. | 9 47 | | | 12 55 | | | 2 5 | | | 6 29 | | | 9 59 | | |
| 66¾ | Lansdowne Junction | arr. | 9 X52 | | | 1 0 | | | 2X12 | | | 6X37 | | | 10 4 | | |
| 67¾ | Cheltenham | „ | 9 55 | | | 1 5 | | | 2 15 | | | 6 40 | | | 10 7 | | |

| Distance. | UP TRAINS. WEEK DAYS ONLY. | | 1 | 2 | 3 | 4 | 5 | 6 | 7 | 8 | 9 | 10 | 11 | 12 | 13 | 14 | 15 |
|---|---|---|---|---|---|---|---|---|---|---|---|---|---|---|---|---|---|
| | | | Passenger. | Passenger. | Goods. | Passenger. | Goods. | Passenger. | Passenger. | Goods. | Passenger. | Passenger. | Passenger. | Passenger. | Passenger. | | |
| | | | AM. | AM. | AM. | AM. | AM. | PM. | PM. | PM. | PM. | PM. | PM. | PM. | PM. | | |
| | Cheltenham | dep. | 6 50 | | | 10 0 | | | | 2 5 | 3 25 | | | 6 50 | | | |
| 1 | Lansdowne Junction | „ | 6 53 | | | 10X 3 | | | | 2X 12 | 3 28 | | | 6X 53 | | | |
| 3 | Leckhampton | arr. | 6 58 | | | 10 8 | | | | 2 21 | 3 33 | | | 6 58 | | | |
| | | dep. | 7 0 | | | 10 10 | | | | 2 31 | 3 35 | | | 7 0 | | | |
| 4½ | Charlton Kings | arr. | — | | | — | | | | 2 38 | — | | | — | | | |
| | | dep. | 7 5 | | | 10 15 | | | | 2 46 | 3 40 | | | 7 6 | | | |
| 7¾ | Andoversford | arr. | — | | | — | | | | 3 1 | — | | | — | | | |
| | | dep. | 7 15 | | | 10 25 | | | | 3 15 | 3 50 | | | 7 17 | | | |
| 12½ | Notgrove and Westfield | arr. | — | | | — | | | | 3 35 | — | | | — | | | |
| | | dep. | 7 26 | | | 10 36 | | | | 3 43 | 4 1 | | | 7 29 | | | |
| 17½ | Bourton-on-the-Water | arr. | 7 35 | | | 10 45 | | | | 3• 58 | 4 10 | | | 7 38 | | | |
| | | dep. | 7 37 | | | 10X 47 | | | | 4 45 | 4• 12 | | | 7 41 | | | |
| 19¾ | Stow-on-the-Wold | arr. | — | | | — | | | | 4 59 | — | | | — | | | |
| | | dep. | 7 44 | | | 10 53 | | | | 5 3 | 4 19 | | | 7 49 | | | |
| 24¼ | Chipping Norton Junction | arr. | 7 53 | | | 11 2 | | | | 5X 18 | 4 28 | | | 7 58 | | | |
| | | dep. | 8 X11 | 8 50 | | 11X 20 | 11 35 | 1 0 | 3 20 | | 4X 41 | 5 X25 | 6 55 | 8X 13 | 9 X0 | | |
| 26 | Sarsden Siding | | — | — | | — | — | — | — | | — | — | — | — | — | | |
| 28¾ | Chipping Norton | arr. | 8 23 | 9 X5 | | 11 32 | 11 50 | 1 13 | 3 35 | | 4 54 | 5 40 | 7 10 | 8 24 | 9 13 | | |
| | | dep. | 8 X24 | | | 11 34 | | | | | 4X 56 | | | 8X 26 | | | |
| 35¼ | Hook Norton | arr. | 8 40 | | | 11 51 | | | | | 5 13 | | | 8 43 | | | |
| | | dep. | 8 41 | | 10 30 | 11 52 | | | | | 5 14 | | | 8 44 | | | |
| 39¼ | Bloxham | arr. | 8 49 | | 10 40 | 12 0 | | | | | 5 22 | | | 8 52 | | | |
| | | dep. | 8 50 | | 10 43 | 12X 2 | | | | | 5 23 | | | 8 53 | | | |
| 42¼ | Adderbury | arr. | 8 57 | | 10 51 | 12 9 | | | | | 5 30 | | | 9 0 | | | |
| | | dep. | 8 58 | | 10 55 | 12 10 | | | | | 5 31 | | | 9 1 | | | |
| 44¼ | King's Sutton | arr. | 9 3 | | 11 2 | 12 16 | | | | | 5 36 | | | 9 6 | | | |
| | | dep. | 9 4 | | 11 3 | 12 17 | | | | | 5 37 | | | 9 7 | | | |
| 48 | Banbury | arr. | 9 11 | | 11 10 | 12 24 | | | | | 5 45 | | | 9 15 | | | |
| | | dep. | | | | 12 26 | | | | | 5 47 | | | 9 17 | | | |
| 51½ | Cropredy | arr. | | | | — | | | | | — | | | — | | | |
| 56¾ | Fenny Compton | „ | | | | 12 45 | | | | | — | | | — | | | |
| 61¾ | Southam Road | „ | | | | — | | | | | — | | | — | | | |
| 67¾ | Leamington | „ | | | | 1 5 | | | | | 6 17 | | | 9 48 | | | |

**All Local Trains between Chipping Norton and Chipping Norton Junction convey Goods Wagons and call at Sarsden Siding if required.**

*GWR Service Timetable, July 1877.*

of the village called East End. The purpose was to extract ironstone and send it principally to smelting works in South Wales. The means of transporting it was the Banbury & Cheltenham Railway.

A significant aim of the new railway was beginning to be realised.

## WINDING UP

So, at last, the Banbury & Cheltenham Direct Railway came into its own. It had been hugely ambitious and extremely costly, a consequence of the fact that the ideals of its construction were always ahead of the available technology. Nevertheless, the aims of the company never faltered, despite constant challenges.

By the time construction ceased, nearly £1,800,000 had been issued by way of shares and various other stocks. Of this, £250,000 had been issued in satisfaction of arrears of interest and other indebtedness, but a significant part of the excess must have been absorbed in legal expenses and Parliamentary fees to cover the eight Enactments that were necessary for its completion.

One of these was passed in 1887, when, some ten months after the opening, a settlement was agreed for various sums, including payment for the cost of the Act, payment of liabilities incurred by trustees in the construction of the railway beyond the sums that had been available, and payment for company administration and expenses. The Board agreed to pay £1,000 in first series class A debenture stock to the trustees for liabilities.

The line continued to develop over the next few years, including additional siding accommodation at Hook Norton under agreement with the Great Western, the land being conveyed from the Hook Norton Ironstone Partnership. In May 1890, new sidings were provided at Adderbury, the work on which was approved by Col. Rich on 18th July.

Within two years of the opening, a development was occurring around the western end of the line that would have a major impact on the operating of the railway. Whilst the B & CD was struggling to complete the eastern part of its line in the latter 1880s, another harassed company was battling north towards Cheltenham.

The origins of the Midland & South Western Junction Railway stemmed from the desire to connect the port of Southampton with the industrial North-West, to provide a quicker import of raw materials and export outlet for its manufactured goods than could be provided locally.

Its partial realisation came in the form of the Swindon, Marlborough and Andover Railway, which was eventually opened throughout between those towns in 1883. As was often the case with struggling companies, the SM & A had greater ambitions with which to make its fortune, and launched a nominally-independent company – the Swindon & Cheltenham Extension Railway – to connect the Midland Railway's metals at Cheltenham with the London & South Western at Andover, thus providing a direct link between industry and port. In addition, the company had designs on

South Wales' coal traffic destined for the south-western part of England, then largely in the hands of the GWR.

In this scheme, the S & CE would join the Banbury & Cheltenham Direct at Andoversford and exercise running powers over Great Western metals as far as Lansdown Jct., as conferred by the Swindon & Cheltenham Extension Act of 18th July 1881, and then run onto Midland metals for the short distance into that company's station at Cheltenham. However, its ambitions far exceeded its finances, and in late 1884 the receiver was called in. This occurred shortly after the amalgamation of the SM & A and the S & CE to form the M & SWJ, in June 1884, by which time the railway had reached as far north as Cirencester. The arrangement to run over the B & CD was approved by the Great Western in preference to another proposal by the S & CE for running powers over their Swindon to Standish Jct. (Gloucester) section.

Despite its parlous financial situation, the M & SWJ was able to continue north towards Andoversford in 1888.

On 9th April 1889, tracings of the proposed junction plans at Andoversford were submitted to the B & CD; the matter was referred to the Engineer, Mr. MacIntyre (because of his extensive knowledge of that part of the B & CD route) and his solicitor.

Agreement with the M & SWJ was not easily arrived at. During 1889, a claim had been made by the B & CD against the M & SWJ, and the latter company had asked for arbitrators to be appointed and the subject to be approved – a Mr. Samuel Wacker was appointed to that end.

On 16th March 1891, the Midland & South Western Junction completed its connection with the Banbury & Cheltenham. On that date, they commenced a goods service over their extension to Dowdeswell station, about half-a-mile to the south of the new junction.

The terms of the agreement between the two companies to allow running rights between Andoversford and Lansdown Jct. was submitted for sealing on 2nd June 1891, and an M & SWJ goods timetable into Cheltenham was in operation by July. The constant wrangling over terms, together with the non-completion of facilities at the Midland's Lansdown station, held up the M & SWJ's passenger services over the B & CD line until 1st August 1891.

Although traffic ran, legal difficulties continued, and a full agreement between the B & CD and the M & SWJ had still not been effected by December 1891. This was because the purchase price of the lands acquired by the M & SWJ from the Great Western, including solicitor's fees, remained outstanding. In addition, the original dispute surrounding the 1889 claim also remained unsolved. By November 1892, it had been agreed that the sum of £800 should be awarded to the B & CD; however, at a B & CD Board meeting, the directors expressed their dissatisfaction that the Great Western had continued to retain the moneys.

Working arrangements between the B & CD and GWR were also the cause of some disagreement. The problem concerned the routeing of north-eastbound traffic over the

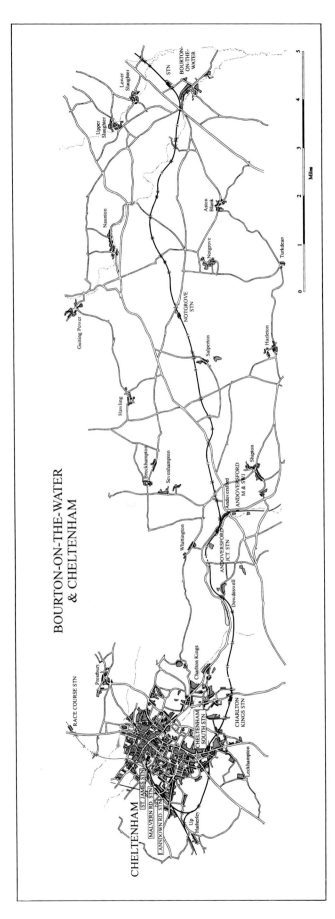

BOURTON-ON-THE-WATER
& CHELTENHAM

B & CD, which was inexplicably being diverted via Oxford and Banbury. The situation was made clear when William Bliss's son, who now ran the family's cloth manufactory in Chipping Norton, approached the Great Western because he had been unable to come to a suitable working arrangement with the B & CD over the supply of coal for his mill from Banbury, via the B & CD line. By the time the meeting between Bliss and the Great Western had been arranged, another problem affecting the conveyance of goods from his business had come to light: 'consignments of cloth intended for the North of England were being delayed owing to the necessity of so many transhipments.'

Matters were cordially resolved. In the case of the cloth transhipments, the Great Western 'has arranged for all those consignments to pass over the Banbury & Cheltenham line to Leamington, where they are put into the Manchester Station Truck.' As regards the coal traffic, the GWR and B & CD came to a clear understanding that where Bliss's coal was consigned via the B & CD route, then it would be carried over it.

Difficulties in the general conveyance of goods were also agreed by the two companies. The Great Western concurred that, in the event of traffic consigned via the B & CD not being passed over it, the B & CD would be credited with their proportion at the rate as though the traffic had been carried over the line.

While the B & CD were struggling over the working arrangements with the GWR and the M & SWJ, relations between the company and its shareholders were also becoming difficult. During the latter part of 1892, a lengthy and hostile correspondence shuttled back and forth between the company offices in Finsbury Square, London, and Mr. E. Brydges of the Public Offices in Cheltenham, who felt strongly that he, on behalf of the debenture holders, had been misinformed and not properly represented. A considerable number of issues were raised, but it is clear that the company had been pre-occupied by changes in the Board to the extent that they failed to acknowledge the duty of representing the investors with propriety. In concluding his final letter, Mr. Brydges penned a stern warning:

'I write in no spirit of hostility to the Board – if only they will abstain from tampering with the respective priorities of Debenture holders, which they have no right whatsoever to do – and will co-operate with them in any way…to get better treatment from the Great Western Railway…I must give you formal notice that if any attempt is made to exchange stock under the Act of 1887 to my prejudice, I shall apply for an Injunction to stop it.'

Evidently the difficulties were again resolved, at least personally, because Edward Thomas Brydges went on to become a director of the B & CD, albeit for a short period. He announced his intention to retire from the Board in February 1894.

Problems concerning working arrangements with the Great Western and the M & SWJ continued to arise throughout the latter 1890s. The M & SWJ presented various proposals to terminate their original agreement, and to negotiate revised terms.

From 1896, the B & CD began to take steps to sell the company. Absorption by the Great Western was inevitable, but it was in no hurry to fully acquire the company. Initial proposals were put forward in May of that year, the Chairman, Augustus Godson, reporting the result of his interview with the Great Western 'with reference to the sale of the undertaking to them in accordance with the resolution of 20th October 1894.' The arrangements for another meeting with the GWR were discussed, the purpose being to 'endeavour to induce them to modify their views.'

Terms of the sale of the line were further considered, and negotiations continued between the two companies throughout the following two years. On 13th August 1896, the agreement was finally made, subject to the approval of the Chancery Division of the High Court.

The transfer of the company to the Great Western was finally made as from 1st July 1897 by the Great Western Railway (Additional Powers) Act of 6th August 1897 S. 82., at which time the Receiver, appointed in 1881, was released.

The principal terms of agreement were made on 6th May of that year. All that remained to be done was the transfer of stock and capital.

As agreed, the price paid by the Great Western was £450,000, a quarter of the issued capital. In the winding up of the B & CD company, the holders of the several classes of debenture stock received various amounts according to their rights, and a nominal £2 per £100 was paid to the holders of the ordinary and deferred stock.

The acquisition by the Great Western Railway occurred at a significant time, for the GW was on the verge of a major development of its own system. The Banbury & Cheltenham Railway, now incorporating the previous lines between Chipping Norton and Bourton, would form part of that system. Indeed some of the B & CD's original proposals, long abandoned, would come to fruition in the exciting years of the great Edwardian enterprise which lay just around the corner.

PHOTO BY A. W. WHEELER.       PRODUCED BY B.-R. MORLAND, BANBURY.

**THE VIADUCT, HOOK NORTON.**

SOLD BY SPATCHER, HOOK NORTON.

*An early view of Stow-on-the-Wold station, looking west c.1890, presumably taken during an overlap of shifts judging by the number of staff present. The distinctive design of the 'Carpenter Gothic' style station building was repeated at Bourton and Chipping Norton junction. Notice the alternating slate bands, the carved timberwork and tall chimney stacks.*
COLLECTION R. SHARP

# CHAPTER SIX
# UNDER THE GREAT WESTERN
## 1881–1913

WHEN the first section of the Banbury & Cheltenham Direct Railway opened in June 1881, its operation was managed by the Great Western Railway, in accordance with the terms of agreement made between the two companies. The locomotives and stock were Great Western, as were the railway staff; the B & CD was, in practical terms, part of the GWR. For the next sixteen years, the line was operated in this manner, connecting with the GWR's Chipping Norton and Bourton branches, until the company was purchased by the Great Western in July 1897. At this point, the Banbury & Cheltenham Direct company ceased to exist. For convenience, this chapter covers the working and development of both company's lines, from 1881 onwards, as one railway, which is, of course, what they became.

In 1881, the line was worked by five passenger trains in each direction between Cheltenham and Chipping Norton Jct., with two goods services over all or part of the route. The line was single throughout, with sidings and loops at the two ends, at Bourton, and also at Andoversford, the only new intermediate passing place. The Great Western continued to run its Chipping Norton branch in the same manner as previously.

Chipping Norton Junction was officially provided with an engine shed in 1881 to house the Cheltenham branch goods engine. Situated in the fork of the main line and the Chipping Norton branch, it was a single-road structure some 33 feet in length, built of timber on low brick walls, with a 22 ft turntable at the entrance also giving access to a pit road. The shed and turntable were quite adequate for the usual tank engine provided at the time. A timber coal stage was located near the shed entrance.

Although the Great Western was proud of its safety record, like any concern involving human and mechanical usage it was susceptible to accidents. On 21st December 1881, the 11.20 a.m. Cheltenham to Chipping Norton Jct. (running as the 11.44 a.m. from Andoversford) was involved in an accident between Stow and the junction station, at a point about 1½ miles east of Stow. The train consisted of a tank engine, running bunker first, and four coaches, operating at a speed of about 30 mph. It would appear that, owing to a landslip to the west of Andoversford, trains were working eastwards from that point only. The engine type, from the official description, would appear to have been an 0–6–0ST, in place of the usual four-coupled tank design. The driver's evidence indicated that both he and his engine were based at Oxford, and although this duty on the Cheltenham line was only his second day, he had worked over the road on previous occasions.

In the official report, the engine had appeared to 'burst the railway, and after pushing the rails and chairs from 1 to 4 inches alternately to the right and left, it broke the road, ran down the bank on the left side of the line and fell over on its right side. The carriages became uncoupled from the engine, and ran down the bank on the right side of the rails.'

Driver Joseph Newport and fireman Thomas Thomas were cut and shaken in the accident, though no passengers complained of being hurt. The two centre coaches had fallen over on their right-hand sides, and the last coach, in which the guard, Mark Gunner, was riding, tipped partly onto its side. He was knocked against the partition, stunned, and the luggage in the van fell on him.

The permanent way was pushed out of alignment over a length of about 80 yards, beyond which seven or eight lengths of the 27 ft sections of track were broken up. Several rails were broken. In replacement, 7½ pairs of rails, 120 chairs and 50 sleepers were used.

In his evidence, Col. Rich stated that the formation of the trackbed was somewhat softer at this point than further back along the line, 'owing to the rails being nearer to the level of the surface of the ground in the valley'.

His findings pointed to

'a heavy tank-engine running at greater speed than the permanent way was able to bear. No complaint had been made of the state of the permanent way, which, although light, was certainly in good order. The engine had been sent to work over this part of the line when a part of the Banbury & Cheltenham was shut up by a landslip.'

In his suggestions, he proposed the use of tender engines of 'not too heavy a class' over the line; that turntables should be provided at each end to turn the engines without the necessity of uncoupling them; and that so long as any portion of the line consists of a light permanent way, the trains should be worked at moderate speed.

The GWR General Manager, James Grierson, responded to the Board of Trade in a letter of 19th January 1883:

'I have to state, with regard to passenger traffic being worked by tender engines, that since the accident took place the passenger trains on this branch have been worked by engines of the class employed to work this Company's trains on the Metropolitan Railway, and our Locomotive Superintendent states that they have worked most satisfactorily and, in his opinion, are more suitable for this branch than any of our tender engines.

'A turntable has been provided at Chipping Norton Junction, in accordance with the undertaking given to the Board of Trade on May 25th, 1881, and there being one also at Cheltenham, the requirements of the Board of Trade in this respect have been complied with.

'With regard to the permanent way, the line between Bourton-on-the-Water and Chipping Norton Junction has recently been relaid, and the Company's Engineer certifies that "the line from Cheltenham to Chipping Norton Junction is sufficiently strong to allow of trains being run at the usual rate of speed".'

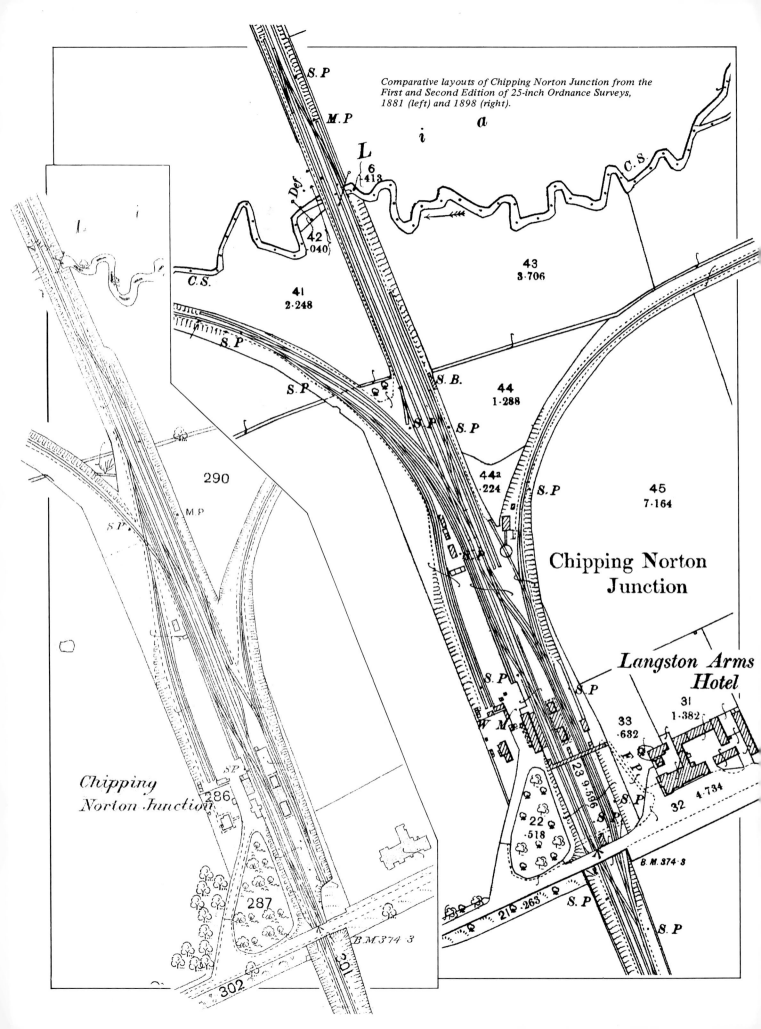

*Comparative layouts of Chipping Norton Junction from the First and Second Edition of 25-inch Ordnance Surveys, 1881 (left) and 1898 (right).*

*A postcard view of Chipping Norton Junction before construction of the Direct Loop (1905).*
COLLECTION CHRIS TURNER

It would appear that this response satisfied the Board of Trade.

In 1884, Chipping Norton Junction station handled twelve branch arrivals and departures daily (with one more on Saturdays) between 8.0 a.m. and 9.0 p.m. in addition to twenty or so main-line services between those hours. The passenger station had changed little since the opening of the Bourton line, although the platforms had been widened and lengthened around 1872. The Chipping Norton branch had its own bay on the eastern (outer) face of the up platform, but there were no such provisions for the Cheltenham branch trains, which had to use the main-line platforms. Any movement between the two branches was somewhat tortuous. Passengers still had to cross over the main lines to gain access to the opposite platform, there being no footbridge; there was a considerable danger in this, as the public were invariably around the station at times when train arrivals and departures were taking place.

The main alterations to the station in 1884 were the building of a third platform on the east side of the site, and the connection of the pair of branch bays thus formed to the Cheltenham line by a series of two double junctions through the main lines, and another on the roads into the branch platforms. The branch bay lines were extended southwards to connect with the up main line to the south of the road bridge; this required the building of a new bridge to carry the Bledington road over the new lines, immediately to the east of that over the main lines.

This layout enabled the Cheltenham trains to arrive and depart efficiently from their own bays with the minimum of disruption to main-line running, and also anticipated the through running of passenger services between Cheltenham and Banbury which occurred three years later.

A substantial new building in yellow brick with a generous canopy was provided on the down main platform, with a small shelter on the eastern platform. The platforms were connected by a long covered footbridge of lattice construction, which extended to the station boundary to give direct access to the Langston Arms Hotel, just to the east of the station.

Rail access to the sidings around the loading bank on the down side of the station had originally been by a trailing connection from the down main, but these were re-aligned and extended to connect to the Cheltenham branch instead. A down loop siding was constructed to the north of the Cheltenham junction, whilst that opposite on the up side was extended northwards.

Movements were controlled from two new signal boxes, North (on the east side of the main line and sidings, opposite the curve of the Cheltenham branch) and South (squeezed between the north side of the road bridge and the south end of the island platform). The original box, believed to have stood at the northern end of the island platform, was demolished in the rebuilding.

The new works were inspected by Col. Rich, who made his report on 24th November 1884. Full details of the new arrangements were included on accompanying plans, and his written submission was short and to the point:

'I have inspected the alterations and new connections at Chipping Norton Junction on the GWR. The station and yard have been extended and thoroughly re-arranged and signalled.

'The points and signals have been interlocked and are now worked from two raised cabins, one at the north and the other at the south, each side of the station.

'I submit that these alterations and new works may be approved.'

In that year, a new signal box was also approved at King's Sutton, alongside the site of the B & CD line junction; this

*Adderbury staff group in 1892. The gentleman on the right was almost certainly Henry Brown who, born at Stoke Poges in 1839, was Adderbury's first station master. At that time the position was station inspector. He lived at Hook Cottage on the Deddington Road, between the station and the village, and remained at Adderbury until his retirement in January 1906, by which time the post had been upgraded to station master. Brown was replaced by Albert Cotterels c.1907.*

*Bloxham's first station master William Herbert Baughan, whose tenure was from the opening in 1887 to 1907. He arrived from Worcester, where he also served on the railway, taking up the Bloxham post at the age of twenty-six. He and his wife Fanny, together with their three children, Alfred, Edwin and William, almost certainly lived in one of the Railway Cottages. None of the children served on the railway. In 1907 William Herbert Baughan emigrated to Canada. He died there in 1922.*
COLLECTION S. McCLOUGHRY
CTY. ALL SAINTS SCHOOL,
BLOXHAM

*Dr. Hyde's footbridge, looking west, with the South Newington road bridge and the buildings of Bloxham station beyond. This photograph was taken by members of All Saints School, Bloxham, Camera Club c.1890. Dr. Jonathan Hyde, a prominent Bloxham citizen who owned land crossed by the railway at the south end of the village, requested that the Banbury & Cheltenham Railway Company provide him with, and maintain, a footbridge over the new railway, giving access to his fields. In describing the footpath which led to Dr. Hyde's fields from the South Newington Road, one source claims a chief delight 'was the wealth of spring flowers which bordered it'. He was granted access via a footbridge, which was a graceful, long, shallow-arched lattice girder structure, which spanned the cutting between the Barford and South Newington road bridges. Dr. Hyde made full use of the bridge during his lifetime. In the rook season he was often seen returning to his home at the junction of the South Newington and Tadmarton roads with rooks shot in the elm trees which grew in his fields. He also used to take shooting parties to the osier-beds between Bloxham and Milcombe, which were approached along a bridle path running close to the railway. Here again, rooks abounded. Rook pie was a delicacy of which, it is said, Dr. Hyde was particularly fond.*          COLLECTION S. McCLOUGHRY, CTY. ALL SAINTS SCHOOL, BLOXHAM

*Bloxham station, looking west, c.1893, with Butler's timber yard on the extreme left. The uniformed staff member posing on the down platform was almost certainly William Herbert Baughan. Both views feature the original Gloucester Wagon Co. signal cabin in the distance.*
COLLECTION S. McCLOUGHRY, CTY. ALL SAINTS SCHOOL, BLOXHAM

*Bloxham station, looking east c.1893 while under B&CR ownership. Note the original station sign and the small Gloucester Wagon Co. ground frame hut behind the platform fence beyond the station building. The ground frame controlled the points at the east end of the crossing loop which were beyond the reach of the lever frame in the original Gloucester Wagon Co. signal box which can just be glimpsed in the distant background of the previous photo.     COLLECTION S. McCLOUGHRY, CTY. ALL SAINTS SCHOOL, BLOXHAM*

*Butler's timber yard from the south c.1893, with Bloxham station buildings in the background. For several years after the opening of the railway, Butler's timber yard occupied a large site immediately south of the station. The business was begun by James Butler in the late 19th century, as a family-run business of carpenters, employing some twenty men. Towards the end of the 1890s, the company fell into financial difficulties which led to its closure in 1902. For a further eight years the site remained unused, one of the villagers recalling that 'the field was left in a mess'. In 1920, George Allen, a London solicitor, gave the land to the village and on 7th November of that year it was formally handed over to the trustees of the recreation ground. The villagers cleared the site with great endeavour, piling the debris into a large mound which was then set alight. The photograph also shows a row of cottages and a lane towards the right-hand side of the view. Before the railway arrived, this lane was the main road to South Newington, which continued in a straight line towards the position of the photographer, and joined the alignment of the present road at the edge of the playing field. The cottage closest to the camera was actually two dwellings. Tom Tyrell lived in the left-hand cottage and Herbert Hawtin occupied the right-hand one. 'Durg' Hawtin, as he was known, was a thatcher by trade. He kept twelve hives of bees; hence the name of his property was Beehive Cottage. These cottages have since been demolished. Edgar Barbour lived in the cottage behind the telegraph pole. He was an engineman stationed at Banbury who lived with his mother and two sisters, Cicely and Wyn.*

COLLECTION S. McCLOUGHRY, CTY. ALL SAINTS SCHOOL, BLOXHAM

HOOK NORTON STATION

*Hook Norton station c.1890 showing the station entrance and Railway Hotel alongside the Hook Norton to Milcombe road. Hook Norton station was constructed on an embankment in part of the village called East End. The land had formerly been part of Hyatt's Orchard.*

COLLECTION M. QUARTERMAIN

*An 1890s view of Hook Norton station, looking south, showing the early track arrangement with weighted hand-lever-operated sprung trap points in the entry to the down loop in the foreground.*
COLLECTION M. QUARTERMAIN

*Frank Beechey, station master, was almost certainly second from the left in this view of Hook Norton station c.1900. Frank Beechey was born in Bristol in 1857. In 1877 he married Lucy Allen at Kingham and was described as a switchman, probably at Chipping Norton Junction. The 1881 census for Kingham refers to him as a switchman (pointsman) and in 1882 as a railway porter. The original Gloucester Wagon Co. signal cabin is seen here on the right, on the down platform, whilst the single-aspect arm of the Gloucester up starting signal above had been replaced by a standard GWR arm and spectacle plate. Notice the construction of the station platform brickwork supported on wrought-iron beams, doubtless to combat potential movement of the fresh earthworks.*
COLLECTION M. QUARTERMAIN

*The earliest view discovered so far of the new B&CD station at Chipping Norton c.1895. The original terminus had been situated in the right background. Here the original shortlived Gloucester Wagon Co. single-aspect signals feature at the end of the down platform, whilst the Gloucester signal cabin survived until 1964 when the line was closed.*

COLLECTION ALAN BRAIN

would replace the original structure to the south of the down platform.

The Cheltenham line was formally operated by the Great Western under agreement by virtue of the Great Western Railway Act, 25th June 1886, S.41.

With the opening of the Banbury section in 1887, through passenger running commenced between Banbury and Cheltenham, which necessitated a reversal at Chipping Norton Jct.

A goods trains service between Banbury and Hook Norton was introduced at the opening of that line. In addition to general merchandise and coal, the train was soon conveying iron ore from quarries around King's Sutton and Hook Norton. The goods services were expanded as greater quantities of ore were demanded, and through running to and from Wolverhampton with this traffic (and return empties) was introduced.

*The approach to Chipping Norton, with the Worcester Road bridge in the 'Common Hollow' centre of view.*
AUTHOR'S COLLECTION

*The Worcester Road crossed the line on this substantial brick overbridge, the first to have been built by the Banbury & Cheltenham Direct Company. This view was taken looking south-east over the station with the tunnel behind the photographer.*
PERCY SIMMS, CTY. ALAN BRAIN

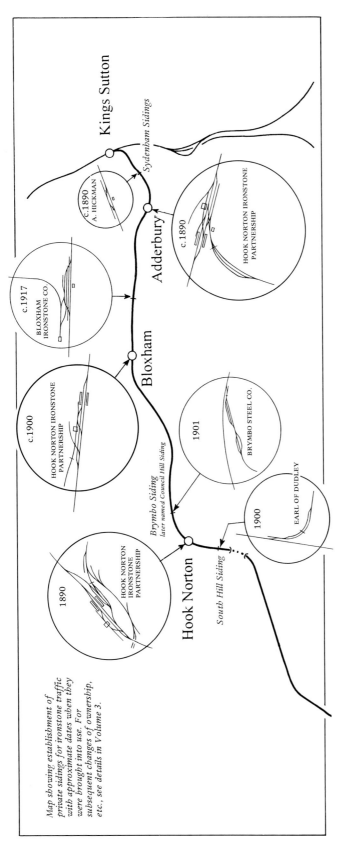

Kings Sutton

Sydenham Sidings

c.1890
A. HICKMAN

c.1890
HOOK NORTON IRONSTONE PARTNERSHIP

Adderbury

c.1917
BLOXHAM IRONSTONE CO.

c.1900
HOOK NORTON IRONSTONE PARTNERSHIP

Bloxham

1901
BRYMBO STEEL CO.

Brymbo Siding
later named Council Hill Siding

1900
EARL OF DUDLEY

1890
HOOK NORTON IRONSTONE PARTNERSHIP

Hook Norton

South Hill Siding

*Map showing establishment of private sidings for ironstone traffic with approximate dates when they were brought into use. For subsequent changes of ownership, etc., see details in Volume 3.*

Quarries had been in operation around King's Sutton since the 1860s, with the Adderbury Ironstone Co., and from the late 1880s, with Alfred Hickman, conveying ore by canal, then rail, from the station area or close by. Hickman's Sidings, on the north side of the B & CD line, were opened in 1890, though a canal and railway interchange for ore to the south of the line seems to have existed too.

Further west, the Hook Norton Ironstone Partnership had commenced work on quarries to the north-west of Hook Norton station, and ore was being dispatched by the early 1890s. This was connected with the railway at sidings on the south side of the down platform at Hook Norton station.

Additional quarries came into operation at Hook Norton in the late 1890s, when Brymbo Steel Co. purchased land around the station at Hook Norton. Consignments to Wrexham commenced in 1899. The company soon had quarrying operations in hand on the north, east and south sides of the station, connecting to the branch some ¾-mile to the east of the station, at a site that came to be known as Council Hill Sidings.

Yet another company began to arrange for quarrying operations at Hook Norton around 1899 when the Earl of Dudley, who had massive industrial interests in the Black Country, requested a connection to the railway at South Hill, to the south of the No.2 (southerly) viaduct. The Board of Trade report dated 2nd December 1899 indicated that 'the points are worked from a ground frame containing two levers which are locked by the key on the electric train staff.' Quarrying and production work commenced in the area around this viaduct in 1901, though it ceased in 1916.

At Cheltenham, the B & CD services ran into the Great Western station at St. James, which had its frontage on St. James's Square, and the River Chelt passing under the station throat. The station comprised two platform faces, between which were four terminal roads, with a goods shed and an engine shed to the west, both on the north side of the running lines. By the early 1890s it was found that the station was becoming increasingly unable to deal efficiently with both the Gloucester and B & C traffic, with a total of over sixty passenger and goods arrivals and departures taking place between 6.50 a.m. and 1.0 a.m. the following morning, plus numerous empty stock and shunting movements. Sanction was therefore obtained from the Board of Trade to rebuild the station with four platform faces, construct a new goods shed and greatly increase siding accommodation. In order to accommodate the larger facilities, the line was extended a further 150 yards or so towards St. James's Square from the site of the old station. Work had been largely completed by August 1894.

It was not until December of that year that the Board of Trade inspector, Lt. Col Yorke, visited the site, and he submitted his report on Christmas Eve.

'The old station at this place has been demolished, and a new station, built 150 yards nearer to St. James' Square, the line having been extended through this new station. An extensive goods yard has been laid out,

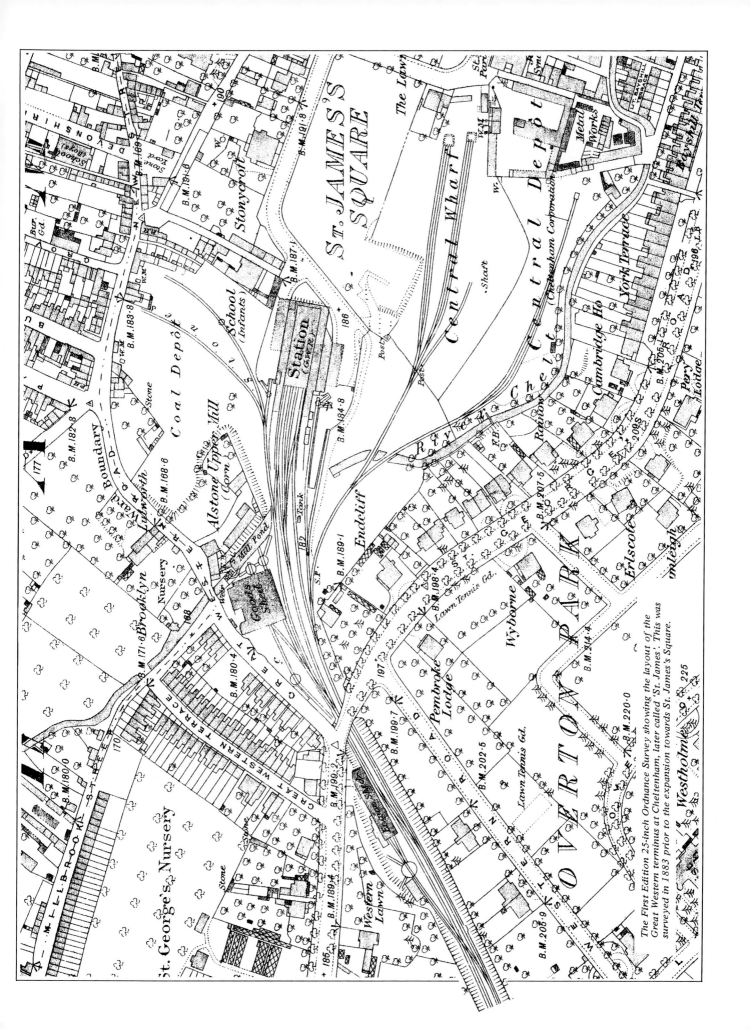

The First Edition 25-inch Ordnance Survey showing the layout of the Great Western terminus at Cheltenham, later called 'St. James'. This was surveyed in 1883 prior to the expansion towards St. James's Square.

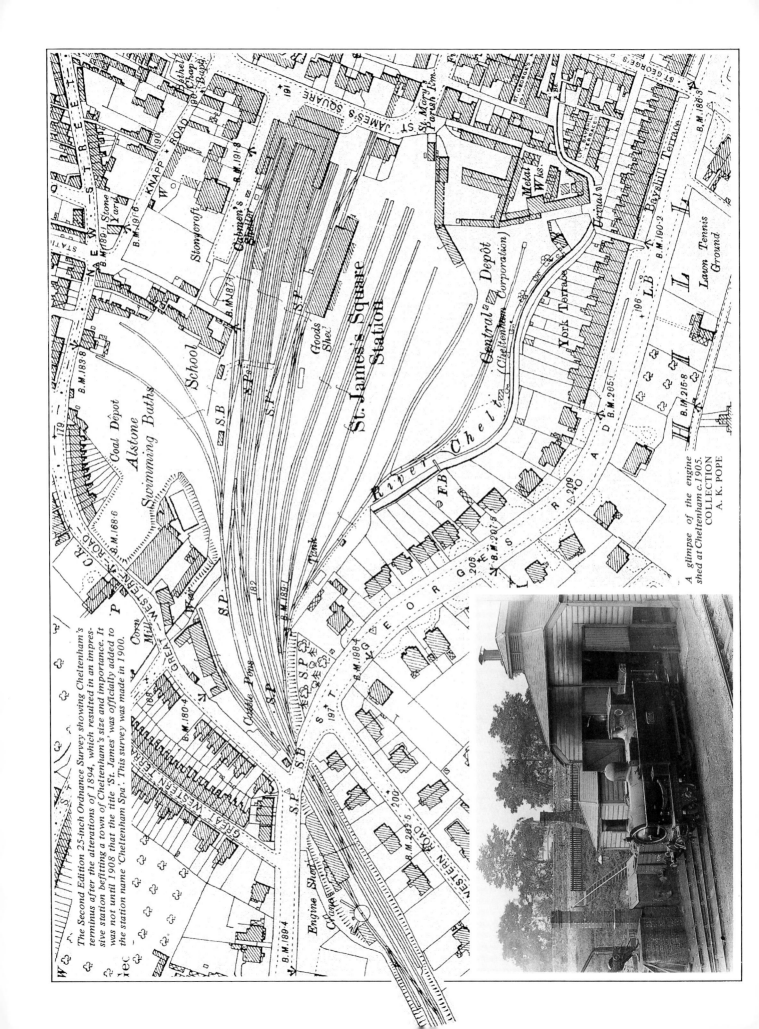

The Second Edition 25-inch Ordnance Survey showing Cheltenham's terminus after the alterations of 1894, which resulted in an impressive station befitting a town of Cheltenham's size and importance. It was not until 1908 that the title 'St. James' was officially added to the station name 'Cheltenham Spa'. This survey was made in 1900.

St. James's Square Station

Central Depôt (Cheltenham Corporation)

River Chelt

Alstone Swimming Baths

Coal Depôt

School

Goods Shed

York Terrace

Bayshill Terrace

Lawn Tennis Ground

Engine Shed

A glimpse of the engine shed at Cheltenham c.1905.
COLLECTION
A. K. POPE

& the facilities for dealing with both passenger & goods traffic largely increased.

'The new passenger station contains two arrival and two departure platform lines, besides carriage sidings &c. The accommodation for passengers is ample & commodious, & includes waiting rooms & conveniences for both sexes. I would, however, suggest for the consideration of the company that a few screens placed on the platforms would add to the comfort of the passengers waiting either for arrival or departure of trains, as owing to the absence of any side walls, the platforms, despite the fact that they are roofed over, are much exposed to wind and rain.

'The signalling arrangements are carried out in two new signal boxes, viz – The Bays Hill signal box, which contains 30 levers in use & 5 spare, and the Cheltenham Station box, which contains 37 levers in use and 4 spare, and the interlocking is correct.'

The only requirement from Col. Yorke was the movement of the safety catch point, leading from the engine shed, backwards by half-a-rail's length, to prevent the likelihood of a derailed engine at that point fouling the down main. This was operated from Bays Hill box. Rather than move the point, the Great Western decided instead to replace it by a short shunting spur, and completion of this was notified to the BoT in May 1895.

As regards the provision of platform screens to provide shelter against the elements, as suggested, the company decided that, for the time being, they could not entertain the idea. In view of 'the very heavy outlay the company have incurred in the construction of the new station at Cheltenham', they decided to wait until some experience of the effects of weather had been gained. Nevertheless, they did admit in internal correspondence that the new station was 'exceedingly drafty'.

The Midland & South Western Junction Railway (in the form of the Swindon & Cheltenham Extension Railway) had obtained running rights over the Great Western line between Andoversford and Lansdown Jct. by its Act of July 1881. It was not until March 1891 that the M & SWJ were in a position to commence a goods service over their extension and, with modifications taking place at the Midland's Lansdowne station, passenger services into Cheltenham could not be introduced until 1st August 1891. The agreements also gave the M & SWJ the right to call at the inter-

*An Edwardian view of Cheltenham Spa station from St. George's Road.*
COLLECTION
S. BOLAN

*An unidentified 'Metro' class 2–4–0T with a train of clerestory stock alongside Platform 3 at Cheltenham Spa c.1905.*
CHELTENHAM
REFERENCE
LIBRARY

mediate GWR stations through which it passed, and also gave the Midland Railway running powers over the M & SWJ, including that section of GWR metals between Cheltenham and Andoversford. The M & SWJ quickly exercised their right to call at Charlton Kings and Leckhampton stations – from 1st April 1899 – but it was not until 1st October 1904 that their trains called at Andoversford too.

## THE DOUBLING WORKS

The insertion of M & SWJ traffic into that of the Great Western between Andoversford and Cheltenham in 1891 made a considerable impact on working over that section. Immediately prior to that time, the GWR ran four passenger and one goods trains in each direction over the single line between Cheltenham and Chipping Norton Jct., a usage that could be comfortably accommodated by the facilities and

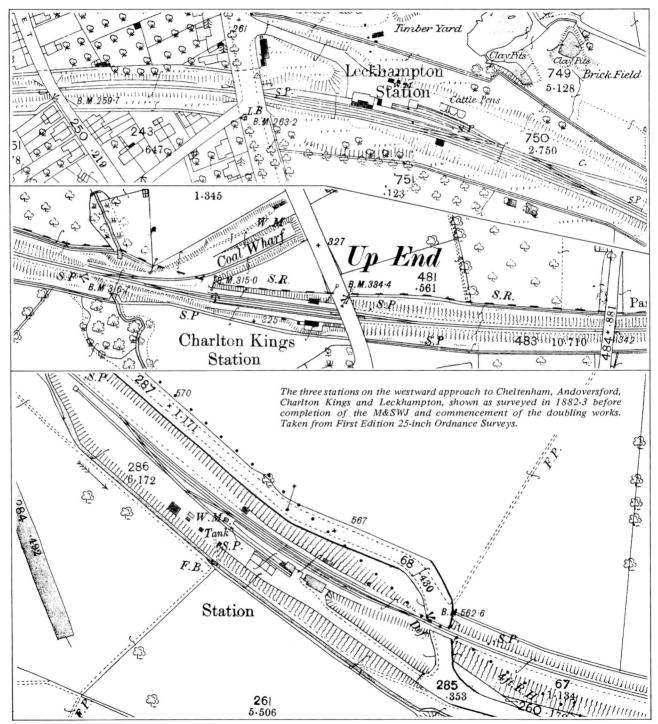

The three stations on the westward approach to Cheltenham, Andoversford, Charlton Kings and Leckhampton, shown as surveyed in 1882-3 before completion of the M&SWJ and commencement of the doubling works. Taken from First Edition 25-inch Ordnance Surveys.

passing places provided at intermediate stations. Of those passing places occupying the shared route west of Andoversford, the loop at Leckhampton was some 305 yards, and at Charlton Kings around 220 yards; these loops had been added to the original single-line stations around 1880. The loop at Andoversford was 285 yards in length.

With the introduction of M & SWJ goods services, another two trains ran daily each way over the section. In August 1891, these were joined by five passenger services in each direction, more than doubling the previous traffic flow. The timetable was arranged so that most conflicting trains passed at either Andoversford or Cheltenham, before entering the section, and only passed once intermediately, at Charlton Kings (though twice when the up afternoon conditional GWR goods ran).

Resolving the accounts of railway companies, as with any large concern, was a complex procedure. This was particularly so when third parties were closely involved, as was the case with the B & CD, with both the Great Western and the Midland & South Western companies concerned. A dispute over the advances of monies between the B & CD and the GWR in 1892 showed some of the gross figures involved, and serve to illustrate income and expenditure:

Gross Receipts, 1st June 1881 to 30th June 1892     £27,444 14s 8d

| | |
|---|---|
| Plus Cheltenham Station Rent Charge | £3,894 3s 7d |
| Less the Terminals at Cheltenham | £304 13s 6d |
| Plus Interest at £133 per annum, 4th April 1887 to 30th June 1892 | £697 1s 4d |
| | £4,286 11s 5d |
| TOTAL | £31,731 6s 1d |

Towards the end of the decade, there were in excess of thirty regular movements over the section daily, with six or so conditional trains in addition, as well as occasional specials. The potential for traffic delays over this single-line section had now become significant, to the extent that future traffic expansion of both companies could be affected. The M & SWJ therefore proposed that the section between Andoversford and Lansdown Jct. should be doubled to ease congestion; it was the M & SWJ who appeared to have the greater need, as they were in the process of doubling their own line between Cirencester and Dowdeswell, whilst the line was already double track from the south end of Dowdeswell station to the junction at Andoversford, a distance of some half-mile. Largely in order to apply pressure, the M & SWJ proposed its own direct line from Andoversford to Ashchurch, on the Midland main line about seven miles north of Cheltenham, thus bypassing the B & CD line. This proposal was a revisitation of an original idea put forward by the Northleach & Cheltenham Railway

*The tunnel at Sandywell Park, or Dowdeswell, was constructed to take a double line of rails, although only the single track was laid. This view of the western portal, with the trees towering above the crest of Dowdeswell Hill, shows an eastbound goods train climbing the 1 in 70 incline towards Andoversford.*
COLLECTION M. BARNSLEY

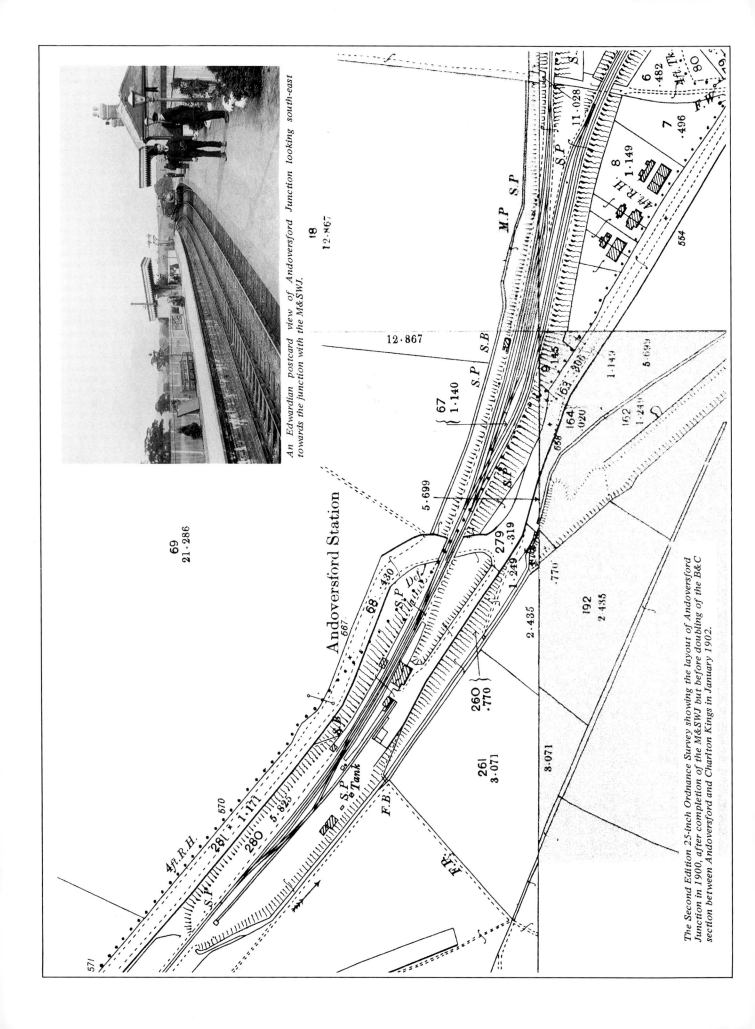

An Edwardian postcard view of Andoversford Junction looking south-east towards the junction with the M&SWJ.

The Second Edition 25-inch Ordnance Survey showing the layout of Andoversford Junction in 1900, after completion of the M&SWJ but before doubling of the B&C section between Andoversford and Charlton Kings in January 1902.

of 1860. However, it was not an idle threat; an embankment to take the proposed line on from Andoversford was actually built, and it remained isolated in a field to the north of the B & CD line, for many years afterwards.

The Great Western approved the doubling of the common section, but insisted that the upgrading was dependent upon the Ashchurch scheme being abandoned.

No immediate moves were made to deal with the doubling. As the 1890s drew to a close, the level of hostility between the Great Western and the M & SWJ rose – eventually it would reach overbearing proportions, a product of inherent difficulties experienced by two companies separated by status and means, but sharing similar ideals, and both running over a common section of line.

The first decade of the twentieth century marked a short period of intensive consolidation for the Great Western Railway, the culmination of many years' commitment to improving the efficiency of the system. The developments ranged through the general upgrading of facilities, improved designs of locomotives and rolling stock, and a large-scale programme of new railways to reduce the distances between major centres; the latter involved the construction of more than 250 miles of new line, and the upgrading of secondary routes to main-line standards, allowing a significant improvement in services. Perhaps the most impressive of the 'cut-off' routes had occurred in 1886 with the completion of the Severn Tunnel, but those of the early twentieth century had an overall greater effect. The Great Western was thus turning

around from its 'old fashioned' image to one of a progressive, modern company.

As far as the Banbury & Cheltenham route was concerned, the new works commenced with the doubling of the line between Andoversford and Lansdown Jct., providing relief to the traffic flow over that section.

The original double-track section through Andoversford station had earlier been extended eastwards to a point some 650 yards beyond the junction, giving good lengths of running line for GW traffic to be held clear of the 'joint' section.

By January 1902, the section between Charlton Kings and Andoversford was well in advance of that into Cheltenham. The Great Western advised the BoT that the work 'would be so far completed as to admit of double line working being commenced on the 2nd proximo [next month].' However, this did not seem to be the case, and a delay of a week was soon being announced, and even this was optimistic. It was not until 29th March that Col. H. A. Yorke produced his report on the section:

'I have the honour to report for the information of the Board of Trade, that in compliance with the instructions contained in your Minute of 31st Decr. 1901 I have inspected the doubling between Charlton Kings and Andoversford and also the temporary connections at the former place on the Great Western Railway.

'One additional line of rails has been laid between the places named, but in some places the existing line has been slewed so as to improve the gradients and curves and there both lines are new. The doubling is 3 miles 44.3 chains in length. The steepest gradient has an inclination of

*The 192-yard Dowdeswell or Woodbank Viaduct seen during the widening works to accommodate the double line of rails. This view was taken looking west from the slopes of the Chelt valley.*
COLLECTION M. BARNSLEY

*Double tracks at the eastern portal of Sandywell Tunnel in 1914.*     COLLECTION M. BARNSLEY

1 in 68.83 and the sharpest curve has a radius of 24 chains. The rails are of two different sections, some being 77 lbs per yard, and the remainder 80 lbs per yard, the chairs in all cases being 35¼ lbs each. The sleepers are of the usual dimensions and the ballast is of broken stone and slag. The permanent way is in good order, but speed over it should be restricted to 20 miles an hour until the engineer in charge is satisfied that the road is sufficiently consolidated to render such a restriction unnecessary.

'The deepest cutting has a maximum depth of 50 feet, and the highest embankment a height of 46 feet. Both the cuttings and embankments will require watching for some time to come as the soil is treacherous.

'There are four bridges, three with segmental arches and one with wrought iron girders and jack arches. And there are four under bridges, three with segmental brick arches and one of 12 ft span with steel troughing resting on abutments of brickwork. This last has sufficient theoretical strength and gave moderate deflection under test.

'There is also a viaduct with 12 arched openings each of 40 ft span, which seems to be standing satisfactorily, and there is a tunnel which was originally built for a double line and remains unaltered.

'The station platforms and buildings at Charlton Kings remain unaltered, but a new signal box has been built, containing 20 levers in use and 5 spare levers. The number plates on the levers require correction, and the company's officer said should at once be attended to. A new temporary connection has been laid in here to facilitate the extension of the doubling towards Cheltenham.

'The platforms at Andoversford are being extended, but the work was not completed at the time of my visit. Otherwise this place remains as it was. The signal box has been enlarged and a new locking frame provided, containing 25 levers in use and 2 spare levers.

'Andoversford Junction box was also inspected by me, a new cross over road having been laid in here. It contains 30 levers in use and 5 spare levers.

'The interlocking in all cases is correct.

'Subject to the restriction in speed over the new lines to which reference has already been [made], I can recommend the Board of Trade to sanction the use of the doubling between Charlton Kings and Andoversford for passenger traffic.'

Colonel Yorke's brief mention of a viaduct referred to the 192-yard Dowdeswell (or Woodbank) viaduct, which was enlarged by the building of a new, identical structure alongside, and bonded into, the existing 1880 viaduct.

A small alteration in connection with the doubling was the modification of the junction into Lansdown station from the Great Western line by the replacement of the existing diamond by a single compound (slip), to provide a crossover

road for the Great Western at that location. This was brought into use in March 1902.

Construction on the other section had in the meantime proceeded well, and the Great Western informed the Board of Trade on 30th May 1902 that 'the work will shortly be completed.' Six weeks later, they were again in contact concerning the use of the new line: 'It is desired to bring the new line into use as a single line so as to allow of certain alterations and improvements being made to the old line.'

Sanction was granted to use the new line on 31st July.

Work continued throughout the year. Then, on 17th January 1903, Col. Yorke made his written report on the western section of the widening.

'I have the honour to report for the information of the Board of Trade, that in compliance with the instructions contained in your Minute of 27th November 1902 I have inspected the additional line of rails which has been laid between Charlton Kings and Lansdown Junction on the G. W. Rly.

'This completes the doubling of the railway between Andoversford & Lansdown Jn; the portion between Andoversford & Charlton Kings having already been inspected & reported and in use in March 1902.

'In some places the old line of rails has been slightly altered in position for the purpose of improving the gradients & curves.

'The length of the widening is 3 miles 3.33 chains.

'The steepest gradient has an incline of 1 in 74.24 & the sharpest curve a radius of 20.20 chains.

'The permanent way is laid with rails weighing 80 lbs per yard, in lengths of 44 ft 6 in. The chairs weigh 35¼ lbs each. The line is well ballasted & is in excellent condition.

'The fencing, where new, is of the post & wire type, there being 8 wires supported on timber posts 4 ft 6 in apart.

'The deepest cutting is 25 ft in depth & the highest embankment 20 ft in height.

'None of the bridges are new, all of them having been built originally for a double line of track. One under bridge is constructed with wrought iron girders & cross girders with jack arches between them. This gave very moderate deflections under load.

'There are two stations in the widening, viz Charlton Kings & Leckhampton.

'Charlton Kings was originally a passing place on the single line & therefore has a double sided station with up & down platforms. The platforms have now been extended to a length of 400 ft. There is a waiting shed on the up platform, & booking office, waiting rooms & conveniences for men and women on the down platform.

*Charlton Kings, looking towards Andoversford in the early years of the 20th century.*
LENS OF SUTTON

*An Edwardian picture-postcard scene of Leck-hampton station, looking east towards Charlton Kings.*
LENS OF SUTTON

'Leckhampton station had formerly a single platform. It has now been doubled. The up platform has been extended in both directions, & the down platform is altogether new. On the former, a booking hall, waiting rooms & conveniences for men & women are provided. On the latter a waiting shed, and conveniences for men have been built.

'The signal boxes are at Lansdown Junction, Leckhampton and Charlton Kings.

'Lansdown Junction branch box is a block box only, there being no connections with either line of rails. It contains 7 levers of which 4 are in use.

'Leckhampton Station box is new, & contains 10 levers in use, and 5 spare levers.

'Charlton Kings box is practically new, & contains 20 levers in use & 5 spare levers.

'In all cases, the interlocking is correct.

'The new line of rails being in good order, & the arrangements being in all respects satisfactory, I can recommend the Bd. of Trade to sanction the use of the work for passenger traffic.'

Charlton Kings was initially a single-line station with one platform, though by the addition of a loop at some time after the opening, it became a passing place for a passenger and a goods train. In the early 1880s it received a second platform, and the loop was lengthened around the same time. As indicated in the report, Leckhampton retained its single platform until the doubling, though again it had become a passing place for passenger and goods trains by the provision of a loop. Before the arrival of the M & SWJ, there were no scheduled crossing of passenger trains on this part of the branch, these being effected where necessary at crossing stations between Chipping Norton Jct. and Andoversford, or at Lansdown Jct.

Other small modifications were made to various other sections of the line. In 1903, the passing loop arrangement was extended at Bourton to measure some 500 yards overall.

DOWDESWELL VIADUCT.

*Dowdeswell Viaduct, viewed from the east, showing the newly-completed brickwork bonded into the original structure behind. A southbound M&SWJ goods train is seen ascending the Cotswold escarpment towards Andoversford Junction.* COLLECTION PAUL STRONG

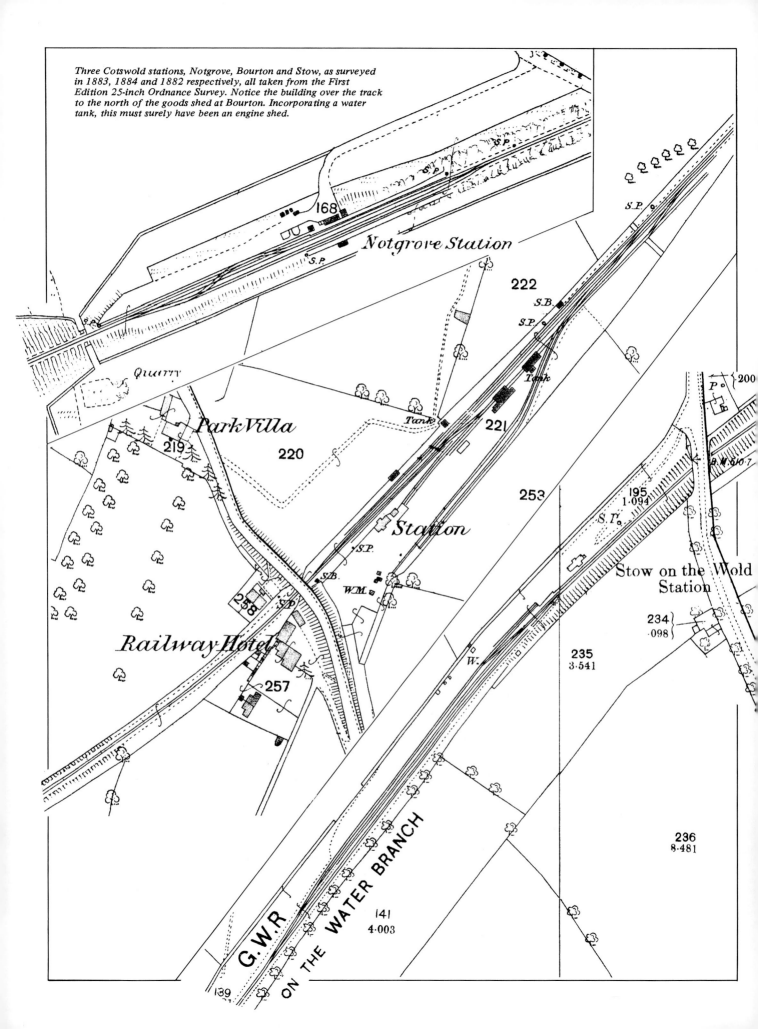

*Three Cotswold stations, Notgrove, Bourton and Stow, as surveyed in 1883, 1884 and 1882 respectively, all taken from the First Edition 25-inch Ordnance Survey. Notice the building over the track to the north of the goods shed at Bourton. Incorporating a water tank, this must surely have been an engine shed.*

168

*Notgrove Station*

S.P.

S.P.

222

S.B.

S.P.

*Quarry*

Tank

Tank

221

*Park Villa*

219

220

253

195
1·094

S.T.

*Stow on the Wold Station*

234
·098

258

*Station*

S.P.

S.B.

W.M.

*Railway Hotel*

257

W.

235
3·541

236
8·481

G.W.R

141
4·003

139

ON THE WATER BRANCH

200

P.o

B.M. 6/0·7

The small 33 ft engine shed at Chipping Norton Junction, along with its 22 ft turntable, had served the needs of the tank engine allocated to work the Cheltenham goods and other local duties since 1881. By the early years of the twentieth century, a tender engine was increasingly being used on that duty, and both shed and turntable were inadequate for the 51 ft-long '2301' class 0–6–0s that was now favoured. In 1904, the turntable was changed for a 44 ft 9 in unit, which could accommodate the 39 ft 3 in overall wheelbase of the 0–6–0.

## MODERNISATION 1905/6

With the gradual removal of the broad gauge from its system, the Great Western had increasingly become involved with through traffic, both to and from 'foreign' companies, and eventually as a route between different 'foreign' con-

*Unlike Chipping Norton Junction or Stow, the 1863 'Carpenter Gothic' style station building at Bourton was fitted with a decorative canopy over the platform. Only the portion over the main doorway projected sufficiently to provide shelter all the way to the carriages. This view is believed to have been taken c.1900.*
COLLECTION
M. STRATFORD

*'1016' class 0–6–0ST No. 1018 may well have been photographed here at Bourton in the 1890s while on the daily Chipping Norton Junction to Cheltenham goods. The guard and brakesman for this duty were based at Chipping Norton Junction, the 1896 duty book recording: 'On duty at 7.30 a.m. Off duty 6.30 p.m. No meal time. In charge of Branch Goods running daily between C. Norton Jc and Cheltenham. Commence duty at 7.30 a.m. to do shunting and form train. Leaves C. Norton Jc 9.10 a.m. runs to Cheltenham and is due back at 5.35 p.m. Puts train off and does what shunting is required. No Sunday duty.' The engineman featured here may have been Charlie Davis who was regularly rostered on the duty from 1899. By 1901 this engine had been transferred to South Wales. This picture shows another of the Gloucester Wagon Co. single-aspect signals whilst the Gloucester ground frame cabin by the bridge controlled the adjacent points which were beyond the reach of the lever frame in the original Gloucester signal box featured on page 127.*
COLLECTION M. STRATFORD

*A turn-of-the-century view of Bourton-on-the-Water station forecourt and goods yard from the road. Burlingham's coal merchants in the right foreground originated at Adlestrop station on the Oxford–Worcester and Wolverhampton Railway until about 1860. Thereafter the business operated from Bourton.*

COLLECTION M. STRATFORD

*Up and down trains crossing at Bourton in 1905. Notice that by this time a standard GWR signal arm had replaced the single-aspect arm on the down starting signal.*
LENS OF SUTTON

*Bourton station view, looking north-east, and featuring the original Gloucester Wagon Company signal box in the left distance.*
LENS OF SUTTON

Frank Packer was a prolific photographer based in Chipping Norton in the early years of the twentieth century. Here in this Edwardian scene his wife Grace poses for the camera on the parapet of the Worcester Road bridge at Chipping Norton station. The footpath led down to the station from the Worcester Road. The Mill road, leading to the Bliss Tweed Manufactory, features in the right background. It appears that the photograph was taken after arrival of the 'mixed' train from Chipping Norton Junction. The locomotive is seen shunting wagons of wool 'bales' bound for the Bliss Mills, whilst the passenger coaches had been left at the down platform.

F. R. PACKER, CTY. ALAN BRAIN

cerns. One of the major occurrences in this respect was the arrival at Banbury of the Great Central Railway on 1st June 1900 (for goods trains), and for passenger services from 13th August. The possibilities for through traffic had expanded massively, and the General Manager, Sir James Inglis, was soon to harness them. In his report to the directors of 20th July 1904, he indicated that

'The time has arrived when the single portions of the Banbury & Cheltenham lines should be doubled in order that advantage may be taken of the shorter route which it affords between the Northern and Eastern Counties and South Wales. With this view it is recommended that the section between King's Sutton and Adderbury, a distance of 1 mile 61 chains, should be taken in hand at an estimated cost of £8,175.'

In the next paragraph, Inglis re-introduced the original proposal of a direct east-west link at Chipping Norton Jct., abandoned 28 years previously:

'In order however to take full advantage of the shorter route it is essential that a direct junction should be provided at Chipping Norton [Junction] between the east and west sections of the line, the cost being estimated at

*An Edwardian postcard view of Chipping Norton taken from the Worcester Road near the entrance to the Mill road.*    LENS OF SUTTON

*The forecourt at Chipping Norton with the coach which met passengers for the White Hart Hotel in the town centre.*
COLLECTION
ALAN BRAIN

*Looking east from the upper floors of the Bliss Tweed Mill, showing the layout of the goods yard on the site of the original terminus, the original 1855 engine shed featuring to the right of the standard GWR goods shed added in 1887. To the left we can see the weighbridge and stable block. Bliss's private siding in the left foreground looks a little overgrown — by this time the family had sold the business and the firm was being run by Messrs. Fox Brothers of Wellington. The loco shunting was an unidentified '517' class 0—4—2T. Note the chimney of the original Bliss Upper Mill (centre), with the town spread along the hillside beyond.* PERCY SIMMS, CTY. ALAN BRAIN

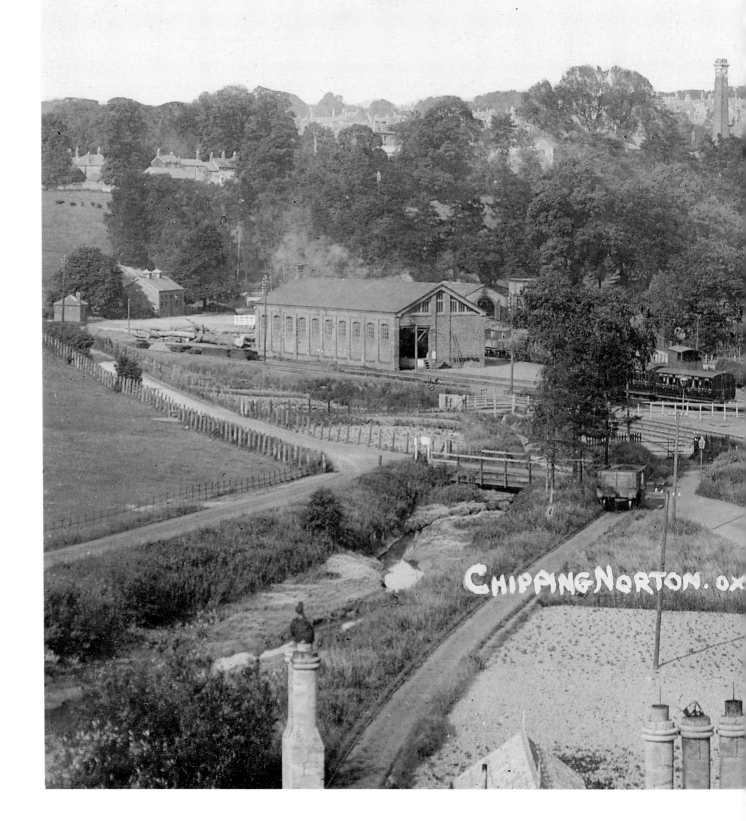

CHIPPING NORTON. OX

£25,950. In connection with this scheme it will be necessary to acquire 8 acres, 1 rood and 31½ pecks of land valued at £1,575, a portion of which will be required for the site of a new engine shed.'

The proposal was approved by the Board.

At a meeting on 4th January 1905, the General Manager also revived plans to construct a southern loop at King's Sutton from the B & C line, giving direct running to and from the Oxford direction, and also for the Bicester cut-off route then in the early stages of construction. He noted that '…a considerable saving should be effected if the surplus spoil to be excavated in connection with the doubling work were deposited on land to be acquired for the loop.'

Again, the proposal to acquire the land (1 acre, 2 roods) was approved, as was the expenditure at Adderbury station in connection with the doubling. However, the southern spur at King's Sutton was never completed.

On 10th May 1905, the General Manager turned his attention again to the trackwork at Chipping Norton Jct., in particular to the short sections between the proposed junctions at either end of the new direct loop line, and the station. He stated that:

'it is desirable that the existing single lines between the Banbury & Cheltenham lines and the Oxford & Worcester line at Chipping Norton Jn. should also be doubled, the cost being estimated at £6,245.'

Discussions were by this time taking place with the Barry, Great Central and North Eastern Railways with a view to introducing a through service between the ports of Barry and Newcastle, utilising the Banbury & Cheltenham line via Gloucester, which was some 16 miles shorter than the main line route via Didcot, Swindon and the Severn Tunnel. As has been seen, the Banbury & Cheltenham Direct had not been constructed to carry fast or heavy traffic, despite its early pretensions. At that time, the line possessed only 6¾ miles of double track at the western end of its 43-mile run between King's Sutton and Lansdown Junction, with short station loops, steep gradients and speed restrictions abounding. Further, trains could not run the whole length of the line without reversing at Chipping Norton Jct., so the operation of an express would have been inconceivable. Nor was there a direct run from the branch towards Gloucester at the Cheltenham end capable of carrying passenger traffic; a loop had been provided to Hatherley at an earlier date, but this was unsuitable as it stood.

An envisaged increase in iron ore traffic between the quarries along the eastern section of the B & C and South Wales also stimulated the desire to carry out the improvements over the route.

And so it was that the Adderbury doubling, the Chipping Norton Jct. direct loop and doubling, and the construction of the Hatherley curve at Cheltenham were approved by the Board and put in hand. It was also recommended that a number of running loop extensions be carried out at some intermediate stations along the single-line sections.

Of the alterations that took place on the branch around this time, the direct loop was the largest single project. It was

built rapidly during 1905, and drew considerable interest around the locality. The two bridge abutments were built first, and it is said that Ernest Lainchbury, the manufacturer of agricultural machinery from nearby Kingham, placed a gold sovereign on one of them as construction began.

An estimated 100,000 cubic yards of material made up the volume of the approach embankments; the western side contained 66,000 cu yds, and the eastern side 34,000. The material was almost certainly a waste product of the coal mining industry in South Wales, and many years later part of the loop caught fire, apparently spontaneously. This took hold with such an intensity that it aroused much speculation as to the composition of the embankments.

*One of the plate girder spans, which carried the Direct loop line over the OW&WR, being lifted into position.*

A. W. LAINCHBURY
CTY. ALAN BRAIN

THE NEW LOOP LINE

*This picture shows the bridge in position in the distance on the right and the new loop line under construction, with the new Kingham East box in the foreground. Notice also the elusive Chipping Norton Junction North signal box on the skyline. The McKenzie & Holland structure was shortly to be superseded by a new one further south — perhaps seen above the roof of East box.*
COLLECTION
ALAN WATKINS

The 'Metro' class 2–4–0T in the centre of this undated photo was at the head of a Cheltenham-bound train, probably in the late 1890s. A handwritten book of station duties for Chipping Norton Junction in 1895 lists the staff complement as 1 station master, 2 clerks, 2 goods guards, 1 foreman porter, 6 porters, 5 signalmen and 1 charwoman. Only four up and four down trains are listed as 'not met by the station master' who had every other Sunday off but was obliged to 'visit the station occasionally when off duty at irregular intervals and see that the staff are at their posts and that proper discipline is maintained.' The porters' duties reveal most about the life at the station: 'Day duty alternate weeks:– On duty at 8.30 a.m., Off duty 8.30 p.m. Meal times: dinner from 1.10 p.m. to 2.10 p.m. Tea 4.0 p.m. to 4.15 p.m. (if the work will allow). To assist with the loading and unloading, counting &c of all Grain, Oil cake, Hay, Straw and Live Stock, and to checking and roping that which requires it. Does the shunting that has to be done with the Passenger trains when Yardsman is engaged with the Goods trains. Assists with taking out the lamps and with cleaning windows, platforms &c and with all the platform work connected with the trains. Also to clean cattle pens and cattle wagons if required. On duty 2 Sundays in 7 in turn with the other six porters from 8.0 a.m. to 12 noon and from 5.30 p.m. to 7.30 p.m. Night duty alternate weeks:– On duty at 8.0 p.m., Off duty 8.30 a.m. To do the shunting with the passenger trains and assist with the platform work until all the passenger trains have gone. Then put out all Station and Waiting room lamps and lock up the Station. Fetch in the Branch signal lamps and attend to all the yard work. Shunting and Roadside goods during the night and in the morning fetch in all the Main line signal lamps as soon as it is light enough for the lamps to be dispensed with. When on day duty assists with Electric Train Staff for C. Norton Branch. Off duty at 5.30 p.m. on Wednesdays when on day turn ...' 'Two of the porters were given specific duties – '...'. Has charge of all parcels to and from Main line, to and from Branches and parcels to and from this station. Cleans and ventilates the Closets Urinals etc. and Waiting Rooms on up side and trims all Waiting Rooms and Office lamps. Assists with cleaning windows, platforms and also with Roadside goods and all other Station work in connection with trains and the station in any way . .' and another porter ' . .' Has charge of all Roadside & Transfer Goods from Branches to Main line and Main line to Branches also all Carted Goods to and from this station and checks all invoices and consignment notes for Carted Goods. Lad Porter – Has charge of the Cart Weighbridge and is responsible for Cleaning, Balancing and keeping the Machine in proper working order. Has charge of the Fire Buckets at the station and is responsible for keeping them properly filled with water. Collects tickets from all trains when on duty and assists with the station work generally. Also assists with cleaning windows, platforms etc. and with taking out and fetching in the Signal Lamps . . ', the other lad porter ' . . . To attend to the heating of footwarmers and supplying them to the branch trains. To assist with cleaning lamps, taking them out and fetching them in, cleaning windows, platforms, and with all platform work in connection with the trains. Also to assist with the Sheeting, Roping, Loading and Unloading of Goods traffic when required.' Charwoman's duties: 'To light the fire and to clean and dust the Booking Office, Ladies Waiting room every morning and to wash and clean all the Waiting Rooms once every week.'

NATIONAL RAILWAY MUSEUM

*The duty book names two of the six porters as being responsible for the transfer of goods at the junction — 'they are assisted in the work by the whole of the staff when necessary as this work is often heavy.' There was no parcels agent at Chipping Norton Junction — 'The people in the villages here pay a man to deliver their parcels. He does it with a Donkey and Cart and parcels outside his delivery we advise.'*

COLLECTION ALAN BRAIN

*John George Brecknell, who was responsible for the duty book, served as station master at Chipping Norton Junction from c.1881 to at least 1906. The picture shows him seated with his little son Albert and wife Rhoda. Emily was missing when this picture was taken but the other members of his family standing behind were Thomas, Walter, Annie, Charles, Rhoda, Jack, Alice and George.*

BLEDINGTON LOCAL HISTORY SOCIETY
Cty. SYLVIA REEVES

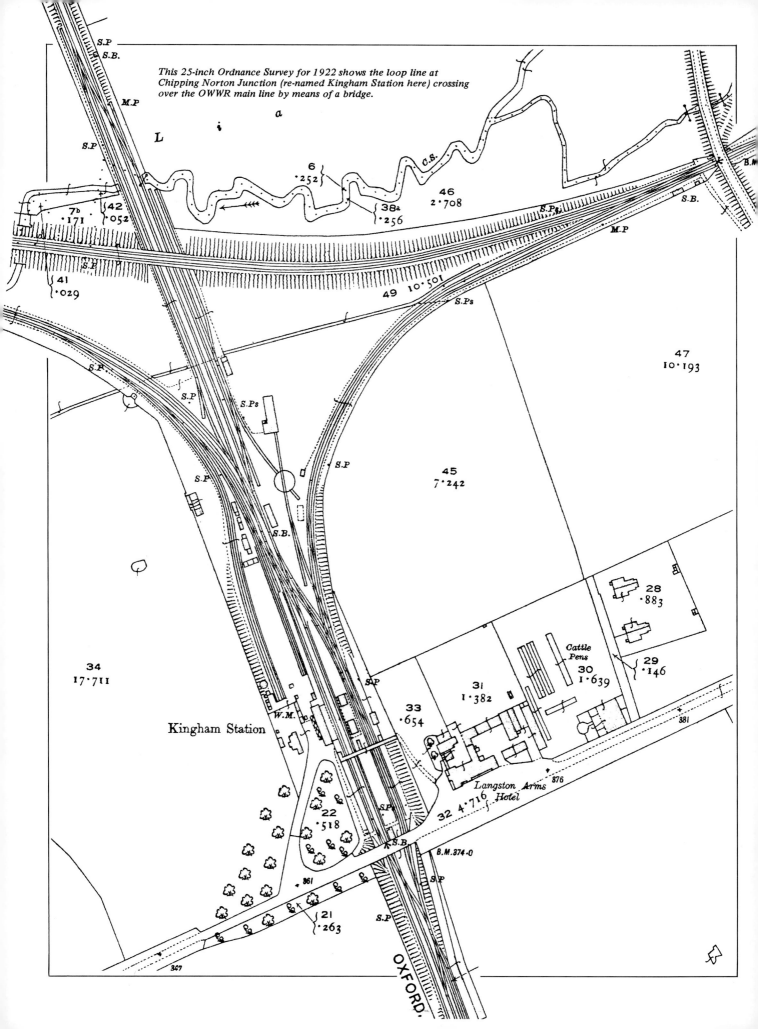

This 25-inch Ordnance Survey for 1922 shows the loop line at
Chipping Norton Junction (re-named Kingham Station here) crossing
over the OWWR main line by means of a bridge.

Kingham Station

Langston Arms
Hotel

Cattle
Pens

OXFORD.

*This picture was taken from the elusive South Signal Box, the brick base of which features in the background of the picture on page 134. The Langston Arms Hotel, which features in the background of the same photo was linked to the station via the foot-bridge, the extension of which can be seen leading off to the right-hand edge of the photo. The duty book records 'There is also an extension of this [foot-bridge] to the Hotel premises and this gate has to be locked up nights and Sundays and the key kept by the Station Master.'*
COLLECTION
ALAN BRAIN

At the meeting of 20th December 1905, Inglis recommended that the three sites be opened for passenger traffic when ready, and that the Board of Trade should be approached for sanction.

Board of Trade inspections at the three main sites took place in the latter half of January 1906, and were carried out by Col. H. A. Yorke. The first element was the loop at Hatherley, which connected the B & C branch with the Cheltenham & Gloucester line some 55 chains (just under ¾ of a mile) to the west of Lansdown Jct. Col Yorke described the new loop as follows:

'This loop, which is 39¾ chs. in length, forms a direct connection between the lines from Cheltenham to Gloucester and from Cheltenham to Chipping Norton Junction. It was formerly constructed as a single line goods loop, but was little used, and has now been doubled and relaid as a passenger line.

'The steepest gradient on it is 1 in 73, and the sharpest curve has a radius of 18 chs. It is mostly carried on an embankment which, having been tipped for many years, is stable. [The permanent way was of standard construction, and details had previously been given in a letter from the Great Western to the BoT.]

'There is one bridge under this line, constructed of wrought iron plate girders with jack arches between, and resting on brick abutments. This bridge is substantially constructed, and gave very slight deflections when tested.

'There are no stations on the loop, but a new signal box has been built at the east end, called Gloucester Junction Loop Box, which contains 17 levers in use and 8 spare levers. At the west end, the junction of the new line with the Gloucester – Cheltenham line is controlled from the Hatherley signal box, which now contains 18 levers in use and 7 spare levers.'

Col. Yorke recommended that the Hatherley loop be sanctioned for use by passenger traffic.

The loop line at Chipping Norton Jct. was authorised by the GWR Additional Powers Act, 1905, and Col. Yorke's reports on the new arrangements were presented on 25th January 1906. The first concerned the doubling of track on the two branches from their junctions with the ex-OW& W lines at the station to the new loop line junctions.

'The object of the doubling is to enable double junctions to be formed between these lines and the new Chipping Norton Junction loop line, which forms the base of a triangle of which the two branch lines now doubled form the sides. The doubling on the Cheltenham branch is about half a mile in length, and that on the Banbury branch is about a quarter of a mile.

'The new lines of rail are parallel in each case to the existing line, with similar curves and gradients.

'The connections have been altered, the signalling re-arranged, and a new signal box built at the north end of Chipping Norton Junction Station to suit the new conditions. The signal box, which is known as Chipping Norton Junction North Box, contains 73 levers in use and 15 spare levers. There is also a ground frame containing 12 levers bolted from the signal box for working points on the main line.'

At the same time, the new loop line was inspected by Col. Yorke.

'This loop, which is 57.8 chains in length, forms a direct communication between the lines from Chipping Norton Junction to Banbury and Cheltenham respectively, with each of which it is joined by means of a double junction, and is carried over the main line from Chipping Norton [Junction] to Worcester by means of a bridge.

'The line is double, and is on embankment for nearly the whole of its length. The gradients are 1 in 80 on the Banbury side of the bridge, and 1 in 62 on the Cheltenham side.

'There are three bridges under the line, two being built with semicircular brick arches, and one, which carries the new line over the main line, of steel plate girders with cross girders and rail girders; the abut-

*The 9.42 a.m. Barry to Newcastle passing the up platform at Hook Norton station c.1906 behind an unidentified 'Bulldog'. The GCR stock during the first few years of the 'Ports' carried the brown and French grey livery, though from 1909 that company's coaches were turned out in teak. The figure on the platform alongside the engine was collecting the single-line train staff whilst one of the men beneath the canopy is seen holding up the train staff for the section ahead ready for the fireman to collect. This was before the provision of lineside exchange apparatus.*
F. R. PACKER

ments in all cases are of brick. The girder bridge, which has a square span of 86 feet 10 ins., gave moderate deflections when tested.

'There are no stations on the line, but two signal boxes have been built, one, called East Box, at the junction with the Banbury line, and the other, called West Box, at the junction with the Cheltenham line. Each of these boxes contains 17 levers in use and 6 spare levers, and the interlocking is correct.

'As the embankments of the new line have not yet had time to settle, the speed will have to be reduced to what the Engineer in charge considers a safe limit. Subject to this condition I can recommend the Board of Trade to sanction the use of the new loop line for passenger traffic.'

Col. Yorke appears to have transposed the gradients on the loop line, for an official GWR map shows them to be 1 in 62 at the Banbury end, level for the crossing of the main lines and an adjacent culvert, then 1 in 80 on the Cheltenham side.

Unusually for the Great Western, the final plans of the new junctions had either not been sent to, or received by, the Board of Trade, and Col. Yorke had consulted earlier sheets showing the temporary connections required for the construction of the loop lines. However, this did not affect his ultimate decision.

The description of the new permanent way was cursory, having been 'laid in accordance with the standard permanent

way construction of the G. W. Rly.', though details were further amplified in other communications between the company and the BoT.

The new direct loop at Chipping Norton Jct. was opened for through goods traffic between Banbury and Gloucester on 8th January 1906, creating a new, through route.

On 1st May 1906, the inaugural Barry & Newcastle express and its balancing service from Newcastle passed along the length of the line without entering Chipping Norton Junction station.

Access to the engine shed at Chipping Norton Jct. had originally been from a trailing connection with the up main line, but with the double junction connections between the main and branch line platforms in the 1884 rebuilding, this conflicting connection had been altered across to the branch lines. This was retained, though with the removal of the shed around 1906, an additional connection from the turntable was made to the up sidings that ran under the new girder bridge taking the avoiding loop across the main lines.

The major alterations at the eastern end of the line concerned the doubling of the section between Adderbury and King's Sutton. The Great Western informed the Board of Trade on 12th January that the works had been completed.

Col. Yorke once more reported his findings on 25th January 1906:

'The line is at present single and one additional line of rails has been laid in between the places. The length of the doubling is 1 mile 41 chains.

'The curves and gradients are similar to those on the existing line.

'There are three bridges under the line, of which one has bricks and segmental arches, one has 3 arch spans and one girder span, and one has steel trough flooring. The abutments in all cases are of brick-work. The

works appear to be substantially constructed, and the girders under the line gave moderate deflections when tested.

'There are no stations on the line, but some alterations have been made at Adderbury, where the platforms have been extended, and the siding connections re-arranged; the station buildings, however, remain unaltered.

'The Kings Sutton Branch signal box, where the double line formerly joined the single line, has been abolished, and a new signal box has been built at Adderbury Station, where the junction between double and

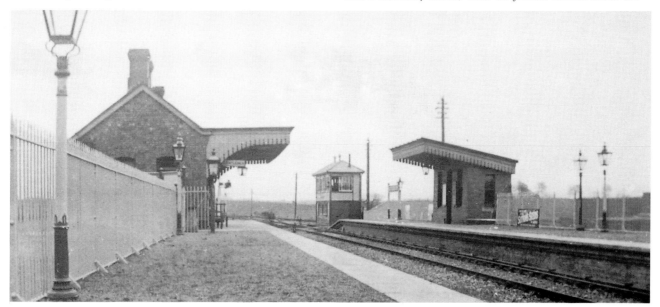

*This pair of photos of Adderbury station were probably taken at the time of the 1906 alterations. They show the new siding connection in the foreground, the new signal box and extended platforms.*
COLLECTION B. J. DAVIS

single lines now occurs. This new box contains 29 new levers in use and 6 spare levers. The only requirements I noted was that No.3 lever should lock levers Nos.8 and 9 in both positions.

'Subject to their alteration being made within a month, I can, as the arrangements are otherwise satisfactory, recommend the Board of Trade to sanction the use of the doubling of the line.'

Kings Sutton Branch box had been located a few chains around the corner from the junction with the main lines,

between the Cherwell flood arches and the Cherwell/Oxford Canal viaduct, where the double track from that junction became single.

The Great Western reported on 27th February that the alteration at Adderbury signal box had been carried out. Colonel Yorke's recommendations had thus been carried out in full, and the three sites were duly sanctioned for use.

In the meantime, running loop extensions were in hand at Notgrove, Hook Norton and Bloxham, with a view to providing passing places for longer goods trains and other traffic.

*The Ports-to-Ports express approaching the easternmost bridge over the Sor Brook, Adderbury, on 14th April 1907.*
MAJOR GEORGE NORRIS, CTY. J. FOX

*An unidentified 'Metro' class 2–4–0T alongside the down platform at Notgrove with a train for Cheltenham. The top of the original timber-built Gloucester Wagon Co. signal box was relegated for use as a garden outbuilding outside the railway boundary fence on the skyline in the centre of this view. This also appears in the photograph on page 193. This photograph was probably taken from the steps of the new GWR brick-built signal box which had opened on 24th April 1906.*
*COLLECTION M. STRATFORD*

*An unidentified staff group at Stow station c.1906. Note the poster advertising the new Newcastle–Barry service.*

The loops at Chipping Norton and Bourton-on-the-Water were considered to be quite sufficient for this purpose already.

On the western section of the line, approval for work at Notgrove was given at a Board meeting in December 1905. The company requested the Board of Trade's sanction on 12th May 1906, when it was reported that alterations at Notgrove had been completed. Col. York once more carried out his inspection, the report of which was presented on 6th June 1906.

'The line is single, and is worked on the electric train staff system, Notgrove being a passing place and staff section.

'The new works comprise the extension of the loop at both ends, the alteration in position of the siding connections, the construction of a new signal box, and the re-signalling of the whole place.

'The signal box contains 20 levers in use and 5 spare levers, and the interlocking is correct.

'The facing points at both ends of the place are 250 yards from the signal box, and the plungers as well as the switch blades are fitted with detectors.

'The line through the station is level, but falls towards Bourton at an inclination of 1 in 60. Owing to this gradient, no mineral trains should be brought to a stand at the down home signal unless it has an engine in the rear, in other words no such train should be allowed to leave Bourton for Notgrove unless the line is clear for it to run into the loop at Notgrove.

'Subject to these conditions, I can recommend the Board of Trade to sanction the use of the alterations at this place.'

The stipulation that a heavy westbound goods train should either require the expense of an assisting engine, or be held back at Bourton until the loop at Notgrove was clear, was taken as an unacceptable working imposition by the Great Western. On 12th July, they responded with a compromise solution:

'I beg to state that to satisfactorily carry out the conditions of working required in the penultimate paragraph of the report would very materially minimise the utilisation of the station as a crossing place, and I have to request that, by way of an alternative condition, permission may be given to the company to work trains in either direction towards Notgrove on the undertaking that any goods or mineral train from Bourton have a 20 ton brake van in the rear.'

The Board of Trade approved this suggestion.

Another station undergoing loop extensions was Bloxham, and work was under way by June 1906. A new signal box was also to be provided. On completion, the Great Western again applied to the BoT for approval, and following his visit, Col. Yorke submitted a report on 16th February 1907.

'The alterations comprise an extension of the passing loop to the full extent of 250 yards from the signal box in each direction, the construction of a new signal box, and the re-signalling of the whole place.

*This view, looking north across the viaduct, provides some idea of the earthworks built up to provide the site for the station at Hook Norton. It also shows the ironstone sidings behind the down platform and the approach from the east.*

F. R. PACKER, CTY. ALAN BRAIN

'The facing points at each end of the loop are provided with detectors on the facing point lock, as well as on the switches. The signal box contains 24 levers in use, and 5 spare levers. The interlocking being correct and the arrangements satisfactory, I can recommend to the Board of Trade to sanction the use of the alterations at this place.'

Four miles to the west, work had been taking place at Hook Norton with improvements in the running line. The Great Western sought provisional sanction for the work in May 1906, and on 15th February 1907 was able to report to the BoT that Col. Yorke, 'when in the neighbourhood yesterday, took the opportunity of inspecting the work.' His report was completed on 18th February.

'The line is single, Hook Norton being a passing place, and the alterations comprise the lengthening of the loop in both directions, the construction of a new signal box, and the re-signalling of the whole place.

'The loop points are now 250 yards from the signal box, and detectors have been provided on the facing point locks as well as on the switches.

'The signal box contains 27 levers in use and 6 spare levers.'

*This picture of staff lined up on the up platform at Hook Norton shows the GWR signal box which opened on 8th February 1907, replacing the Gloucester Wagon Co. cabin formerly situated on the down platform.*

F. R. PACKER
CTY. ALAN BRAIN

*This postcard of the south end of the station not only shows a little more of the ironstone sidings behind the down platform but also provides a rare glimpse of the goods yard and coal office.*

F. R. PACKER, CTY. ALAN BRAIN

BIRDS EYE VIEW
OF HOOK NORTON          54

*Churchill village street scene.*

F. R. PACKER, CTY. ALAN WATKINS

*Churchill Crossing c.1908 with Arthur and Alice Watkins and their first child, baby Nancy, born 28th April 1907. Note the rendered walls of the building.*

COLLECTION ALAN BRAIN

As with Bloxham, the interlocking was correct, and with other arrangements satisfactory, Col. Yorke was able to recommend the alterations.

With the completion of the loop extensions, the official working lengths of the crossing loops at single-line stations was given as follows:

| Station | Length (Yds) & Details | |
| --- | --- | --- |
| Bloxham | 308 | |
| Hook Norton | 370 | |
| Stow-on-the-Wold | 253 | For 1 goods and 1 passenger train, or 2 goods trains only |
| Bourton-on-the-Water | 293 | |
| Notgrove | 366 | |

Chipping Norton was later specified as 462 yards.

## THE HALTS

From the time that the B & CD had opened its first section in 1881 to the improvements completed in 1906, the line had changed dramatically from a lengthy branch into a significant through route. However, it still retained many of the original drawbacks, including steep gradients, so in effect the line could best be described as 'much-improved' rather than 'rebuilt'.

There were to be further improvements during the second half of the opening decade of the twentieth century, as the early influence of competing road traffic prompted the Great Western to increase passenger facilities over the eastern part of the branch, in line with similar developments elsewhere.

This provision was met with three new halts, all opened between July 1906 and January 1908. The first was at Sarsden, located on the north-western outskirts of Churchill, between Chipping Norton and the Junction, beside the disused Churchill mill. The halt at Churchill was not strictly without precedent, for it had long been the site of the minor goods accommodation known as Sarsden Siding.

The Great Western requested the usual provisional sanction for the construction on 21st June 1906, and work commenced shortly thereafter. Following his visit, Col Yorke submitted his report on 11th September 1906:

'The line is single and worked on the electric train staff system. The stopping place consists of a single platform, 150 feet long, 7 feet wide and

*The railway passed within a stone's throw of Churchill Mill where Mill Lane crossed the railway and entered the mill yard, with its attendant outbuildings and the miller's house. In 1859 this lane only continued beyond Churchill Mill, as a bridleway known as the Miller's Path, which terminated in Daylesford, some two miles to the north-west. Whether the railway crossing over Mill Lane was manned or not is unclear. The earliest track layout is shown on the 1880 Ordnance Survey which shows a drop platform and a small brick building, perhaps an office, positioned some distance behind the platform, close to the boundary. Very little is known about the early life of Sarsden Siding. The main development affecting the locality was the purchase of Kingham Fields Farm, together with 180 acres of land, in 1888 by C. E. B. Young, to construct Kingham Hill Homes, one mile north-west of the siding. 'Squire' Young constructed a private road linking the farm (which he renamed Stratford House) with the Swailsford Carriageway, and Churchill Mill, thus opening up a through road to Churchill. This view shows the level crossing with the entrance to Sarsden Siding on the right. The entrance gate to the new halt was on the other side of the line. The miller's house features on the left.*

COLLECTION ALAN WATKINS

SARSDEN HALT. 23.

This early view of Sarsden Halt shows a '517' class 0—4—2T waiting alongside the wooden platform with a train from Chipping Norton Junction. The earliest reference to the existence of Sarsden Siding is in 1859. The origin of its name is obscure for this tiny little outpost is some 2½ miles distant from the hamlet of Sarsden and would seem to have been more appropriately named after the village of Churchill, whose centre was no more than a mile away. Local legend claims that the owner of Sarsden House, James Houghton Langston, MP for Oxford, who offered much of the land required for the original Chipping Norton Railway at little more than an agricultural price and who helped to steer the Act for the railway through its readings in Parliament, requested that the company provide him with a picking-up and setting-down point named after his residence. The original intention might well have been to name the proposed siding after Churchill, but as there was already a station of the same name on the OWWR with which the Chipping Norton branch was amalgamated in 1860, Sarsden may have been chosen to avoid confusion.

F. R. PACKER

3 feet high. It is provided with a waiting shed, lamps and name board.

'There is a siding connection, the points of which are locked by key on the electric train staff, and there is also a level crossing provided with gates and a distant signal. The two latter works are old, and have already been inspected.'

Col. Yorke duly recommended the opening of the halt. He did not, however, refer directly to the small signal box opened in 1893, and reduced to a ground frame six years later.

For some villages, the new passenger facilities could not come quickly enough. The community of Great Rollright, located a half-mile to the north of the line between Hook Norton and Chipping Norton, was an obvious candidate for a halt. Representations had been made as far back as 1875, when a Mr. Saunders had launched his single-minded campaign, which he renewed with vigour in September 1884.

Evidently, the villagers of Great Rollright felt strongly about the need for a station; their situation, being close to

*Sarsden Halt c.1907, looking north-east, with crossing gates open for a train. The small brick building close to the signal box, which dated back to the days when Sarsden was a siding, was already old when the photograph was taken. In the 1920s the shed was left unlocked, and a cat, which was able to get in and out through a hole in the door, lived inside on a bed of hay. The large board advertising services provided by the halt is now in Winchcombe Museum.*
        CTY. MRS. M. HOWELLS

*Coal being unloaded into William Peachey's coal wagon. He was publican of the 'Chequers' and coal merchant, supplying to the village school.*
COLLECTION
ALAN WATKINS

SARSDEN HALT.

This view of Sarsden Halt was probably taken shortly after it opened in July 1906. The miller's house can just be glimpsed between the passengers standing on the platform. Mr. Barlow, who lived there, was a painter at Kingham Hill School. Churchill Mill, by this time disused, is seen on the right. The pulley wheel just showing behind the railing of the platform ramp, was added by the miller, 'Noggy' Williams, to drive the mill machinery by means of a steam engine for use in times of drought. He became tenant in 1887, and was described as a 'short, stout man with a taciturn and intractable manner'. He also obtained a threshing machine which was also powered by the steam engine. When this was set up in the yard, it effectively blocked the road. On one occasion when 'Squire' Young was manoeuvring a load of coal which he had collected from Sarsden Siding, 'Noggy' Williams refused to shift his threshing machine to let the coal wagon pass. 'Squire' Young was not accustomed to encountering opposition, and an accumulation of incidents such as this appears to have convinced him to round off his Kingham Hill estate by purchasing the mill with its adjacent 20 acres. The purchase from Lord Ducie of Sarsden House was completed in 1897. 'Noggy' Williams left before the purchase was completed in 1897, and the mill, which remained tenantless after his departure, never worked again. Abandoned mills are fascinating places for schoolboys. Charles Roper, who lived at Kingham Hill Farm from 1898 to 1906, recalled returning from Churchill village school as a small boy and slipping into the deserted mill to set the machinery in motion. However, he had to make a run for it, as the sound of the mill wheel turning quickly brought the Sarsden Siding signalman on the scene.

F. R. PACKER

THE AUTOCAR.

'517' class 0—4—2T No. 1470 with a Banbury to Chipping Norton Junction autocar, probably c.1907. The engine, seen here in lined chocolate brown livery, was shedded at Banbury from 1907-1910. The driver, just inside the cab, is said to have been Ted Parry.

COLLECTION ALAN WATKINS

*Rollright Halt in the final stages of preparation before opening in December 1906. Limekiln House is seen to the left of the halt.*
AUTHOR'S COLLECTION

the railway without being able to use it, must have been frustrating in the extreme, as expressed in a letter from a correspondent signing himself 'Common Sense':

> 'Such a station would be very largely used for both passenger and coal traffic. Beside Great Rollright there are Long Compton, Whichford, Ascott and Little Rollright, all of which places have to drive distances varying from three to seven and a half miles to get to a station. It seems to me a very shortsighted policy ... I think steps should be taken in all the villages by getting up petitions.'

The Great Western approved the provision of a halt, which was constructed just to the east of the bridge carrying the line over the Great Rollright to Over Norton road, beside Limekiln House. It was opened for traffic on 12th December 1906.

Yet another halt was proposed for Milton, between Adderbury and Bloxham, and expenditure was approved by the Board in October 1907 for the purpose. The halt was opened to traffic on 1st January 1908.

The social implications of the railway on the communities close to it were considerable. Generally speaking, it was the larger and more prosperous villages that had been provided with stations, and they continued to flourish. Indeed, housing developments accompanied the opening of the stations at Bloxham and Chipping Norton, extending the existing limits of those communities nearer to the railway.

Conversely, the smaller, poorer villages remained without direct railway access, being reliant upon the services of local carriers to and from the nearest stations into the late 1930s, and even beyond. The situation was lamented by H.A. Evans in his topographic guide *Highways and Byways of Oxon*:

> 'South Newington and its neighbours Wigginton & Swerford, higher up the stream, may be taken as the poorer Oxfordshire village, a type which presents a marked contrast to the well-to-do and populous Adderbury or Bloxham. Swerford, it is true, has its park and great house ... but Wigginton & Newington consist chiefly of rows of humble cottages, which have suffered little change for generations. As you wander down the village street you are made to feel that times are bad, and that the flower of the rising generation has taken this to heart and has departed to seek its fortune elsewhere.'

Clearly, the social problems of South Newington could not be rectified by the provision of a railway station – it was too far away to be of direct benefit.

However, the inhabitants of Milcombe, Wigginton and Swerford had a chance to do something about their circumstances. Anything was possible if they were prepared to pay for it. The following account describes the unsuccessful attempts by the villagers of Wigginton to petition for a station to serve their locality. The village was situated about a half-mile to the south of the railway, approximately halfway between Hook Norton and Bloxham stations. Negotiations for a halt on the branch, which commenced in 1905 and continued for nearly five years, are faithfully set out in the Parish Council records.

PANORAMIC VIEW OF MILCOMBE

*A panoramic view of Milcombe from Fern Hill, looking south c.1930. The railway passed by in the cutting in the foreground.*
COLLECTION B. WOODWARD

*Paradise Lane, Milcombe, with the railway cutting beyond.*     COLLECTION B. WOODWARD

## NEGOTIATIONS FOR A STATION

- an unsuccessful attempt to open a station for Wigginton     (Extracts from the Wigginton Parish Council Minute Book, 1895 to 1918)

**25th November 1905:**
The GWR was asked by the Parish Council to provide a siding near Wigginton.

**26th January 1906:**
The Chairman of the Parish Council was instructed to enquire about the provision of a 'Motor Halt' instead of a siding.

**3rd June 1907:**
The village of Swerford, located about 1½ miles to the south-west of Wigginton, was asked to support Wigginton's application. Swerford was about 2½ miles by road from Hook Norton station, and a halt at Wigginton would have been slightly closer.

**14th August 1907:**
Swerford refused, hoping 'to gain a halt of their own on the other [south-west] side of Hook Norton station.' Wigginton Council renewed its application to the GWR.

**16th October 1907:**
The Council was informed that a visit was to be made by '3 GWR gentlemen'. They were told that a halt at the railway bridge over the Heath road (north of Wigginton) would cost £250. Afterwards, they 'alighted at a place near the top of Dashlake Hill' and said that although a halt there would cost less, they doubted if it would prove as convenient. The Chairman, Rector Mozley, offered to grant all free public right of way across the [Glebe] field to a halt there. The GWR representatives asked if the Parish Council would bear part of the £250 cost of a halt at the bridge. The Council preferred the Dashlake Hill site.

**25th November 1907:**
A further visit was made by GWR officials, when they showed plans for a halt on the Heath road. 'They did not much approve of the place near Dashlake – a halt there would cost £200, and there must be a road up to it kept in good order and lighted. A right of way across the field would not be enough.' The GWR would expect 5% or 6% interest on any outlay by the company.

**December 1907:**
The Council enquired as to how Milton secured its halt, and were told by the vicar of Adderbury that interest in outlay must be guaranteed by pur-

chases of season tickets and goods conveyance. Two farmers alone at Milton each paid £5 a year for milk carriage. Inquiries were to be made of the Adderbury stationmaster.

**24th February 1908:**
The Council met the GWR Superintendent and Assistant Engineer, who urged that the parish should offer to contribute towards the costs of a halt.

**April 1908:**
The Council decided to 'take round a paper', seeking support and promises of patronage of a halt from 'persons having some stake in the parish or neighbourhood.'

**May 1908:**
As a result, Lady King's £10 was proposed to be offered to the GWR, but the company did not respond to the letter asking if this sum would be acceptable.

**June 1908:**
The GWR estimated the cost of the halt at £215, so, 'taking 5% interest and 4% maintenance, we should require a turn of £24 a year', plus 10s a week for the 'cost of lad porter', a total of £50 per year. 'I presume you are not prepared to guarantee this each year. If not... the matter must drop.' The letter was signed by G. Cooke (Superintendent).

**November 1909:**
The Council resolved that 'an effort be made to raise the £50 guarantee required by the GWR.'

**26th January 1910:**
The GWR were still not prepared to promise the halt even if £50 was forthcoming. The company required £50 guarantee for 10 years; receipts to be reckoned to Banbury and Kingham; no season tickets would be available, but market tickets issued to Banbury and Chipping Norton; any fall-off of receipts at Hook Norton and Bloxham to be debited against Wigginton sales; and each year's receipts to stand alone, and no carry over if more than the guaranteed amount was received in any year.

The rector offered personally to guarantee 15% of any annual deficiency. But the matter was dropped.

## IMPROVEMENTS 1905–1913

Since the opening of the Cheltenham extension, the sections between Chipping Norton Jct. and Lansdown Jct. had been worked by the train staff and block telegraph system, with intermediate staff posts at all stations except Stow and Leckhampton. With the opening of the branch from King's Sutton in 1887, a similar arrangement was in force over the eastern half, with all intermediate stations as staff posts. In the latter 1890s, the route between Kings Sutton and Chipping Norton Jct. and that between Andoversford Jct. and Lansdown Jct was converted to the electric train staff system.

In May 1905 it was decided to convert the Chipping Norton & Andoversford Jct. sections to the electric train staff. The signal box at Sierford (GWR spelling – Syreford being the nearest village), situated a half-mile east of Andoversford Jct. box, and opened six years earlier, was also included. Stow was added to the list around 1906, with staff exchanging apparatus approved in December of that year. With the doublings at either end, and around Chipping Norton Jct., the electric train staff system now stretched from Adderbury to Chipping Norton Jct. (East), and from Chipping Norton Jct. (West) to Andoversford Jct. The installation comprised Webb telegraph instruments.

Although the two original signal boxes at Chipping Norton station were not rebuilt, the signalling and telegraph instruments were replaced at this time, as elsewhere. Fred Warren, who worked at the station box from 1946 to 1954, recalled one 'very old' instrument in the underframe, which may have been in existence since the opening in 1887.

Another major change affecting the character of the extreme western part of the route occurred in 1906 with the completion of the Cheltenham section of the GWR's new Birmingham & Bristol route, a project that had been developing since the turn of the century. Central to this scheme was a twenty-mile section of new main line from Honeybourne to Cheltenham, to join the existing line from St. James' station to Gloucester at a point called Malvern Road Junction. This junction was immediately to the west of the Cheltenham station. Work began firstly on the southern half of the new route, and preliminary construction work around Cheltenham was in evidence from 1904. On 1st August 1906, a service of steam railmotors commenced between Cheltenham St. James and Honeybourne, reversing direction at Malvern Road Jct.

The Birmingham & Bristol route was completed with the opening of the various sections to the north of Honeybourne

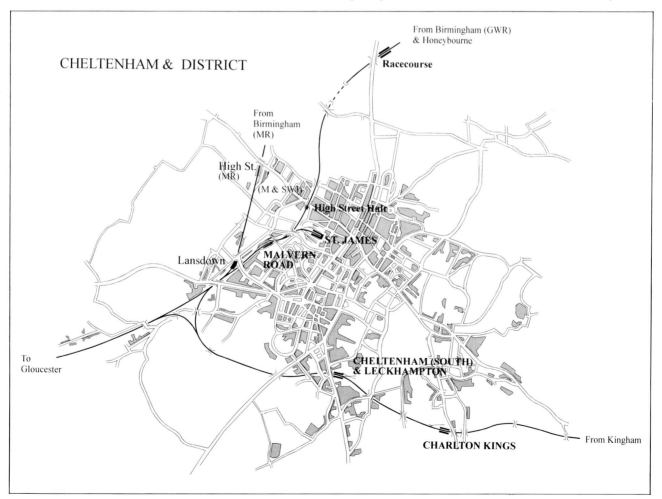

*A postcard view of Malvern Road station, Cheltenham, viewed towards St. James station shortly after opening.*
LENS OF SUTTON

during 1907; through goods traffic commenced on 9th December 1907 and through passenger trains between the Midlands and the West Country on 1st July 1908.

In conjunction with this new route, a station was built at Malvern Road, to the west of the new junction of that name, and a mere 30 chains (660 yards) from the terminus at St. James. Col. Yorke once more carried out the inspection of the new station, and submitted his report on 4th June 1906:

> 'The station consists of an island platform, upon which are provided Waiting Rooms, and lavatory accommodation for both sexes. The approach road to the station, and the Booking Office, are situated on the east side of the place, and access from the Booking Office to the platform is afforded by means of a footbridge.
>
> 'A Bay for rail motor-cars has been provided at the east end, and siding connections and a crossover road have been laid in at both ends of the place.
>
> 'Two signal boxes have been built. One, called Malvern Road East, controls the connections at the east end of the place and also the new double junction between the lines to Gloucester and the line to Honeybourne. This box contains 49 levers all in use. The view of the up platform from this signal-box is partly interrupted by the side of the cutting between the over-bridge and the platform, and also by a wooden support which has been erected under the over-bridge during certain alterations that are being made thereto. Steps should, I recommend, be taken to improve the view by widening the cutting, and removing as soon as possible the wooden support referred to.
>
> 'The other signal-box is the West Box, which contains 29 levers in use, and 8 spare levers.'

The Colonel also pointed out that two signals (Nos. 3 and 6) controlled from East Box were duplicated with the idea of improving the view of these from the footplate of an approaching engine. He did not think that these were necessary, or even desirable, 'as drivers will get a sufficiently early intimation of the condition of these signals by means of the distant signal.' Owing to the curve through the new station, he thought that the speed of trains approaching from the

Gloucester direction should in any event be moderate, thus removing the necessity for such duplication.

As the problems were of a minor nature, he had no hesitation in recommending the opening of Malvern Road station. The Great Western wrote to the BoT later that month to confirm that the wooden supports had since been removed from the overbridge, and the cutting sides flattened, thus improving the view of the up (north-eastbound) platform from the West Box. The duplicate signals had also been removed.

In October 1908, Cheltenham was provided with a halt at High Street a half-mile to the north-east of Malvern Road on the new main line to Honeybourne. There were now three Great Western stations within a half-mile, although the halt was closed with the manpower shortages of the Great War. In 1908, there were also the Midland stations at Lansdown and at High Street (a quarter-mile west of the GWR halt), and the B & C station at Cheltenham South & Leckhampton, giving a total of six passenger stations positioned around the town within a distance of about two miles.

Work on additions and improvements continued along the B & C with a request to the Board of Trade for two new siding connections into the single line at Great Rollright on 9th May 1908. The loop siding, located about 200 yards east of the halt, was completed in March 1909, and the site was visited by Col. Yorke the following month. As with Sarsden, his report indicated that the single line was worked by electric train staff. The report of 20th April continued:

> '...the points of the new siding connection are worked from two ground frames, each containing two levers locked by the key on the electric train staff.
>
> 'Owing to the gradient, instructions have been issued by the company that all up trains must draw past the gradient post marking the

summit of the incline before coming to a stand for the purpose of doing work at the siding.'

At the same time, some additional work was carried out at King's Sutton. The platforms were extended by 100 feet, a footbridge constructed, two new siding connections with trailing points on the up line laid in, a crossover road provided between the mains, and a slip point connecting the up main on the through road from the up sidings with the down main added. The signal box of 1884 remained, though it now contained 33 levers, all of which were in use.

Significant changes occurred at Chipping Norton Jct. from 1909. As the railway system from the Junction had gradually expanded over the fifty years since its opening, the title 'Chipping Norton Junction' had become increasingly irrelevant. Since the opening of the Bourton line in 1862, the junction had ceased to relate to just the one town, and

*King's Sutton station c.1910 with station master Harry Gardner seventh from the right.* COLLECTION MISS B. PROBERT

*Station master Harry Gardner, posing in the up side waiting shelter at King's Sutton c.1910.*
COLLECTION
ALAN BRAIN

Scenes from Chipping Norton station. Porter Charlie Parsons with the parcels delivery dray. COLLECTION ALAN BRAIN

Unidentified station staff c.1912. Note 'Wallace', the station cat, on a porter's shoulder. The station master is thought to have been Mr. Drew. COLLECTION ALAN BRAIN

No material was regarded as too trivial for the camera's subject! 'Wallace' with his prize. COLLECTION ALAN BRAIN

*The GWR parcels delivery van (centre) one Fair Day on 'Top Side', Chipping Norton.*    COLLECTION ALAN BRAIN

the extensions to Cheltenham and Banbury had further exacerbated the situation. The duplication of the place name also caused some confusion, especially with traffic from places far removed from the GWR system. Stories are told, though not officially verified, of passengers unfamiliar with the area alighting at the Junction, having purchased their tickets under the misapprehension that they would arrive at Chipping Norton, to be informed that their intended destination was still four-and-a-half miles away!

On 1st May 1909, Chipping Norton Junction's name was officially changed to Kingham, the name of the nearest village, approximately one mile north of the station. The name 'Kingham' thereafter became synonymous with the railway.

As has been discussed, the timber engine shed at Chipping Norton Jct. was officially closed in 1906, and subsequently removed, though the site, along with the 44 ft turntable, had remained a stabling point for the Kingham engines. It was decided in 1912 to provide a replacement shed, and this was constructed on the same site in brick to a length of 75 ft, with a slate roof. An office annexe was provided on the south-western corner, adjacent to the shed doors. The new shed was opened in 1913.

The use of the telegraph had been long associated with the Great Western Railway, the first example being in operation during 1839 between Paddington' and Hanwell. Telephones were a much later addition, and it was not until 1879 that the first public system opened in Great Britain, with eight subscribers. By the mid-1890s, around 50 stations were served by the 'official' GPO system, mostly in the cities and larger towns, though this was predominantly to the goods departments at those places. By 1897, Cheltenham Goods Department had received its connection, and a call to 'Cheltenham 120' would provide instant communication with the goods agent. Within the first decade of the twentieth century, this had been joined by Banbury ('45' Goods, '46' Passenger), Chipping Norton ('13'), Stow ('19'), and Leckhampton ('Cheltenham 187'), whilst the passenger station at Cheltenham had also been connected ('392').

By the end of the first decade of the twentieth century, the Banbury & Cheltenham railway was able to provide a very respectable service to both local and national interests. Ironstone trains bound for the West Midlands and beyond, and for South Wales, were a daily occurrence, as were goods trains running between Banbury and Gloucester, as well as local services between Banbury and Kingham, and Kingham and Cheltenham.

Into the mix should be added the Midland & South Western Junction's through traffic, which included north & south expresses. Surely the culmination of these developments was the inauguration of the Barry & Newcastle service – the 'Ports to Ports' express – in May 1906. With the Banbury & Cheltenham, the GWR demonstrated that it possessed the infrastructure for a route of some importance; the successful running of the 'Ports' express, that 'elegant and prestigious' service, against the backdrop of what had been merely a rural branch line, proved that it had.

This undated view of Bourton-on-the-Water station was taken c.1912 after the replacement of the original Gloucester Wagon Co. signal box. It shows the crossing of an up passenger train with the down pick-up goods, the engine of which is glimpsed beneath the water tank in the course of its shunting the yard.

# CHAPTER SEVEN
# CHANGE AND CONTINUITY
## 1914–1939

DURING the reign of King Edward VII, there began a short period when the railway companies ruled supreme. Powered flight was in its infancy, lorries and omnibuses were slow and inefficient, and the age of the motor car was still a long way off. Apart from the trams that abounded in the large towns and cities, nothing threatened them.

The golden age of the railways coincided with another development, and one which reached a state of some maturity at that time – photography. This versatile medium was seized upon by enterprising photographers, and a new business – the community photographer – flourished in towns throughout the country. In the Cotswold region were the studios of Butt's at Bourton-on-the-Water, Tooze at Stow, Percy Simms, and most prolific of them all, Frank Packer, at Chipping Norton. The Edwardian railway provided perfect material but almost any subject could be turned into an elegantly composed photograph through the lens of these masters. Scenes depicting village life from this period show a considerable variation in social order across the region.

Apart from the changes which were effected across the region by the presence of the railway, other, more sweeping changes were affecting society on a national level. Old systems were making way for more democratic processes, and a growing unease was reflected in the enginemen's strike of 1911 and the coal strike of 1912, the latter lasting some seven weeks. An increase in military traffic using the line was also recorded.

On 4th August 1914, following the assassination of Archduke Franz Ferdinand in distant Sarajevo, the Kaiser's army invaded Belgium, and at midnight Prime Minister Asquith announced that Britain had declared war on Germany. So began the bloodiest conflict the world had known.

At that moment, the railways came under Government control, and the Railway Executive Committee, formed in 1912 to take over in the event of a national emergency, was activated. The committee was formed of ten General Managers of the largest railway companies, with Frank Potter the representative from the Great Western.

One of the first problems confronting the committee was the return of those Territorials from their annual summer training camps to their home stations before general mobilisation could take place, and 186 special trains were run accordingly over the Great Western. The area around Tidworth and Ludgershall had seen a great expansion in army facilities from the turn of the century, whilst a large camp was being established at Chiseldon. The Midland & South Western were therefore heavily involved in these movements, and many trains ran over the line from Andoversford to Cheltenham conveying the Territorials en route to the Midlands and the North of England.

Immediately afterwards, Salisbury Plain was again busy with the preparation of both regular and territorial troops for transfer to France, and continuation training for others. Men, horses, luggage and stores were carried in great abundance. On the Great Western, 632 trains ran within the initial 15-day mobilisation period, a number of which would doubtless have run over the western end of the branch. Although excursions were suspended during that period, the regular services operated normally.

Whilst the rest of the branch was relatively unaffected by these operations, the main lines at the two extremes were. On Monday, 17th August, for example, Swindon was the centre for very heavy military operations, which necessitated the diversion of South Wales expresses onto the Bicester,

*An unidentified '517' class 0–4–2T approaching Cornwell bridge with a Banbury to Kingham autocar in 1913.*

AUTHOR'S COLLECTION

ENGLAND DECLARES WAR ON GERMANY. — CHIPPING NORTON BRANCH ST JOHN AMBULANCE LEAVING FOR SERVICE. AUG 9 1914. 1.
PACKER. PHOTO

COLLECTION ALAN BRAIN

CHIPPING NORTON MUSEUM

ENGLAND DECLARES WAR ON GERMANY - 2
CHIPPING NORTON BRANCH OF ST JOHN AMBULANCE BRIGADE ENTRAINING

DEPARTURE OF ST JOHN AMBULANCE BRIGADE CHIPPING NORTON BRANCH

COLLECTION JOHN BRICE

*The legend on this card reads 'Chipping Norton welcomes some Belgian refugees 1914'.*

COLLECTION ALAN BRAIN

"THE CALL TO ARMS"
CHIPPING NORTON NATIONAL RESERVE SERVICE SECTION
LEAVING FOR SOUTHAMPTON NOV 26. 1914

COLLECTION
ALAN BRAIN

COLLECTION ALAN BRAIN

A BUSY SCENE AT CHIPPING NORTON STATION SHOWING ONE OF THE SPECIAL TRAINS AND THE CADETS ENTRAINING

COLLECTION JOHN BRICE

CHIPPING NORTON TERRITORIALS FOR ACTIVE SERVICE

COLLECTION ALAN BRAIN

Stratford and Gloucester route. The diverted up trains thus passed Lansdown Jct., and 1 hour 25 minutes later ran past the opposite end of the B & C at King's Sutton, en route to Paddington. No attempt was made to cut the mileage by diverting these trains over the B & C, which would in any event have required an engine change and reversal at Banbury; had the proposed south loop at King's Sutton been constructed, then perhaps consideration may have been given. Nor could they run via Oxford and the western half of the B & C, as that station was already congested with regular and military movements at the time.

Iron ore traffic peaked during the Great War, and iron-stone workings expanded in response to the increasing demand for steel, to supply the war effort. The area between

*More views of military activity, this time in the goods yard at Chipping Norton. Notice the empty coaching stock alongside the engine shed, no doubt for troop movements.*
COLLECTION JOHN BRICE

PERCY SIMMS, CTY. ALAN BRAIN

*This undated photograph shows a Banbury auto-car alongside the up platform with another coach in tow behind the engine. It was probably taken in the late 1920s.*
AUTHOR'S
COLLECTION

*The Banbury & Cheltenham Railway was particularly vulnerable to the effects of bad weather, particularly snow. These scenes, taken several years apart, are typical of winter in Chipping Norton during the early 20th century. Right: The Bliss Tweed Mill strike in 1914 with policemen as pickets standing guard. The Chipping Norton West signal box is seen at the far left.*
AUTHOR'S COLLECTION

REAL
WINTER —
AT CHIPPING NORTON

*The first serious snowfalls to affect the Banbury & Cheltenham Railway were those of March 1916. George Allen, who lived at Coldharbour Farm overlooking the railway between Rollright and Hook Norton, recalled the scene — "The hedgerows — you could just walk over them". The southern portal of Hook Norton Tunnel was blocked, with a locomotive stranded in a snow drift at the entrance. As George remembered, "There were all these men dodging around . . . with shovels" to free the train.* AUTHOR'S COLLECTION

King's Sutton and Adderbury received new siding accommodation in late 1914. These were located on the up (north) side of the branch, a little to the east of the site of the old Hickman's Sidings. The quarry, once again owned by Alfred Hickman Ltd., was opened in March 1914, and was worked by a tramway which fed the sidings, alongside which a set of kilns were used to calcine the ore. At the east end of the site, a facing connection had been added on the down line with a single slip forming a trailing connection on the up, whilst at the west end, a new trailing connection had been added on the up line. The points and signals were worked from a new signal box – Sydenham – which contained a frame of 23 working levers and 6 spaces.

By January 1916, enemy air raids had started to penetrate beyond the South-East of England, and the Birmingham area was increasingly targeted. On receipt of an air raid warning, all train services were halted and lights extinguished. On 31st March 1916, the Banbury & Cheltenham line was affected by an air raid alarm when Zeppelins had been sighted in the vicinity. The restrictions lasted from around 9.0 p.m. to 3.0 a.m., with four or five goods or mineral services probably being brought to a halt. Subsequently, the Banbury area was affected rather more with air raid warnings than was the branch itself.

If enemy action over the branch was having little effect, the same could not be said of staff who had been drafted into the army from the branch stations. Amongst these, Mr. E. Mosby, a PW packer from Adderbury, had been killed in the early part of 1915, and others wounded.

Another new quarry which opened at the height of demand for iron during the Great War was that between Adderbury and Bloxham at Milton, owned by the Bloxham Ironstone Co., and later the Bloxham & Whiston company. The sidings were loops on the north side of the single running line (one of which was termed a goods passing loop), controlled from a signal box on the south side of the line called Bloxham Iron Stone Sidings. Plans were approved in June 1916, and the sidings were opened some months later, though regular production did not commence until early 1918. The new signal box divided the electric train staff section between Bloxham and Adderbury, and it was necessary to make special arrangements for switching out. During the time the new box was switched out, the through section (Bloxham to Adderbury) was worked by train tablet, all contingencies having been provided for by means of interlocking between staff, tablet, and locking frame.

Also in 1916, new kilns were built for the Brymbo Ironstone Company at Hook Norton.

By January 1917, some 20,000 Great Western staff had been 'called to the Colours', around a quarter of the number usually employed, though the number of their replacements was far short of that figure. The company had therefore to

*GWR 2-6-0 No. 5354 passing through King's Sutton with the GCR stock of the Swansea to Newcastle express circa 1922. This engine was based at Gloucester shed from 1921-4. At that time Gloucester 43XXs worked the Newcastle train from Gloucester to Banbury and returned with the opposite working for Swansea.    L&GRP*

close stations to release staff for other, more pressing duties, and Cheltenham (Malvern Road) was temporarily closed on 1st January of that year for the duration.

Shortages of men and materials due to the increasing demands of the war effort caused the withdrawal of the 'Ports' express, and of the slip coaches serving the Cheltenham line, in January 1917. A basic service of four local passenger trains over each half of the line now operated.

The postwar era was a difficult one for the railway; the war effort had drained national resources, and there was a lack of investment generally. A short period of boom occurred after cessation of hostilities, which was reflected in new ironstone workings alongside the Tadmarton road, close to Bloxham station, owned by the Northamptonshire Ironstone Company.

Also in the immediate postwar period, the Great Western formulated proposals to double the line; two surveyors were sent on a reconnaissance mission, but the idea did not develop further.

Recovery was replaced by stagnation in many industries. The railways came in for a great deal of criticism, as the reduction of passenger services to some 44% of those operating in 1913 was only slowly being rectified – amongst other things, governmental control and a shortage of rolling stock were still imposing restrictions on what could be achieved, whilst limited availability of coal was also causing concern. The men drafted into the armed forces were now returning in some numbers, and by the end of 1919, some 19,000 of the 25,500 men who joined the Colours from the company had returned. In the conflict, over 2,100 had been killed, and even more wounded, some of whom were unable to return to their jobs with the company.

During the summer of 1920, the Ministry of Transport issued an outline of proposals as to the future of the railways, and these amounted to the formation of seven new companies by amalgamation and absorption, based along geographical lines. As the date for the end of Government control

over the railways – 15th August 1921 – approached, the proposals had been adjusted to four companies. The retention of the 'Great Western' title for one of these allowed the GWR to effectively expand its system with the railways of its much smaller constituents, and engendered the company with a forceful individuality not seen in the other three.

With the Great Western in the 'Western' group was placed the Midland & South Western, also fiercely independent, which was to be absorbed, and not amalgamated as a constituent. The Railways Act 1921 (11 & 12 Geo. 5) had set the date of 1st January 1923 for the effective completion of the scheme, although constituents could voluntarily agree to amalgamation before that date. The absorption of the M & SWJ was, however, delayed beyond that date due to a dispute with the new LM&SR over loans made to the M & SWJ by the Midland, one of its own constituents. This was eventually resolved, and the M & SWJ became part of the Great Western Railway on 1st July 1923. It was the last of the pre-grouping main-line railways to retain its identity; doubtless, feelings amongst its loyal staff ran high when at last it succumbed to Great Western ownership.

Life gradually began its return to normal, with the reintroduction of the 'Ports' in July 1920, and the London slip coaches in the following year. The reinstatement of the full local passenger services took place in 1921/2. Malvern Road station had partially re-opened to serve the Wolverhampton & Penzance trains (and one branch connecting service) in mid-1919, although it did not assume full operation until 1921.

Engineering responsibilities over the B & C were shared by two divisions: the section from Cheltenham to Stow-on-the-Wold came within the remit of the Gloucester Engineer's Division, whilst the remainder came into the Wolverhampton Division. Permanent way depots were established at Cheltenham, Kingham and Banbury, whilst their gangs were spread over the branch; each might consist of a ganger, a sub-ganger and one or two undermen/length-men. Kingham, for example, also had the services of other tradesmen – a bricklayer, a carpenter and a painter, with a labourer.

Accidents over the branch requiring the assistance of a breakdown crane or other special equipment were handled by three gangs. The Banbury breakdown gang would handle any derailments or other problems over the line to Kingham (exclusive), whilst the Gloucester gang were responsible from Kingham (exclusive) to Cheltenham. Kingham itself was handled by the Oxford gang.

During this unsettled period of the interwar years, a number of minor closures were effected along the line. The most significant from an operational perspective was the closure of Chipping Norton shed in July 1922 after a working life of 67 years.

*The old engine shed lingered on after closure, this picture showing it on 27th August 1939. It was a stone structure with brick facings, a slate roof and, more unusually for a shed of this size, 10 roof-lights (5 each side) instead of the customary windows. Internal dimensions were 68ft 7in long, 18ft 2in wide, with heights to the ridge and wall plate of 21ft 3in and 15ft 3in respectively. A simple brick-built sand furnace was situated at the far end of the shed, on the right-hand side, and an engine-men's cabin on the left just inside the entrance shown, whilst a small lean-to behind the rampant foliage housed a WC. The inspection pit inside was 62ft 8in long and three chimneys ventilated the full-length smoke trough.* W. A. CAMWELL

*This view of the engine shed in 1933 provides a rare glimpse of the coal wharfage.* C. L. MOWAT

*For some reason, Adderbury did not receive as much attention as the other stations between Banbury and Kingham, but this 1920s view shows the very neat flower beds and the recently planted conifers which, in later years, grew to dominate the platforms.*

A general lack of investment prevailed within industry, which reduced productivity and demand, and therefore the amount of traffic carried on the railways. This was reflected in closures at the Bloxham & Whiston workings at Whiston; the Northamptonshire Ironstone company at Bloxham (though the quarrying continued under new management, Clay Cross Ltd.); and Alfred Hickman at Sydenham. There was also considerable fluctuation in the output of the largest of the B & C-served workings, the Brymbo company at Hook Norton.

By far the most serious long-term effect for the railway was the growth of road transport competition, particularly the omnibus, with its cheap fares and flexible operation, although the use of private lorries was also expanding. Ownership of motor cars was also increasing, though this did not form a particular threat at the time.

*A Midland Red bus and an AEC 'Y' type belonging to the City of Oxford company waiting in the Market Place at Chipping Norton on 11th August 1921.*
R. K. COPE

*A 1920s view of the station gardens at Bloxham.*

PERCY SIMMS

These three pictures, believed to have been taken in 1924, show the station gardens at Bloxham developed by station master Herbert Lloyd. The date at which he took up the station master's post at Bloxham is not clear, although he was certainly there in 1923. Born on 15th March 1878 on the outskirts of Worcester, he began his railway career as a porter at Worcester Shrub Hill station and progressed through the clerical grades to become a relief station master based at Worcester. He married Alice Hall, daughter of the Shipton-under-Wychwood ganger Charles Hall in 1912. The family moved from Worcester, initially living in Milton for a short while before taking up residence in one of the new council houses in Bloxham. His posting at Bloxham was a relatively short tenure of seven years, yet in that time his name became indelibly linked with Bloxham station. A keen Anglican churchman, like Frank Coppage before him, he was a man of high moral character, strict, firm, and respected as well as being well-liked by all who knew him personally. He is remembered for his hard work combined with a meticulous attention to detail. In winter months a fire always burned in the waiting room. In summer a vase of fresh flowers was invariably seen in the ladies' room. His favourite motto was borrowed from Young's Night Verses: 'Procrastination is the thief of all time' and nowhere were the sentiments of this maxim more clearly expressed than in the magnificent station gardens, which became something of a local attraction, drawing people from miles around. Herbert began work on the gardens at the earliest opportunity, working day and night to complete them. He incorporated lawns, paths and treillage, rose borders and rock gardens. Everywhere was the meticulous attention to detail which was his hallmark. The stones for the rock garden, for example, came from Cheddar Gorge in Somerset. He said that if he had not been a station master, he would like to have been a landscape gardener. He entered Bloxham station gardens in the annual Worcester Division competition and won year after year. When Herbert Lloyd moved to a higher grade post at Hanborough station on the Oxford–Worcester line, he dismantled the treillage and rockery piece by piece and reassembled them there. This view, taken from South Newington road bridge looking west, shows the station name picked out in white stones on the right and, more prosaically, Palmer's coal wharf and office, and the replacement GWR signal box.

AUTHOR'S COLLECTION

*Another view of the gardens from the up platform, looking east, with Herbert Lloyd and his children.*

*A closer view of the staff grouped on the eastern barrow crossing in front of the engine of a Banbury–Kingham goods. The figure with the shunter's pole was 'Nobby' Clarke, followed by an engineman believed to have been Harry Butler, then Herbert Lloyd and on the far right Basil Packer, the photographer's son. The number of the engine is not recorded but at the time Banbury had two of these '2361' class 0–6–0s, No. 2369 shedded there almost entirely from 1920-37 and No. 2378 which was mostly at Banbury between 1920 and 1942. The Banbury–Kingham goods was more commonly worked by '2301' class 0–6–0s.*                        COLLECTION ALAN BRAIN

Looking towards Kingham from the down platform on a glorious summer day in the 1920s. The neatly laid out rock garden is clearly visible on the up platform.

Chipping Norton. Railway Station.

Yet another example of the classic general view of Chipping Norton station, this time probably in the 1920s, by which time the platform fencing along the rear of the platform in the foreground had been largely removed south of the footbridge to provide land for the development of the station gardens which were particularly in vogue at the time.

*Although Bloxham station regularly took first prize in the Worcester division gardens competition, the quality across the region was of a uniformly high standard. Chipping Norton's station gardens took second prize.*
PERCY SIMMS

*A closer look at the rock garden.*

F. R. PACKER, CTY. ALAN BRAIN

*This picture, taken at Chipping Norton during the 1926 General Strike, shows Mr. Johnson, brother of the local saddler, serving as fireman, Fred Morse, foreman at Kingham, and Mr. Rowell, engineman. Fred Morse began his railway career c.1909 as a porter at Chipping Norton, then Kingham, Kidderminster and Worcester. During the Great War he was shot in the right arm, which left him with a twisted hand which he could not use properly. He continued as a nursing orderly and on return to the GWR he became foreman at Kingham. He lived in The Leys, Chipping Norton. The engine, No. 2445, spent a lot of time based at Kingham shed between 1923 and 1926.*

Of significance to the Great Western in the mid-1920s was the growing unrest of workers faced with alterations in working practices, largely brought about by the industrial situation, which culminated in the General Strike of May 1926. The position of coal as the principal fuel was beginning to be threatened by an increasing demand for oil or alternative power in many areas of industry, and a slump occurred in the mines. The growing crisis was centred on South Wales, the main coal-producing area, to which the Great Western was inextricably linked as a major carrier of coal products, as well as a user. The company put forward proposals to its workforce to cut working expenses following the continued reduction in coal traffic, and it was eventually agreed that dismissals of staff would occur when necessary, rather than a cut in hours or reductions in pay.

A government subsidy to the coal owners gained time, but could not ward off the inevitable miners' strike.

Allegiance to the Great Western among its staff was strong, but there was a growing sympathy towards the miners' cause. The General Strike was called for Monday, 3rd May 1926.

The Great Western began to prepare for an anticipated shutdown in communications, and organised the distribution of essential supplies, particularly milk and other perishables.

Felix Pole, the GWR's General Manager, issued the following notice to the staff:

'The National Union of Railwaymen have intimated that railwaymen have been asked to strike without notice to-morrow night. Each Great Western man has to decide his course of action, but I appeal to all of you to hesitate before you break your contracts of service with the old Company, before you inflict grave injury upon the Railway Industry, and before you arouse ill feeling in the Railway service which will take years to remove.

'Railway Companies and Railwaymen have demonstrated that they can settle their disputes by direct negotiations, The Mining Industry should be advised to do the same.

'Remember that your means of living and your personal interests are involved, and that Great Western men are trusted to be loyal to their conditions of service in the same manner as they expect the Company to carry out their obligations and agreements.'

At midnight on 3rd May, the General Strike began. From the outset, there was a general cessation of traffic, though some stopping trains worked on the first day, including a service from Oxford to Paddington. There followed a steady stream of volunteers presenting themselves for service.

However, the strike had bitten hard in the B & C area. The *Gloucester Echo* of that day reported a total rail stoppage in Cheltenham: 'Not a single puff of smoke sends up a message of hope, and not a porter's truck disturbs the quietude of empty platforms.' The only railwayman at work was one who looked after the horses, 'the poor dumb beasts who have no union to look after their interests.'

At various stations along the line, the company responded to the effects of the strike. Arthur Plackett, proprietor of an enterprising omnibus company operating from Adderbury, removed the seats of the bus to carry milk from the station to depots in London. Across at Chipping Norton, Mr. Rowell, an ironmonger from the town, drove the train from Kingham to Banbury, his fireman being a Mr. Johnson, brother of the local saddler. The Brymbo company at Hook Norton stepped in to help by providing two engine drivers.

However, at Kingham station the strike took on a deeper perspective. Lovdin Farmer had been the stationmaster for only a month when the strike was announced; his previous position had been at Charlbury, where he had served since 1917, and was promoted to Kingham when William Insall retired. Mr. Farmer held an active interest in local politics, and at Charlbury he had become a member of the local Parish Council, the Rural District Council and the Board of Guardians.

On Saturday, 1st May, the stationmaster was walking over the station footbridge while his wife and son were inspecting the station house in preparation for their imminent move (he had already taken up his post). A young porter approached him there and asked his advice concerning the strike.

'What should I do tomorrow, sir?'

The stationmaster replied: 'I can only tell you to come to work if you ask me that question on station premises.'

This reply was diplomatic, but revealed his own political persuasion. As the stationmaster explained later, the answer was given to the man in such a way so as not to influence him while they were at work; he was not yet a member of the union, and would expose himself to certain unemployment if he went on strike.

On Monday, 3rd May, the staff arrived at Kingham for their normal duty. In the booking office, a large room containing a telephone and three single-needle telegraph instruments, the clerks were going about their usual business when the telephone rang. It was answered by a young clerk called Bert Lane, who found himself talking to a representative of the NUR, calling the men out on strike. He wrote down the message and passed it on to the stationmaster.

'What's it mean, Mr. Farmer?'

'They're going on strike tomorrow.'

The stationmaster went on to ask Bert and his colleague, a clerk named Lodge, what they intended to do. Bert told him they would not strike.

On the following day, Tuesday, 4th May, Lovdin Farmer did not arrive for duty at the station, nor did a large number of other railwaymen including Engineman Charlie Davis, Guard Sydney Warren, and John Allen, one of the porters.

A handful of trains were running by 7th May, operated by volunteers, including one afternoon return branch trip from Cheltenham to Kingham. The LMS also put on a couple of trains between Gloucester or Birmingham. By Monday, 10th May, there were four or five trips each way between Cheltenham and Gloucester, and a couple to Honeybourne. The M & SWJ ran a morning return trip to Swindon, and added an afternoon return train the following day.

A deputation of striking railwaymen arriving at St. James's station on 13th May were met by officers of the company and informed that their services were not required at present, and that they would be sent for when required. A

*Bourton-on-the-Water station in the 1920s, looking towards Stow. The lattice-post down starting signal in the foreground, probably provided by Stevens & Co., replaced the original Gloucester Wagon Co. wooden post seen in previous photos. The station master on the boarded crossing has not been identified.* COLLECTION F. A. J. POOLE

*This picture of the signal box was taken at the same time.*

COLLECTION F. A. J. POOLE

reinstatement form which included a phrase to the effect that the striking men were 'not relieved of the consequences of having broken your terms of service' formed another obstacle.

The strike finished on Friday, 14th May with the agreement between the railway companies on one hand, and the NUR, ASLEF and the RCA (Railway Clerks' Association) on the other, in which the unions admitted that they had committed a wrongful act against the companies in calling a strike where there was no dispute between the two sides.

There was little extra movement the following day, and it was assumed that work would resume as normal from the Monday. However, it was to be several days before any degree of normality was attained.

On the same day, the GWR published its terms of settlement for 53 members of staff who were to be transferred to other positions without loss of pay, when a suitable position arose. The Kingham stationmaster's name was listed along with 15 others of similar rank. Mr. Farmer undertook a long battle for reinstatement, and three months after the cessation

*The view of the station from the signal box on the same occasion.* COLLECTION F. A. J. POOLE

*Bourton-on-the-Water station, looking towards Kingham in 1929.*

D. THOMPSON

of the strike, he was re-appointed as a 5th grade clerk at Pershore; ironically, the clerk in charge of the office where he was working was a man he had trained some twenty years previously.

Mr. Farmer went on to Droitwich Spa from that autumn (a move apparently opposed by senior clerks in the Divisional Office at Worcester) and served as a grade 2 stationmaster until retirement in 1938. In Droitwich, he enjoyed retirement by tending his small garden with its gold-fish pond. He became a Town Councillor and a Justice of the Peace, from which he was elected as Chairman of the Bench. Lovdin Farmer died in 1951.

The manual process of keeping the permanent way and surrounding areas in a good state of repair had required the services of many men. In an effort to increase the efficiency of maintenance, a 'motor economic' system was introduced on the Great Western in 1928. Under this system, manually-operated mechanical trolleys were provided for conveyance of men and tools, and for use by gangers when inspecting their lengths, thereby effecting considerable saving in time which would be otherwise occupied in travelling.

The Kingham gang were originally responsible for the station area, with separate gangs maintaining the main line, and the length between Kingham and a point midway

*A local bus for Banbury waiting in West Street, Chipping Norton.*                    AUTHOR'S COLLECTION

*The Great Western attempted to counter local bus competition by introducing their own bus service arranged to coincide with trains. Commencing on 1st July 1929, services ran from Banbury, through Hook Norton and Great Rollright, to Chipping Norton, Kingham station and Bledington, though the destination board of this vehicle only lists Bledington, Kingham and Chipping Norton.*
COLLECTION
J. CUMMINGS

*No. 6362 pulling away from the west end of Notgrove station with the down Ports-to-Ports express in the late 1930s. Wesley Keddle, who was signalman at Notgrove when this photograph was taken, remembered the photographer from Cheltenham asking permission to walk down the line. He promised Wesley a copy of the picture, which duly turned up later. No. 6362 was shedded at Banbury from 1936-9.*

COLLECTION WESLEY KEDDLE

between Stow and Bourton. The Chipping Norton gang worked on the section between Kingham and Chipping Norton, whilst the Rollright gang looked after the stretch between Chipping Norton and Hook Norton.

Following economies, the Chipping Norton gang was abolished and the Kingham gang extended its length to a point midway between Rollright and Hook Norton, while Rollright and Hook Norton gangs were combined.

The lengths maintained by one gang extended to about five miles, but the introduction of petrol-driven vehicles soon afterwards improved the system further.

In connection with the conversion of the ex-M & SWJ section between Andoversford and Cirencester from double to single line in 1928, the 'motor economic' system of maintenance was adopted. This necessitated the installation of a number of token key boxes with telephones, at intervals of

*An undated view of Notgrove station, looking west towards Andoversford, probably in the 1920s.*                                         L&GRP

*The permanent way motorised trolley at Notgrove station, with ganger George Fletcher on the right and sub-ganger Bert Stratford seated. The other man has not been identified. George and Bert, like so many of the Notgrove gang, lived at Naunton. Both men retired from the permanent way, George at Notgrove and Bert at Bourton, where he was later ganger.*                                         WESLEY KEDDLE

approximately one mile, which enabled the permanent way staff, with the concurrence of the signalmen, to withdraw a key, entitling them to occupy a section of the line.

The system was introduced onto the single-line sections of the Banbury & Cheltenham line in 1930. In addition to the necessary line wire, the conversion required 42 occupation key boxes, 40 telephones, and 8 occupation control instruments. The system involved the use of four gangs, each covering lengths of around 8 or 9 miles:

| From | To | Intermediate Boxes | Telephone To |
|------|-----|-----|-----|
| **Gang No.85 Notgrove** | | | |
| Andoversford | Notgrove | Nos. 22–25 | Andoversford |
| Notgrove | 93m 40c | Nos. 19–21 | Bourton |
| **Gang No.84 Bourton** | | | |
| 93m 40c | Bourton | Nos. 18, 19 | Bourton |
| Bourton | Kingham West | Nos.14–17, Stow East GF | Bourton |
| **Gang No.143 Kingham** | | | |
| Kingham East | Chipping Norton | Nos. 11–13 | Ch. Norton |
| Chipping Norton | 94m 40c | | Nos. 7–10 |
| Hk. Norton | | | |
| **Gang No.142 Hook Norton** | | | |
| 94m 40c | Hook Norton | Nos. 5–7 | Hk. Norton |
| Hook Norton | Bloxham | | Nos. 2–4 |
| Hk. Norton | | | |
| Bloxham | 85m 69c | No. 1 | Bloxham |

The staff establishment of most stations along the B & C line at this time was for a stationmaster, one or two porters and two signalmen (or combinations incorporating porter signalmen), as was to be found at Adderbury, Bloxham, Stow, Notgrove, Charlton Kings and Cheltenham South & Leckhampton. Hook Norton had three porters in a total of six staff, whilst Andoversford had more signalmen or porter signalmen for its two boxes in its complement of seven. Bourton warranted a clerk and a goods checker in addition to the other staff members, with a total of eight. Chipping Norton had the largest number of staff with thirteen, comprising clerks, porters, a goods checker, signalmen for two boxes (East and West at that time), and a crossing keeper for Churchill, in addition to the stationmaster. The West box at Chipping Norton was taken out of use during the summer of 1929, and the whole of the signalling concentrated in the 28-lever East box, with a commensurate reduction in staff.

As befitted its main-line junction status, Kingham had a staff of 21 members.

By this time, all stations along the line had been connected to the GPO telephone system. In addition to those having public telephone communication before the Great War, it was now possible for traders and passengers to contact their local branch stations at Adderbury ('Adderbury 30'), Bloxham ('15'), Hook Norton ('11'), Kingham ('14'), Bourton ('19'), Notgrove ('Lower Guiting 31'), Andoversford ('2') and Charlton Kings ('Cheltenham 1286', then '3286'). Of these, connections had been provided to Bourton, Andoversford and Charlton Kings in the first half of the 1920s, and the remainder in the latter half.

The railway itself had telephone systems, and by 1930 the western half of the line was extensively connected by a 'bus' system. Most of the stations were connected to their booking offices and/or signal boxes, though Andoversford also had connections by switch to all the stations on the ex-M & SWJ as far as Swindon.

The economic slump of the early 1930s hit the company hard. In 1929, the receipts from railway and other operations

This picture, taken in the late 1920s, is believed to show the Chipping Norton and Kingham permanent way gangs working together at Kingham. It shows (from left to right) George 'Jobie' Slatter, then at the back Lewis Hall, in front of him John Stayt, then Charlie 'Doggy' Franklin, unknown (possibly George Belcher?), Jack Collett, George Winter, Fred Hill, Dick Warren, John Warren, unknown and Inspector Boulter.

COLLECTION
ALAN WATKINS

*Relaying at Bloxham on 7th April 1935. The brick arch bridge spanning the cutting carried the Barford Road.*    L. E. COPELAND

had totalled £38 million, though this had decreased to £36m in 1930, giving a surplus of income over expenditure of £8m and £7m respectively in those years. In 1931, the receipts had dropped to £32½m, with a surplus of £5½m, and in 1932 to £29½m and a £4½m surplus. The Great Western constantly sought to lower working expenses and search for greater efficiency in the increasingly competitive transport industry. In the difficult situation prevailing, the company had managed to keep the 'profits' at a reasonable level, and, thanks to skilful and prudent management, was able to sustain an overall better performance than many around it. One effect of the economies was staff reductions; by 1934, most of the smaller stations along the branch had lost one member of staff (often a porter), though Chipping Norton had been reduced from fourteen to ten. Kingham suffered a similar cut in staff numbers, being reduced from 21 to 16. Although the company was set fair for the recovery, the laying-off of staff had caused a lot of personal difficulties to many men.

Particularly affected were the junior staff. George Stayt and Fred Warren, both sons of railwaymen serving on the

B & C, and both from Bledington, were laid off from their posts in the cutbacks – George from Kingham, and Fred from Hook Norton, in 1931. Fred had commenced employment at Chipping Norton in 1929. They retained their employment in the company, with George moving to Adlestrop, and Fred acting as relief porter at stations on the Oxford & Worcester section. Their contracts of employment were terminated on their twentieth birthdays.

Fred recalled: 'The GWR kept in touch with us, giving us jobs when they could.'

George viewed the situation with candour: 'You couldn't get another job, They knew that, so they hung onto you and played around with you.'

Both George Stayt and Fred Warren were reinstated some three years later, when a measure of stability and growth returned to the company. However, never did the financial rewards of the 1920s reappear.

The 1920s and 30s bore witness to a programme of relaying operations over the length of the B & C, long overdue, doubtless caused by the diversion of skilled manpower and materials for military use in World War I. Many junior railway staff found employment on PW work during the period of redundancy, including Fred Warren. The relaying gangs at Kingham comprised the ganger, with assistants from the regular PW gangs; the remaining members were made up of casual labour. In the 1930s, the ganger was Charles Hall of Bledington, who was a ganger on the Stow-on-the-Wold length. He replaced Joe Hartland, from Banbury, upon his retirement. Fred remembers that they would 'congregate at Kingham station, get on the train, and the train would stop on the site, drop these men off and then carry on.'

Relaying work was largely a summer activity, supervised by District Inspector Pinnell during the interwar years. His predecessor was a man named Mr. Boulter, whose position was identified by his habit of wearing a top hat on duty. Based at Kingham, Boulter inspected the work of all the gangs from Adderbury on the B & C, and between Handborough and Moreton-in-Marsh on the main line.

*Cheltenham Spa St. James station in 1932 with Platform No. 1 (the arrival bay) on the left, No. 2 (the main line arrival platform) and No. 3 (the main line departure platform) seen here occupied by corridor stock. Kingham trains normally left from Platform 4 (the departure bay), which was on the far side of the platform behind the coaches.*                                                          L&GRP

*Churchward Mogul No. 6341 alongside Platform 1, perhaps in 1936-7 when the engine was based at Malvern Road. The engine may have been about to shunt its stock over to Platform 4 ready for departure as this platform was normally for arrivals.*
L&GRP

Amongst the relaying operations of the 1930s, extensive work was carried out on the Kingham direct loop early in the decade, under Joe Hartland's supervision, and on the double-track section between King's Sutton and Adderbury, together with Adderbury yard.

In this period, motor transport was gradually superseding the traditional horse and cart. William Williams, the Chipping Norton stationmaster from 1932 until his retirement in 1945, recalled the painful transition:

> 'The goods traffic still flowed in by rail, and Mr. Johnson's teams of men and horses collected and delivered goods around the town. The two horsemen were Messrs. William Johnson and Leonard Morris, who had the misfortune to seek quite another form of service when the horse transport was superseded by petrol self-propelled vehicles. These two good men, not being initiated into the new era, had to work as handymen, finding employment at the Post Office and the public institution in London Road respectively.'

One local private carrier who plied the district up to 1933 from Chipping Norton station, and possibly also between Shipton station and Burford, was so caught up in the economic hardships that, according to Mr. Williams, 'he fastened on the idea of reducing the horses' corn and chaff by weekly instalments', with fatal results. On this occasion, as he was steadily making his way up Over Norton hill with two horses and trolley (two horses were needed on the steeply-graded hills) under the burden of a heavy load, one horse stopped in the shafts and fell down, dead. The owner dismounted, stood looking over the animal for a few moments, and made a classic statement: 'Well well, I've never known 'im do that afore!'

During the 1930s, the Great Western introduced its Country Lorry services into the Cotswold area, with vehicles stationed at Banbury, Bourton-on-the-Water and Cheltenham. These delivered grain, flour, manures and other traffic, and collected agricultural produce etc. for dispatch by rail.

The local services to Kingham in the latter 1930s amounted to four auto trips from Banbury, five passenger trips from Cheltenham, and a couple from Chipping Norton. The M & SWJ ran four passenger trips each way. Goods services had been reduced to a couple or so over each half of the line, and three or four on the M & SWJ. The through freights traversing the whole line were by now invariably conditional; they would soon be a memory.

So too would the 'Ports-to-Ports', which ceased at the outbreak of war in September 1939. The service was eventually reinstated in October 1946, but ran via the Severn Tunnel and Oxford (a journey 16 miles longer) 'in order to give a more useful service generally than that formerly given via Gloucester and Kingham', according to the General Manager.

In 1937, proposals were already being considered for the planned evacuation of London to the country districts in the event of Hitler's army launching an attack on the city. Oxfordshire was designated as a reception area. In that year, a surveying body from London visited Chipping Norton to consult the local authority on the possibilities of civilians

*A Banbury '43XX' beginning the 3-mile 1 in 60 descent towards Bourton-on-the-Water with the 7.40 a.m. Swansea to Newcastle express. The summit of the line lay near Salperton, beyond the overbridge in the distance, with a number of deep cuttings in the area indicating the route through the hills. The ex-NER dining car, fourth in the formation of LNER carriages, had a very distinctive underframe, and can be seen in many mid-1930s photographs of this train. The van of the leading Corridor Third Brake conveyed luggage and parcels for York, transfer and beyond, whilst the trailing van contained more general destinations. In the late 1930s, coach working programmes placed the Hull through coach at the rear, although up to 1937 it was scheduled to be formed behind the engine, and left in Sheffield Victoria station as the Newcastle portion behind it departed in the reverse direction behind a fresh engine.*

*The first evacuation train arriving at Chipping Norton Junction on Friday, 1st September 1939.*　　　CHIPPING NORTON MUSEUM

*The same occasion, viewed towards the tunnel.*                    CHIPPING NORTON MUSEUM

being accommodated in the town. A meeting was arranged, and among those present were representatives of the Great Western Railway, a Mr Kenyon of Chipping Norton Rural District Council, Mr Whettam, representing the Borough Council, and William Williams, the Chipping Norton stationmaster.

Much of the meeting involved 'wrestling with the fantastic ideas...about the number of evacuees that could be accommodated in the Chipping Norton area.' A figure of 14,000 people had been calculated, which the townspeople knew was unrealistic. Understandably, nobody wanted to appear to be in contention over a humanitarian programme of such overwhelming necessity. Nevertheless, the stationmaster responded practically, letting it be known that as the railway would be the principal carrier, the responsibility for distributing those people not able to be placed immediately would doubtless fall upon the shoulders of the railway staff. He explained that 'it would be an unbearable headache for the likes of me as stationmaster to sort things out...' and then, flaring up with his 'Welsh temperament', as he called it, he 'gave them to understand that they were being warned against making a huge mistake.' After the air had cleared, Williams was asked how many evacuees could be safely

accommodated in the town, to which he suggested a figure of 2,000 people. He then explained that the same quantity of households had already promised their accommodation to relatives and friends looking for rooms, for wives and children, in the event of an attack. As it was, the number of people evacuated to Chipping Norton was close to that figure.

As the clouds of war gathered, a system of 'schools' teaching air raid precautions were established at centres throughout the Great Western. Although these were mainly aimed at staff in the large centres – those likely to become the target of enemy bomber raids, in an attempt to cripple the transport system – staff at the rural branch stations of the B & C still had to acquire knowledge of effects and precautions, particularly against gas and incendiary attacks. A stand-to mobilisation occurred in 1938, but it was suspended.

From 1st September 1939, the evacuation trains started arriving in the region. Many local centres received trainloads of evacuees, including Banbury, whose first trainload carried 800 children and 80 teachers from schools in West Ham, Camberwell and the Dagenham district. Other stations to receive evacuees were Oxford, Charlbury and Chipping Norton. William Williams takes up the story:

*Evacuees from the East End of London making a hurried exit from Chipping Norton station into an uncertain future. Friday, 1st September 1939.* CHIPPING NORTON MUSEUM

CHIPPING NORTON MUSEUM

'First Friday in that September, two long trains arrived in Chipping Norton with teachers and the children…mainly [from the] East End of London…All went off very well because the teachers accompanying [the children] kept [them] organized and the weather was fine.'

Certainly one of the trains was formed of twelve coaches, containing 800 children from three schools in West Ham: New City Road, St. Antony's Catholic School and Upton Cross.

'Now Saturday dawned very threatening weather and two trains of mothers and small children were scheduled to arrive from Plaistow, and other East Ham areas. People by now 'had the wind up' as they say…the two trains were overloaded and it rained in torrents when the first train of about 14 coaches and vans arrived. Mr Packer took photos of our predicament.

'Our platform being only long enough to take five coaches at a time – we had to unload in three efforts.'

For the first batch, the rain fortunately abated and the effort proceeded.

'The vehicles were outside ready to take the evacuees to the surrounding villages and all were soon overloaded, with some [people] left behind.

'Now the furious rain came down and my HQ were clamouring for the empty train to be returned to Kingham and I firmly refused to disembark the second batch until there were signs of the transport vehicles returning. Our small station shelters were … overcrowded … local people helped to make the chaos complete.

'The police tried to send some away, but there were helpful volunteers … Womens' Voluntary Service etc. [but] no tents to protect them from the elements.'

Stationmaster Williams summed up the historic events with characteristic stoicism: 'We muddled through in good old British fashion.'

From the time when the railways began to affect society to the outbreak of the Great War, they had come to symbolise dynamic change, while at the same time being a catalyst for it. The mode of transport had completely altered the long-established ways of moving people and materials over distance, a process that effectively closed at the end of the 1930s with the demise of the carrier's cart.

Alas, for the railways, the positive dynamism of earlier years gave way to a growing unease as they were caught in the grip of severe economic retrenchment, imposed as a response to increasingly-powerful competition.

Despite this imposition, a sense of continuity prevailed, and did so even as the country entered a war for the second time in twenty-five years. Following the declaration of war on 3rd September, troops began to move in great numbers across the district, munitions and military stores were shifted from place to place, whilst strategies for protecting the railways from aerial attack were put into place. Regular train services were immediately affected.

The continuity of the railway in the face of change was most notably recognized at the point where it interacted with society – at its stations and depots – where, by and large, business continued much as usual. But the political and economic events that were shaping the future of the Banbury & Cheltenham railway were being played on a world stage. Their effect upon the railway, and indeed upon society, would be considerable, not only through the dramatic years of the Second World War but increasingly during the lean postwar era and beyond, as will be seen.

# ACKNOWLEDGEMENTS

Many contributions, large and small, have enabled this account to be written. Most of these are from railwaymen and women who worked on the line although a valuable source has been the recollection of people who lived within sight and sound of the railway, as well as its users, from farmers and local business operators to passengers. I am particularly grateful to the retired staff of the Great Western Railway who shared the experiences of a working life on the Banbury and Cheltenham line. A special debt of gratitude is owed to Fred Warren, Fred Harrison and John Fortnum, three railwaymen who gave their time willingly over many weeks of extensive interviews. It was very special to find friendship developing through this shared interest. I also wish to express my appreciation to Mr Harold Hall for his help on many important matters of detail.

These four railwaymen had astounding qualities of recall. A simple question could open a window onto an extremely detailed past, if I dared pursue it, even down to such minutiae as the number of drawers in a booking office desk, for example. They also had several characteristics in common, beginning their careers in the late 1920s and early 1930s, which was a difficult time for the railways; severe economic crises, coupled with the rise in road competition, brought about stringent measures to reduce expenditure; a great deal of flexibility was required of staff, which gave them an unequalled variety of experience. Fred Warren, in particular, travelled far and wide to many stations in the Worcester Division and held the distinction of having worked at no less than eight stations on the eastern section of the Banbury and Cheltenham line.

These men enjoyed their work. It was a great pleasure to interview people who genuinely loved what they did. As it was, all those interviewed shared a similar view about their careers. They enjoyed talking about the railway, too. The anticipation of visiting them to find out more was one of the special highlights of carrying out this project. The information they volunteered seemed to be drawn from a bottomless well of experience. Of some 120 people approached, only one refused an interview. This was definitely a sobering experience and it served as a reminder that for some people life on the railway may not have been a happy experience.

A final characteristic of these railwaymen was that their fathers were also railwaymen. When they began their service on the railway it was accepted that the subsequent generation would follow the same course as the one that had gone before. Indeed, Fred Warren and his cousin Archie (who has also contributed considerably to this project), both belonged to a large family whose lives were shaped around the railway. Harold Hall belonged to a particularly notable railway family. His father, Charles Hall, was ganger on the Shipton-under-Wychwood length on the Oxford-Worcester line and also on the Stow-on-the-Wold length. Many members of Harold's family served on the Banbury and Cheltenham line and are mentioned in this study. One of the most precious moments during the course of my research was the occasion when, on a visit to Harold's home, he left the room in which I was sitting and returned shortly after, carrying a large family Bible dating from the late nineteenth century. He opened it to the first page and there in handwritten script were the names of all his siblings, together with the dates of their birth and, poignantly, the dates of those who had died, with his father and mother's names, Charles and Alice Hall, along with their siblings, heading the list.

The story of the Banbury and Cheltenham Railway, ultimately, is a story about a railway and the people associated with it. The technical and historical facts and details are an essential part of the account, but they cannot stand in isolation. Therefore the human experience is included. Obviously, this approach is risky: memory can play tricks; certain events, over time, can become exaggerated. Wherever possible, attempts have been made to corroborate the evidence. Fortunately, Fred Warren's and Harold Hall's experience shared a similar path, occasionally crossing over as they worked at the same stations, so it was found that their recollections agreed on many different points. Notwithstanding all efforts to produce a detailed and accurate account, the possibility exists that errors may have arisen. If this has occurred then I accept full responsibility.

I am extremely grateful to Paul, June and Ann at Wild Swan Publications, for the excellent production and the opportunity to see this work published. Thanks are especially due to Chris Turner, for his 'indefatigable exertions' (to use a phrase used later in the narrative), particularly his dedication to interviewing many railwaymen and women, some of whom I have not met. Chris and I set out with very similar aims, at around the same time, neither of us knowing anything about the other. Joining forces was the necessary outcome – after all, we were starting to ask the same people identical questions! Chris has spent many hours interviewing staff and a special mention must be made to Philip and Alice Butt, Doug Cunningham, Frances Flick, Gordon and Dennis Insall, Beryl Johnston and Archie and Violet Warren. I would like to express my appreciation to John Copsey for his assistance with Chapters 6 and 7 and for processing the manuscript. His contribution to the working details has been invaluable.

Special thanks are due to the Rev Ralph Mann. Not only did he make himself available to answer difficult questions, but he very kindly lent me all his material on the railway, particularly his original notes on William Bliss and the Chipping Norton Railway, which provided a very useful starting point. He assured me that these notes were transcribed from historic documents – his son John read them out, while Ralph wrote down the text – and all carried out in the days when the idea of requesting that a laptop be taken into a public record office was pure fantasy!

Particular thanks are also due to three very generous contributors, Alan Brain, Martin Quartermain and Alan Watkins, all of whom have been collecting photographic material for many years. Without their willingness to lend precious and irreplaceable photographs and postcards, this work would have been so much the weaker.

I would like to thank my parents, Bill and Elfi Hemmings, for their encouragement, and to my wife, Pat, who has stood with me through the years that this project has unfolded. I would like to say a special thank you to Pat for her support, especially during the last eight months.

In addition to those mentioned above, I am grateful to the following people who have given assistance: Cyril Aston, Darrill Bailey, John Batts, Jaclyn Bennett, Ron Boyle, Stan Fuller, Mr C.E Heritage, Bert Humphries, Henry Oliver, John Shepherd, Graham Simmonds, Mick Soden, Bob Sutton, George Turton, Janet Bevis, Geoff Judd, Ivy Morbey, Bet Probert, Peggy Adams, Norman Davis, John Fox, David Lynes, Fred Lynes, John Adams, Norman Chainey, John Cordingley, Dorothy Quartermain, Miss C M F Wall, Mary Clarke, Mrs Nora Day, Jonathan Day, Alan Donaldson, David Gibbard, Henry Hirons, Arthur Hosband, Gerald Johnson, Douglas Webb, Barry Woodward, Tom Powell, Peter Turnock, Mrs A Coppage, Miss B Coppage, George Coppage, Paul Eagles, Eileen Green, Sylvia Hannis, Brenda Pickering, George Allen, John Brice, Ken Cox, Alfred Carter, Mr R L Evans, Phyllis Morse, Violet Parsons, Christopher Rayson, Jim 'Cod' Robinson, Geoff Rose, Pete Scarsbrook, Margaret Ward, Les Floyd, Marjorie Howells, Mrs Barbara Seidel, Roger Seidel, May Davis, Harvey Duester, Geoffrey Dix, Bert Field, Mrs E J Hall, Ken Hughes, Dilwyn John, Doreen John, Arthur Jupp, Johnny Langan, Michael Lainchbury, Ted Leadbetter, Phil Lidzy, Eric Millard, Horace Slatter, Michael J. Tattershall, Ivor Townsend, Len Tuffley, Adrian Vaughan, Audrey Viner, John Wilks, Don Williams, Daniel Arthurs, Jack Didcote, Jack James, Bob Sharpe, Lily Cooper, Peter Morris, Mr H Sambell, David Stratford, Bill Ayres, Hilary Davidson Smith, Tom and Joan Handy, Harry Harris, Mike Stanley, Michael Clifton, Stan Cowley, Bert Clapton, Arthur Edginton, George Harris, Dennis Matthews, Ron Moss, Jack Powell, Arthur Payne, Bill and Shirley Rathbone, Bob Small, Tom Steatham, Gordon and Geoffrey Simms, Ron Stares, Eric Thornton.

The following organisations have also been of assistance: Banbury Museum; The Centre for Banburyshire Studies; the staff of Green Pastures Nursing Home, Banbury; Pendon Museum; Bloxham School: Major Shaw McCloghry; Bloxham Village Museum: Mrs Yvonne Huntriss; Hook Norton Historical Association: Mrs Barbara Hicks; The Met Office, National Meteorological Archive; Ian MacGregor; the Mayor and the Clerk to Chipping Norton Town Council, Councillor Jo Graves and Michael Fletcher; Chipping Norton Museum: Mr J Howells; Sworn King and Partners: Steve Busby; Bledington Local History Society: Mrs Sylvia Reeves; Centre for Oxfordshire Studies, Oxfordshire Record Office; Gloucester Record Office; Linnell's: Jamie Sutton; Cassell Illustrated Publications: Ros Webber. I am also indebted to Wild Swan Publications for allowing me to use the original lecture notes compiled by the late John Norris on the Banbury and Cheltenham Railway.

## PUBLISHER'S NOTE
The publishers would particularly like to thank the following for their kind help: Mike Barnsley, Sean Bolan, Alan Brain, Barry Davis, Alan Donaldson, John Copsey, Paul Strong, Peter Swift and Chris Turner.